ERITREA'S WAR

ERITREA'S WAR

Confrontation, International Response,
Outcome, Prospects

By Paul Henze

SHAMA BOOKS
Addis Ababa, Ethiopia

© SHAMA BOOKS

A division of Tranco p.l.c.

Addis Ababa, Ethiopia

First edition 2001

PUBLISHED BY

Shama Books

P.O Box 8153

Addis Ababa

Ethiopia

Distribution in partnership with New Line Press, U.S.A.

ISBN 1-931253-06-4

Printed in Singapore

Other Books by Paul B. Henze

Ethiopian Journeys, Travels in Ethiopia 1969-72,
London: Ernest Benn, 1977.

The Plot to Kill the Pope,
London/New York: Macmillan, 1983.
Warsaw: Fakt, 1991.

Rebels and Separatists in Ethiopia,
Santa Monica: RAND, 1985.

Ethiopia: Crisis of a Marxist Economy,
Santa Monica: RAND, 1989.

Soviet Strategy and Islam, (Co-author)
London: Macmillan, 1989.

The Horn of Africa from War to Peace,
London/New York: Macmillan, 1991.

Aspects of Ethiopian Art, From Ancient Axum to the Twentieth Century, (Editor)
London: JED Press, 1993.

Turkey and Ataturk's Legacy,
Haarlem: Research Center for Turkmenistan and Azerbaijan, 1998.

Layers of Time, A History of Ethiopia,
London: Christopher Hurst, 2000.
New York: St. Martin's Press, 2000.

Paul Henze is well known to Ethiopians as a long-standing friend of the country. He has traveled extensively throughout Ethiopia and written hundreds of articles and several books on Ethiopian history, politics, and culture. He visited Ethiopia many times throughout the 1960s and from 1969 to 1972 he was a political counsellor at the American Embassy. As a member of President Carter's National Security Council, he headed several official missions to Ethiopia and other Horn of Africa countries.

Retiring from the U.S. Government in 1980, he has been a consultant to the RAND Corporation and many NGOs and participated in dozens of research projects relating to Ethiopia. Since the fall of the Derg in 1991, he has given strong support to American and other international programs to help Ethiopia develop, modernize, and democratize. He spends several weeks in Ethiopia every year and continues to write about all aspects of the country's history and development.

DEDICATED
to hope for a future
reconciliation between
the peoples
who live on both sides of
the Mareb

Contents

PREFACE

by Professor Haggai Erlich
Tel Aviv University

Eritrea's attack on Ethiopia in May 1998 surprised nearly everyone concerned. It came as a mystery and as a paradox.

The demise in May 1991 of the military dictator Mengistu Haile Mariam heralded a new period in the relations between Ethiopia's government and the Eritrean nationalist movement. Leaders in newly liberated Addis Ababa and Asmara swore cooperation in the name of mutual recognition and neighborly understanding. For a while they headed in this direction. In 1993, with the blessings of the new regime in Ethiopia, Eritrea declared independence. Constructive, even cordial, relations seemed to have developed. The new leaders belonged to the same Tigrinya-speaking Ethiopian people. They seemed to share not only ethnic affinity but also the Tigrayans' old concept of statehood, that of cultural diversity and political decentralization. Ethiopia's leader, Meles Zenawi, and Eritrea's Isaias Afewerki were said to be in constant touch on stabilizing the region. Western leaders and diplomats defined them as a model and a new hope for the whole of Africa. Keener observers, however, could identify some problems. Lacking resources other than tapping the foreign trade of Ethiopia, Eritrean leaders began to over-exploit their nearly exclusive control of Ethiopia's access to the sea. The long years of common struggle against Mengistu left some mistrust. By 1995 relations were becoming troubled, but workable. New arguments over old boundary lines seemed no more than a side issue, a little family misunderstanding about some barren land. The constant contact between Ethiopian and Eritrean officials seemed likely to keep such problems contained and isolated. A 1997 economic and monetary dispute did not deteriorate into an open crisis.

Then, out of the blue, war erupted. Eritrean forces launched a surprise campaign, invading Ethiopian-administered territories they now claimed. Bloodshed followed inevitably, with tens of thousands of young men losing their lives. Two societies, poor in modern infrastructure but rich in history, conflict and disaster, were plunged back into fighting. Ethiopians and Eritreans were captives again of the vicious circle of violence. Why? For many, including those who have spent their lifetimes studying the region, the war came as a mysterious, bitter surprise. If back in early 1998 I would have been asked to stretch my imagination and provide a hundred different scenarios for the future of the Horn of Africa, an Eritrean-Ethiopian war would not have been on my list.

By that time, however, a historian of the region could already have observed a paradox unfolding. This paradox offers answers.

For centuries Ethiopia's rulers worked to build a centralized state around their personal imperial absolutism. The last two of them, Haile Selassie I (1930-1974) and Colonel Mengistu Haile Mariam (1974-1991), dominated almost two-thirds of the twentieth century. Their methods and sources of legitimacy varied, but in common they avoided modernization of politics. Nothing they built was supposed to balance or check their unrestricted personal power. They sought political absolutism cemented by ethnic-regional subordination and cultural assimilation. In the process they also contributed to the deterioration of the Eritrean problem.

Eritrea, or most of it, had been an integral part of Ethiopia's history and culture prior to this province's takeover by the Italians in 1890. Under the colonialists no unity was enforced on Eritrean society. The Italians applied the principle of divide and rule, and their British successors (the British Military Administration in Eritrea, 1941-52) worked to politicize Eritrean ethnic and political diversity in order to promote their own interests. Eritrean society, experiencing colonialism and responding to its challenges, developed its own political movements and organizations. When the United Nations decided to recombine Eritrea with Ethiopia, a new Eritrean constitution (adopted in 1952) prescribed a full parliamentary political system. By this time, under the British, various political parties, trade unions and other movements had mushroomed. They represented rival groups, different religious communities and sub-provincial interests.

Eritrea's road to political modernization was energized also by imperial Ethiopia's centralization ethos. Haile Selassie's absolutism could hardly co-exist with Eritrea's parliamentary autonomy (1952-62). Systematic Ethiopian crushing of Eritrea's constitutional politics had the effect of deepening the politicization of Ethiopian society. A new form of political modernization, the "liberation front" appeared in the 1960s. Importing organizational concepts from the Middle East, the predominantly Muslim "Eritrean

Liberation Front" (ELF) was later, as of 1969, to face the Eritrean People's Liberation Front (EPLF), dominated by Tigrinya-speaking Christians. The two rival "fronts" went on developing their political organizations. For many they served as a model of grass-roots democratization.

The dichotomy between Ethiopia's absolutism and Eritrea's popular institutions peaked when Mengistu and his Derg captured power in 1974. Mengistu twisted the traditional Amhara concept of centralization and turned it into brutal dictatorship. His military tyranny only helped the Eritreans to regroup around their new nationalist identity. It also alienated the various other forces in Ethiopia. Their resistance to Mengistu was indeed the beginning of Ethiopia's political modernization. In forming their new movements, Ethiopian opposition leaders followed the Eritrean model of the "liberation front". The most effective new movement was the Tigray People's Liberation Front (TPLF) which, not without differences and not without difficulties, worked together with the EPLF. It was due mainly to their combined struggle that Mengistu was toppled, and the year 1991 seemed to have ushered in a new era.

But then a paradox began unfolding. Ethiopia, the land of imperial absolutism and centralization had steadily opened up. Eritrea began closing. The new ex-TPLF leadership of Ethiopia, headed by Meles Zenawi, applied the Tigrayan decentralization concept. Ethiopia was reconstructed as a federation of nine states, each based on a different ethnic combination. A new Ethiopian constitution prescribed institutionalized representative systems on both the federal and state levels. Though Ethiopia's democratization left a lot to be desired, the country's politics turned into a field of many voices and of openly competing factors. For

IV

the first time in centuries Ethiopia had no ruler, and decision-making processes became a matter of checks and balances. Freedom of expression and a free-market economy, with all due problems, have been introduced. Experimenting with their new political decentralization, endorsing the separateness of Eritrea on the same premise of regional pluralism, the last thing Ethiopia's new leaders wanted was a renewed Eritrean war.

But while Ethiopia departed from personal authoritarianism and adopted political diversification, Eritrea turned paradoxically in the other direction. After independence (official as of May 1993), the leadership of the EPLF failed to shed its "liberation front" mentality. Instead of building on Eritrea's proven record of political modernization, Isaias Afewerki seized absolute power. He gave no one else access to power and decision-making, not to the various groups in Eritrea, not even to his closest colleagues. He surrounded himself with yes-men. With no checks and balances, he followed the footsteps of so many other authoritarian leaders. He closed the society, tightened control of the economy, created a military garrison state and discouraged return of the most talented Eritreans in exile. The nearly inevitable followed. As this crude system failed to meet expectations, externalization of problems was the natural outlet. Isaias was quick to pick quarrels with everyone around Eritrea: Sudan, Djibouti, Yemen and then finally Ethiopia. Self-delusion and self-deception, the absolutist's inherent disease, prevailed. In igniting a sudden war with Ethiopia, Isaias must have thought he could control the fire. He gambled disastrously on the welfare of his population and everybody has lost. Isaias' only major achievement has been in the field of global public relations. The war he started was covered by Western media with ignorance.

Major newspapers naively recycled his propaganda. This book is an attempt to provide a balanced analysis.

Nobody is perhaps better qualified to produce the first book on the current conflict than Paul B. Henze. He uniquely combined extensive, panoramic and multidisciplinary academic knowledge of the region, a personal intimate knowledge based on four decades of intensive involvement in Horn of Africa affairs, a rare analytic and insightful mind, and a long record of condemning and staring down dictators. The present volume is a thought-provoking document of little ambivalence and of great importance. In putting the renewed cycle of Ethiopian-Eritrean conflict into comprehensive perspective, as well as in his own personal prism, Henze provides an interpretation that will inevitably be readdressed by everyone concerned. It will surely help to straighten a war picture twisted by global indifference.

Tel Aviv, 25 August 2000

AUTHOR'S INTRODUCTION

Isaias Afewerki sent his army unannounced across the border into Ethiopia in the first days of May 1998 and provoked a confrontation that turned into a war. When it reached its final stage in May-June 2000, this war briefly had the distinction of being the largest war anywhere in the world at that time. Fortunately Ethiopian military prowess brought it to a swift end. The confrontation was a tragedy which cost the lives of tens of thousands of young men. It disrupted the existence of more than a million innocent civilians in both countries. It resulted in massive property damage. Eritrea planted mines over great expanses of territory which will take years to clear. The war set back the economic and social development of both countries. Its effect on Eritrea, whose leaders initiated the conflict, is far more serious and will last much longer than the damage Ethiopia suffered.

Why did Isaias embark on this confrontation? Why did the men around him support him in this illogical venture? Why did the Eritrean people let themselves be drawn into a crusade against the country closest to them in blood, language and religion? These are mysteries. I speculate about them in this book but I can give no final answers. As time passes we will learn more.

There is little mystery about Ethiopia's response to the crisis that confronted it. Ethiopia was unprepared to prevent Eritrea's incursions because it considered an invasion over its northern border among the least likely dangers it might have to face. In keeping with the country's traditions, Ethiopia's leaders turned to the international community to press Eritrea to withdraw and devise a scheme to mediate a settlement. Those who tried – in the UN, the OAU, the EU and in the United States Government – were good-willed, but ineffective.

They failed to understand that equal treatment of the aggressor and the victim of aggression is counterproductive. Journalists failed to report and explain the basic facts about the conflict. Many of them, whether they realized it or not, accepted and repeated Eritrean propaganda. While patiently collaborating in the international peace-making process, Ethiopia prepared for a military solution. When it became clear that Eritrea was going to continue to block any rational cease-fire and mediation process, Ethiopia took matters into its own hands. Its generals had prepared well, applying key lessons of modern warfare in devising their strategy. They overwhelmed the entrenched Eritreans in days and marched deep into Eritrea. On 18 June, Isaias finally ordered his foreign minister, Haile Wolde Tensae, to accept the cease-fire he had long tried to avoid. The speed with which a full final settlement can now be reached depends on Eritrea.

This book is an attempt to describe the course of the conflict primarily through my own lecturing and writing on it during the past two years. The book does not chronicle each diplomatic move in the international mediation process. That and a full account of Ethiopia's military preparations and actions is a task for the Ethiopian authorities, if they feel it is necessary. I hope they may issue a White Book on the confrontation so that we have a detailed record to counter misinformation, Eritrea has published. In my account, I have devoted particular attention to the misguided involvement of American mediators who failed to understand the history and mentality of Ethiopia, on the one hand, and on the other, avoided acknowledging the nature of the authoritarian dictatorship the EPLF has established in Eritrea. Worse still, these officials failed to apply basic American principles and policies to their judgment of the conflict, a failure profoundly disappointing to me as an American long familiar with all the

VIII

peoples of the region. The United States has performed much more effectively in Ethiopia in the past. I have also included a survey of journalists' reporting on the conflict, equally disappointing because so few journalists made the effort to understand the history of the region and its relevance to the confrontation.

I hope readers will find the BACKGROUND section of this book (Chapters Three through Seven) valuable for the light they shed on both the remote and recent factors contributing to the conflict. I present several basic documents that may be valuable for historians. The EPLF has tried to reduce the enormously complex history of Eritrea to a simple mythology. This mythology is designed to justify EPLF domination of Eritrea but it can hardly be believed by most Eritreans. Eritrea is a classic frontier area where varied geography determines ways people earn their livelihood and where ethnic, linguistic and religious groups intermingle. All these factors influence people's attitudes. While foreign powers have long been tempted to exploit disagreements and tensions in Eritrea, the peoples of the region, over centuries, developed techniques for getting along with each other and easing discord, misunderstanding and competition. There are no majorities in Eritrea, only minorities. A true nation has not yet evolved. Eritrea is, at best, a nation in the process of formation. A democratic system in Eritrea would recognize diversity and respect differences of opinion. The EPLF craves uniformity. It has tried to impose uniformity by rigid controls and ceaseless propaganda. It feels it cannot afford to let Eritreans think for themselves. Instead of slowly moving toward democracy, which the EPLF appeared to be doing up to the mid-1990s, Isaias Afewerki has created an authoritarian police state. This is the core of the current Eritrean problem.

The documents that form the Background section, in chronological order, include:

- A record of a visit I made to Eritrea in the late Derg years, *Eritrea in 1987*, during a period when Derg armies had once again temporarily established control over much of the region. My account of this visit provides a vivid picture of Eritreans making the best of their uncomfortable situation, including many who were working hard and purposefully to ease the strains of life in Asmara and Massawa. The visit concluded with a revealing interview with party secretary, Teferra Wonde.

- A talk I gave to a group of Eritreans in the U.S. in late 1990, when it was already clear that the Derg was going to collapse and Eritrea would be entering an era of comparative peace and opportunity, *Eritrea – the Economic Challenge*. I sketched out a design for a successful democratic Eritrea which could become the economic hub of the whole region.

- A record of my experiences in the independence referendum in April 1993, *Diary of an Official Observer*. This was a time of great hope among Eritreans when the future looked promising and most of the population was ready to believe that the EPLF would lead them to a peaceful, democratic future. Even Isaias Afewerki gave that impression in a long meeting I had with him at the end of this visit.

- *Who Lost Eritrea? What has been Lost?* was addressed to Ethiopian centrists who had agitated for "action" to prevent Eritrean independence. The essay was written immediately after my return from service as a referendum observer. It reads ironically now, but at the time the judgments and hopes I expressed were widely shared in the EPRDF leadership and among a significant portion of the Ethiopian population. It was Isaias who shattered them.

- I conclude my Background with a *Short History of Eritrea* which has been adapted from my *Layers of Time, A History of Ethiopia* (London/New York, 2000). I believe that any objective historian of the region will find it honest and accurate. EPLF partisans, of course, will not, for it negates prevailing EPLF mythology and much of the writing of the sycophantic pseudo-scholars who have glorified the EPLF.

I finish this book with speculation about the future of Eritrea and its place in the Horn of Africa. Isaias and the men around him have persisted in denial of the Ethiopian victory and, apparently, denial of the consequences. Nevertheless, they found themselves forced to face the reality of their defeat when they signed the cease-fire and preliminary mediation agreement brokered by President Bouteflika in Algiers on 18 June 2000. Acceptance of this agreement — in particular the provision for creation of a twenty-five kilometers wide demilitarized zone on the Eritrean side of the border to be patrolled by UN peace-keepers — constitutes *de facto* recognition of Eritrean guilt in initiating the confrontation. Eritrean propaganda, on the other hand, continues to vilify Ethiopia and its leaders, foment ethnic hatred, and pretend that Eritrea has somehow come out of the war with a strong economy and an effective military establishment. Self-delusion will not help Eritrea recover.

Washington, D.C.

CHAPTER I

THE COURSE OF THE CONFRONTATION

As the confrontation continued into the year 2000, the search for a peaceful solution by the OAU with the support of the international community continued without result. Reporting by journalists in the international press remained shallow. Eritrean propaganda continued unabated and reached new heights of invective and mendaciousness. Unfortunately, many of the most blatant Eritrean distortions of fact and history were repeated in the dispatches of newspaper and television reporters and even in the editorials of some of the world's most prestigious publications.

Having received little response from the letters I wrote to American officials, congressmen and newpapers from which I give excerpts in the following chapter, I decided at the turn of the year to prepare a series of essays on the conflict under the heading, Eritrea's War. I chose that title deliberately because Eritrea started the war and forced it on Ethiopia. The first of these essays was written in January 2000 and the second in February.[1] These circulated widely in America, Europe and Ethiopia. I completed this series when I returned from my visit to Ethiopia in May and early

June, after the war reached its final stage with an Ethiopian military offensive against Eritrea and decisive victory.

I have combined these five essays to form this chapter, condensing them somewhat to eliminate repetition of the same themes and information. They provide a summary history of the conflict. They include judgments on key aspects of it. The United States Government slipped into the posture —unjustly and ineffectively — of treating Ethiopia and Eritrea as equally responsible for the conflict out of an apparent desire to avoid excessive offense to the aggressor. This approach led Ethiopian leaders and the Ethiopian public to lose faith in the Clinton Administration's judgment and created speculation among some Ethiopians that it was the American intention to favor Isaias. I have found no evidence that this was the case. The result, however, encouraged Isaias' intransigeance.

We still know too little about what mental processes led Isaias to invade Ethiopia. Did he act on impulse in ordering the invasion in May 1998 and then find himself unable to reverse course? Did he have a long-range plan for undermining the EPRDF government and destabilizing Ethiopia? If so, what led him to believe that this was possible? What could Eritrea gain from this course of action? Was he so unsure of his hold over Eritrea that he felt compelled to unleash a war to keep his own population mobilized? What was the origin of the intense rancor Isaias developed against the TPLF? As Ethiopia mobilized itself to resist, did Isaias consider revising his strategy? How did he expect the confrontation to come to an end?

The workings of Isaias Afewerki's mind remain a mystery. Over time we may learn more about his motivation and judgments. It is clear now that his judgment was wrong. He based his actions on poor understanding of the situation in Ethiopia and the effectiveness of Ethiopian leaders.

We know much more about Meles Zenawi's attitude toward the conflict. His judgments and actions can be understood in terms of Ethiopia's history and the traditions of its previous leaders. In an exchange of correspondence in December 1998 Meles wrote to me:

> I want you to know that I will seek a peaceful solution to the problem as long as there is any glimmer of hope of doing so, no matter how unpopular this approach may be. At the same time, if the peace efforts fail I will pursue the military option with the same vigour that I am now pursuing the peace option no matter how unpopular this option may be among our foreign friends...[2]

When I met with Meles in his office in Addis Ababa on 12 March 1999, he described his feelings about the confrontation:

> ...I congratuled Meles on the victory they gained a few days ago at Badme... He said he was confident that they would win, but their problem was the United States... Washington appears to favor Eritrea, he said, and seems to be bent upon saving Isaias, discriminating against Ethiopia to the point of proposing to condemn it. This has deeply hurt Meles but he maintained that at bottom he was more puzzled than angered.[3]

I had a long conversation with Meles again on 14 April 1999 shortly before leaving Ethiopia. We discussed the confrontation with Eritrea at greater length:

> I asked him how he evaluated the situation at the front. He expressed confidence that Eritrea had been

3

defeated but said that it was unfortunate that they refused to recognize their predicament. If they would withdraw from Ethiopian territory, Ethiopia would immediately agree to the establishment of a demilitarized zone, arrangements for international observers, and negotiations on demarcation of the border. In other words the position he stated when I talked to him five weeks ago remains unchanged... I asked him whether there had been any change...in plans for action against Eritrea. He said with considerable emphasis that Ethiopia has no plans to march on Asmara or Assab. Ethiopia wants no Eritrean territory and Ethiopia does not want to undermine Eritrea's sovereignty... It would be completely unrealistic for Ethiopia to aspire to remain in Eritrea. Ethiopia is better off without Eritrea, he said...

"He (again) expressed his regret at the stubbornness of the Eritrean leadership: Their losses in the fighting have been in a population of only three million. Practically every family in Eritrea will have experienced a loss by the time the fighting is over. Our losses are spread among sixty million people and are therefore much less felt in the society. The result could be very tragic, Eritreans could harbor resentment of Ethiopia for years to come, blaming us rather than their leaders for the losses they have suffered. This, in turn, could generate strong negative attitudes in the Ethiopian population and reconciliation between the two peoples — who are really one — would be indefinitely delayed. Nevertheless, it must eventually take place."

Meles Zenawi gave the pursuit of peace a full two years. He spent hundreds of hours with emissaries talking peace. But simultaneously, as a responsible leader must do, he had the country's military leaders prepare for action. They planned systematically and effectively while Eritrea stalled and hurled insults. U.S. Ambassador Richard Holbrooke's entry into the "peace process" in April 2000 brought it to a rapid conclusion in a manner he did not anticipate. He was apparently not briefed on envoys' previous discussions with Meles. Thus, he failed to understand Ethiopian mentality and seems to have known little about Ethiopian history. As a result, Meles reached the end of his patience and concluded there was no alternative to ordering the Ethiopian military leaders to march. Ethiopian forces taught the Eritreans a bitter lesson and brought the confrontation to an end.

As the five essays which follow demonstrate, I was not surprised at this outcome. But I did not expect the confrontation to reach a climax so soon. I went to Ethiopia at the beginning in early May 2000 for cultural research and meetings with the new director of the Institute of Ethiopian Studies at Addis Ababa University. I assumed that the confrontation with Eritrea would probably still drag on for months. But when the situation reached a climax I was pleased as a historian to be a witness to a major historical event. At the same time, traveling extensively throughout the country, I was struck by how little effect Eritrea's war had on daily Ethiopian life. I traveled through both the south, the center and the north of the country. From Awasa to Makelle I saw that Eritrea's invasion had not halted economic, social and educational progress. I was impressed with the strong backing the EPRDF-led government enjoys throughout the country. Nothing demonstrated this better than the long-scheduled national elections which took place the very weekend the offensive against Eritrea began. They represented an important stage of forward movement toward a more open political system and a more open society.

This chapter concludes with analyses of one, the failure of American policy toward Eritrea's war and two, the failure of journalists and commentators representing international media to understand the confrontation and enlighten their audiences on both the background and the unfolding of events.

I - Causes and Effects, Reflections, and Prospects

Puzzle? The standard formulation in international press reports and references to the confrontation between Ethiopia and Eritrea has been:

Two erstwhile friendly African states, both victors in 1991 over the Derg (the oppressive Stalinist regime of dictator Mengistu Haile Mariam, 1974-1991), went to war in May 1998. Both enjoyed support from the United States and other Western countries. Both were regarded as beacons of hope for the war - torn Horn of Africa. The war between them, purportedly over disputed border regions, is bound to cost lives and resources that could better be devoted to economic development of societies that are among the poorest in Africa and are now threatened by famine. To Americans, Europeans and others who know little or nothing about this part of the world, the war appeared to make no sense. Is the war indeed senseless? Are no principles involved? How did it start and why did it continue?

Illusions. Both countries would be better off if this war had not happened. Why did it happen? The answer is very simple: it happened because Eritrea invaded Ethiopia. Without warning, Eritrea sent its armed forces into territory long administered by Ethiopia, then proceeded to confiscate millions of dollars of Ethiopian goods in the ports of Massawa and Assab, and took measures restricting the freedom of Ethiopians resident in Eritrea. Three key questions can be asked: one, Did Ethiopia, as Eritreans now allege, have designs on Eritrean territory that Eritrea had to forestall? Two, Did Ethiopia provoke Eritrea? Three, Were there no contentious issues between them?

The answers to these three questions are, respectively: No, No, and Yes. There are always arguable issues between states. Leaders whose foremost concern is their own people's welfare attempt to settle arguments with neighbors by negotiation, refraining from military force until all other avenues have been tried. I can answer the first two questions on the basis of my own direct observations.

I have been familiar with Ethiopia for almost forty years, having first visited it in 1962. I have traveled in all parts of the country, including Eritrea when it was joined to Ethiopia and at four different periods since it became independent. I have known personally many of the leaders of both countries. For eight years of my service as a U.S. Government officer in the 1960s and 1970s, I was officially involved in relations with the Horn of Africa. I have remained continually interested in the area since I left U.S. Government service at the end of 1980. As a fellow of the Woodrow Wilson Center for Scholars at the Smithsonian Institution in 1981-82 and as a Resident Consultant in the Washington office of RAND since 1982, I have participated in numerous research projects on African affairs. I have published half a dozen books and more than a hundred reports and articles on Ethiopia, Eritrea, and other countries of the Horn of Africa during the two decades since I left the service of the U.S. Government. [4]

I spend several weeks each year in the region now. During a six-week visit to Ethiopia in February and March 1998 I happened to stay for more than two weeks in Tigray for purposes of historical research. I traveled extensively in the northeastern region, including a visit to the town of Adigrat and a long trek on foot into the region inhabited by the predominantly Roman Catholic Irob people in northeastern Tigray. During this entire time I did not see a single Ethiopian soldier and almost no policemen. In frequent contacts with local officials and a wide range of citizens, I heard nothing of strains with Eritrea that could lead to hostilities. I am confident, therefore, that Ethiopia one, did not anticipate an Eritrean attack, two, consequently, made no preparations to defend against it, and three, made no preparations for attacking Eritrea. The Eritrean invasion came as a surprise to Ethiopia.

Contentious issues are another matter. Contrary to common cliches of journalists, the two guerrilla movements that have led the governments of Eritrea and Ethiopia since 1991 were "brothers in arms" for only a small part of the time they fought the communist Derg, more often they kept their distance from each other and were at odds, and for long periods.

The differences lay in their origins and, as they evolved, in the character of their leaders. After he committed two assassinations in Asmara, the Chinese communists selected Isaias Afewerki as a promising prospect for guerrilla training in the early 1970s. When he came back from China he applied communist techniques-intrigue, force and tight top-down control-to create the Eritrean Popular Liberation Front (EPLF) by overwhelming half a dozen other Eritrean groups to form an authoritarian Marxist-Leninist movement.[5] Other EPLF leaders benefitted from training in Syria and

Cuba. The EPLF was nurtured by money and arms from communist proxies and Arabs until it began to capture large amounts of Soviet arms and equipment from the Derg in the late 1980s. Documents from East German archives describe how Isaias was welcomed in East Berlin as "Comrade" when he came in the 1980s to seek help in persuading Moscow to shift support from the Marxist Derg to the Marxist EPLF. He only began to realize the futility of trying to build a communist Eritrea when the Soviet Union was well on its way to collapse in 1989.

The Tigray Popular Liberation Front (TPLF), on the other hand, evolved as a grass roots student movement based on the traditional Tigrayan peasantry. Its leaders were not foreign-trained and never depended on foreign support, though they long claimed they were Marxists too. With little knowledge of the outer world, they took Albania as a symbol of stubborn self-reliance, but when they realized the way the world was developing in the 1980s they changed ideology and under the leadership of Meles Zenawi sought openings to the West. They depended primarily on weapons captured in encounters with Derg forces.

During the major portion of the two movements' struggle against the Derg they seldom cooperated and were sometimes hostile. Resentments and clashes extending back to the mid-1970s reflected rivalries and tensions among competing anti-Derg movements which at various times collaborated with the TPLF and the EPLF, but seldom in tandem. These included the urban-based Ethiopian People's Revolutionary Party (EPRP) and factions of the largely Muslim Eritrean Liberation Front (ELF), seen by the EPLF as its major rival, at times supportive of the TPLF. [6] In the mid-1980s the EPLF for a period blocked TPLF access to Sudan through Eritrean territory during a time when the

TPLF needed access to relief for famine victims. Both depended on Sudan as an avenue for contact with the outer world and Sudan served as a route for emergency food and medical supplies for both.

Both movements gained decisive victories over Derg forces in the late 1980s. In March 1988 the EPLF decimated a large Derg force which included Russian advisers at Afabet in northern Eritrea. Isaias then realized it could be advantageous to provide some of the armor and artillery he captured to the Tigrayans and the EPLF thus contributed to the decisive TPLF victory at Enda Selassie in western Tigray in early 1989. After his forces were defeated at Enda Selassie, Mengistu reluctantly withdrew all Derg forces from Tigray. The EPLF no longer had to fear Derg attacks from the south. From this time onward the two movements set earlier resentments aside and cooperated to finish off the Derg. Meanwhile the TPLF had built a network of cooperating movements among Ethiopians of other nationalities, the Ethiopian Peoples' Revolutionary Democratic Front (EPRDF). While the EPLF became more firmly separatist, the EPRDF adopted an Ethiopian nationalist position.

Sympathetic to the suffering the Eritrean people had to bear under the Derg and recognizing the futility of trying to keep Eritrea in Ethiopia, the TPLF/EPRDF let Eritrea go its own way in 1991 when the Derg collapsed. Militarily speaking, neither it nor any foreign power had any alternative. Isaias Afewerki's original intention had been to defy international norms and declare independence unilaterally. Persuading him that this would be a counterproductive course of action was not easy. Three U.S. diplomats [7] cooperated to broker an arrangement whereby legalities were observed during a two-year interim while the EPLF administered a *de facto* independent Eritrea as a provisional government until a UN-approved referendum was held in April 1993. [8]

Offering only a yes-or-no choice, the referendum was more of a propaganda happening than a genuine test of public opinion. No gradations of attitude were tested. Nevertheless my own observations [9] lead me to conclude that a majority of the Eritrean population at that time accepted independence as *a fait accompli*. They were impressed by the international good will Eritrea (and Ethiopia) enjoyed for separating peacefully and expected that international support would ensure them a better future while close links with Ethiopia would be maintained. In Ethiopia, nationalist opposition to Eritrean independence subsided quickly and a period of cooperative adjustment between the two governments followed. Eritrean ports were used for Ethiopian trade, Ethiopian currency continued to be used in Eritrea, and Eritrean-born Ethiopians who chose Eritrean citizenship continued to live, work and engage in business in Ethiopia. [10]

In power the two guerrilla movements took sharply contrasting approaches to governing. The TPLF reorganized Ethiopia into ethnic federal states and stressed decentralization and devolution of governmental operations to regions. It gave education and economic development absolute priority. It reduced military expenditures drastically. Since 1991 Ethiopia has had a plethora of political parties and a lively private press. The EPLF, on the other hand, put Eritrea under a rigid centralized administrative system giving no recognition to ethnic diversity. It permitted neither political parties nor independent newspapers. All young Eritreans, women as well as men, have been required to undergo military training. Though no neighbor, least of all Ethiopia, threatened Eritrea, Eritrea has used its military forces against every one of its neighbors, including Yemen across the Red Sea, since independence in 1993.

Contrasts in approach to government and society became sharper after official Eritrean independence in 1993. The EPRDF moved systematically to create a new constitution for Ethiopia and remained committed to developing an increasingly open society. Political agitation and journalistic excesses were met at times by comparatively arbitrary security and legal measures. Ethiopia attracted criticism from Amnesty International, Human Rights Watch and similar organizations for jailing politicians inciting violence and journalists who published provocative or false reports. Eritrea avoided such criticism by permitting neither politicians nor independent journalists to operate, a fact international watchdog groups sometimes failed to notice. Nevertheless while progress toward a more open society in Ethiopia has continued and is now apparent to any visitor to Addis Ababa, Eritrea has remained an authoritarian one-party state.[11] Belatedly Eritrea set a constitutional process in motion in 1995, but while Ethiopia's constitution was ratified and came into operation in that year, Eritrea's has yet to be implemented.[12]

Devolution of responsibility to regional governments accelerated steadily in Ethiopia during the late 1990s and has been more successful than most observers anticipated.[13] Meanwhile the EPLF abolished traditional Eritrean provinces and redivided the country into geographic regions designed to minimize the impact of ethnicity and religion. In all respects Eritrea remains a highly centralized, militarized, authoritarian state with few features of democracy.

Though often the subject of comment in both countries, differing patterns of political evolution were not an openly argued issue between the two governments. Economic issues, however became increasingly contentious. Following World Bank and IMF advice, Ethiopia devalued its currency to a realistic rate in May 1993 and inaugurated a successful system to keep official and unofficial rates in tandem. Eritrea continued to offer more favorable rates of exchange for Ethiopian currency than Ethiopia. This issue disappeared when Eritrea introduced its own currency, the nacfa, in November 1997. However, a more contentious issue immediately developed. The nacfa was set at par with the Ethiopian birr. It lacked the backing of the birr, however. Ethiopia henceforth required Eritrea to pay for imports and services in hard currency, judging the nacfa as a currency likely to lose value.[14] Eritrea denounced the requirement as an unfriendly gesture, but Ethiopian leaders were already concluding that they had been overly generous to Eritrea in this as well as several other respects:

- Eritrean businessmen and citizens in Ethiopia were sending profits and remittances to Eritrea in increasing quantity, sometimes disguising earnings to avoid Ethiopian taxes.

- Controversies had developed over Eritrean port procedures and charges in Assab and Massawa.

- Ethiopia found that it could import petroleum products more cheaply through Djibouti rather than depending on the antiquated Assab refinery, which it was, in effect, subsidizing.

- Ethiopians had evidence that Eritrea was re-exporting Ethiopian products such as coffee to the disadvantage of Ethiopian producers.

13

- Border trade issues along the Tigray - Eritrea border occasionally became contentious.

The degree to which all of these practices were actually injuring the steadily expanding Ethiopian economy is difficult to establish. Both officials and private Ethiopians cite a great deal of circumstantial evidence. As relations between the two countries and their governments cooled, the impression that Eritrea was exploiting Ethiopia's goodwill became widespread among Ethiopians. The EPRDF government came under criticism for having treated Eritrea too tolerantly since 1991.

Why resort to military action? Contentious issues between the two governments had long been under discussion when the Eritreans attacked in May 1998. There had been no obstacles to consultation and communication between the two governments at various levels. Both had embassies in each other's capitals and there were many other formal and informal channels of communication between them, including contacts between senior officials and leaders. Independent organizations and foreign governments, if asked, would have been ready to mediate. There were indeed local problems in a few border areas that had never been clearly defined. Maps differed. (Colonial boundaries were of little importance from 1952 to 1993 when the territory on both sides was part of Ethiopia.) long discussions and negotiations had taken place about some remote areas, for example the Bada region in eastern Tigray. [15] But there was no issue deadlocked enough to justify the precipitate and wholesale Eritrean military occupation of border areas that had continually been administered by Ethiopia. **Was acquisition of these economically insignificant border regions actually the purpose of the invasion? What were Isaias Afewerki's calculations?**

One can only conclude that Isaias made a gross miscalculation. He must have known that the border was weakly garrisoned by Ethiopian military forces, and assumed that Ethiopia would either choose not to resist or would be unable to oppose Eritrean incursions. Other motivations — illusions? — must have contributed to his failure to estimate the consequences of his action. These, to judge by subsequent developments and subsequent Eritrean propaganda, included far more fundamental considerations. Isaias apparently convinced himself that ethnic tensions in Ethiopia were much more serious than they actually were or, even after Eritrean attempts to fan them, proved to be. The proliferation of Ethiopian political parties, many of them ethnically based, and the outspoken private press in Ethiopia may have given him an exaggerated impression of ethnic tension and political disaffection. Isaias seems to have assumed that these tensions could be exacerbated to the point where the authority of the EPRDF government would be seriously undermined. What began largely as rhetoric turned into a program of covert support for Ethiopian dissidents, especially the remnants of the Oromo Liberation Front (OLF) whose resort to violence and consistent political miscalculations had resulted in their withdrawal from the Transitional Government in 1992 and exclusion of the OLF from legal political processes.

Some OLF elements took refuge in anarchic Somalia in the mid-1990s. The EPLF developed a major program for supporting and encouraging their attempts to mount incursions into Ethiopia. This crass Eritrean effort to exploit and exacerbate the degenerated political situation in Somalia backfired. Ethiopia sent forces into Somalia which largely eliminated Eritrean-supported OLF and Somali would-be guerrillas and Hussein Aideed shifted his position to cooperation with Ethiopia.[16] Disruptive operations and intense denunciatory propaganda against Ethiopia brought exactly the opposite result from that which the Eritreans intended: Ethiopia has experienced a remarkable surge of public opinion favoring national unity during the past year and a half. As the new millennium opens, there is evidence on all sides in Ethiopia of a heightened sense of pride in the fact that the country enjoys a comparatively open society with wide opportunity for expression of varied political views. Ethiopia has thus experienced a healthy acceleration of public understanding of the practice of democracy and the values of civil society as an unintended consequence of the Eritrean invasion. Meanwhile the EPLF government in Eritrea has had to subject its population to coercive measures to keep it mobilized to support its misadventures.

On the human plane the most tragic consequence of the Eritrean invasion was the expulsions by both sides of citizens of the other. A wave of deep resentment swept the Ethiopian population shortly after the Eritrean attack in the summer of 1998. Responding to public opinion as well as to their own anger at Eritrean actions, federal and regional officials in Ethiopia expelled large numbers of Eritrean citizens. Some of these had never lived in Eritrea but because of Eritrean ancestry had voted in the 1993 referendum and accepted citizenship. Some were highly successful businessmen who were given little time to settle their affairs. Some of these went abroad rather than go to Eritrea. Eritrea responded in kind against Ethiopian citizens, but since the numbers of Ethiopians in Eritrea were far smaller than those resident in Ethiopia the total from Ethiopia was naturally much higher. EPLF leaders dramatized the expulsions as a humanitarian crime, conveniently forgetting about the example they had set in 1991 with the summary expulsion of far larger numbers of Ethiopian soldiers and civilians including women and children.

The Economic Dimension: Isaias' assumption that cutting off commerce through the ports of Massawa and Assab would generate serious economic complications in Ethiopia proved as illusory as his hopes for fanning ethnic strain. Ethiopian imports and exports were smoothly shifted to Djibouti, with a small amount also now transiting Berbera in *de facto* independent Somaliland. Djibouti welcomed the traffic, expanded port facilities, and both countries have steadily improved rail and highway links. Eritrean attempts to intimidate Djibouti have been unsuccessful. Meanwhile Assab has become a dead city. It may be doomed to permanent decline, for Ethiopia recently announced a project to be carried out by a South African firm for construction of a parallel railway line from Djibouti to the center of the country designed for large-scale container traffic. The European Union has supported upgrading of highways from Berbera into Ethiopia.[17]

The overall pace of economic development in Ethiopia has continued brisk in spite of the confrontation with Eritrea, though foreign investment has slowed and tourism has been adversely affected.[18] Tourism in Eritrea is moribund except for foreign visitors subsidized by the government. Completion of the Fincha refinery has enabled Ethiopia to increase its capacity for exporting sugar. Coffee remains Ethiopia's principal source of export earnings. Good rains in 1999 gave good harvests except in the dry southeast. In spite of Eritrea's confiscation of imports consigned to Ethiopia in its ports when it invaded, most resulting problems have been overcome. The Turkish-built cement plant in Makelle, for example, has gone into operation in spite of the fact that Eritrea confiscated the equipment originally shipped to be installed in it. The Ethiopian birr has remained strong. The nacfa has no significant international standing.

Eritrea has attempted to obscure the severe economic difficulties it is experiencing by unverifiable claims of economic growth and new investment. No authoritative economic reporting or evaluating group has endorsed them. Eritrea is a blank in World Bank and IMF reports. Eritrea appears to be living almost entirely off remittances and donations supplied by its diaspora in the Middle East and America. These are understandably reported to be declining. Isaias' travels during 1999 were primarily motivated by the need to keep money from the diaspora flowing and to gain financial support from some Arab countries.

Persistence of Eritrean Aggressive Efforts: Eritrea made concerted efforts to retake the Badme sector in the early summer of 1999 and was decisively repulsed at the cost of considerable casualties to both itself and Ethiopia. Ethiopia's manpower reserves are practically unlimited in comparison with Eritrea's. Isaias has shown little apparent concern about sacrificing Eritrea's youth, for he has continued periodic probing along the front in northeastern Tigray. He has advanced false claims to localities that have always been under Ethiopian administration, such as the border town of Zalambassa. Eritrean military operations in northeastern Tigray have been devastating to the predominantly Roman Catholic Irob people who populate it.[19] Eritrea has used oppressive methods to force Irob under its control to accept Eritrean citizenship. The Eritrean incursion displaced four hundred thousand people in the border regions of Tigray. Though some have returned to the

Badme area, most remain in camps or temporary housing and are being fed by the World Food Program. In spite of these hardships for the people immediately affected, life in Tigray has continued normal outside the immediate border regions. Substantial economic progress has continued, significant new construction has been completed, road networks have been expanded, and schools and higher educational institutions, including the Catholic seminary in Adigrat and the newly-designated university in Makelle, have continued functioning.

Life and economic activity in Eritrea have been much more severely affected by Eritrea's efforts to mobilize its entire population and keep it on a war footing.

Considering Eritrea's intransigence and prevarication, the international community must be credited with remarkable patience for persisting in efforts to work out ceasefire and mediation arrangements without giving offense to Isaias Afewerki. Though Eritrea announced in the spring of 1999 that it accepted the principle of withdrawal from areas it had occupied and would agree to international peace-making and mediation efforts, it has consistently blocked progress toward solid agreement. While, in spite of repeated missions to both countries by U.S. emissary Tony Lake, the original U.S.-Rwandan peace plan fell into *de facto* abeyance, Algeria, operating within the framework of the OAU, worked out an alternate but similar proposal. As a concession to Eritrean intransigence, this proposal waters down the requirement for clear-cut Eritrean withdrawal from formerly Ethiopian-administered areas and leaves arrangements for verification of withdrawal, subsequent policing, and provisions for international supervision of mediation so unclear that Ethiopia has found the plan unacceptable. Ethiopian skepticism is based on mendacious and deceptive Eritrean behavior ever since the original invasion occurred. Thus Ethiopia insists on water-tight provisions.

Continued Eritrean Propaganda: Well aware that international public opinion almost always assumes that a small country in confrontation with a larger one must be in the right, Eritrean propagandists have been skillful in creating the impression that Eritrea is the victim of Ethiopian aggression. Eritreans have also capitalized on impressions left from the long struggle against Derg oppression and military assault. There is no justification for equating the stance of the EPRDF toward Eritrea with that of the Derg dictator, Mengistu Haile Mariam. The EPLF's extensive propaganda network in the U.S. and Europe directed from its embassies embroiders and distorts these allegations, obscuring the fact that all problems derive from Eritrea's invasion of Ethiopian-administered territory. Meanwhile official Eritrean media continue to engage in extraordinarily vicious denunciation of Ethiopia and personal vilification of Ethiopia's leaders,[20] exceeding in virulence the private press in Ethiopia, which is not controlled by the government at all. Both Eritrean official statements and propaganda reflect no moderation, no interest in reconciliation or peaceful resolution of conflict.

What was Isaias' Goal? Did Isaias Afewerki launch this confrontation with any goal in mind? Or did he misjudge what he was doing and fall into a situation from which his inherent stubbornness makes it difficult for him to extricate himself? In the early months of the confrontation Isaias may well have thought he might cause the EPRDF government to lose control of the country. While it is difficult to see how that could be an advantage to Eritrea, Isaias has never displayed much logic in his aggressive actions toward Eritrea's neighbors. Isaias stepped up his program for fomenting dissidence and insurgency in Ethiopia after his forces were defeated at Badme in February 1999. He was unwilling to abandon his conviction that Meles Zenawi's government could be undermined. That has not happened. Eritrean attempts to foment unrest in Ethiopia via Somalia have failed. There is evidence from many directions of the strength of national unity in Ethiopia. Most significant, perhaps, is the commitment of the EPRDF, in accordance with Ethiopia's 1995 constitution, to hold national elections in May 2000 and its encouragement of multi-party participation. Eritrea has never put its constitution into effect, let alone let political parties operate or considered holding multi-party elections.

There is no evidence of a coherent set of Eritrean "war aims". Regrettably the international community has not demanded that Eritrea explain the aims of its confrontation with Ethiopia. Foolish denunciations of Ethiopia such as the letter of Congressman Benjamin Gilman in the *Washington Post* of 3 January 2000 "Ethiopia Needs a Push. Toward Peace" are victories for Eritrea's propagandists. This letter, combined with the continued reluctance of the Clinton Administration to condemn Eritrea's invasion as aggression, has unleashed a wave of protest and resentment in Ethiopia and among Ethiopians abroad. Does American refusal to condemn Eritrea prove that Eritrea is considered more important to American interests than Ethiopia? The notion has become widespread in Ethiopian media.[21] There is nothing serious to substantiate the allegation.

The U.S. Government's handling of the crisis between Ethiopia and Eritrea has been naive but not ill-willed. Officials with little understanding of Ethiopia's history have tried to implement a "balanced" approach, being more concerned with achieving "peace" than doing justice. This approach duplicates the kid-gloved way American officials have first dealt — but in the end always unsuccessfully — with other brutal authoritarian leaders, such as Saddam Hussein and Slobodan Milosevic. If the Clinton Administration were not so preoccupied with other crises and frustrations in the world — Iraq, Kosovo, Chechnya, Haiti, China, Israeli - Syrian peace — the Horn of Africa might be propelled to a higher and more intense level of consideration in Washington where the issues could be seen more clearly by the President and the Secretary of State. That, unfortunately, has not happened.

What is to be done? Isaias Afewerki leads a country too weak to defy concerted international pressure, as his counterparts in Iraq and Serbia have done in recent years. A shift in approach by the United States to direct condemnation of the aggression which Eritrea has committed against Ethiopia, and in which it has persisted, to outright condemnation of Eritrea might well have brought the crisis to a quick end. Ordered to withdraw from occupied territories, Isaias, after an initial display of recalcitrance, would have had no alternative but to accept. The United States would have little difficulty gaining the support of most of its major allies for decisive action, securing UN concurrence (unless Russia or China chose to defend Eritrea which seems unlikely) and going so far as to threaten or impose sanctions for failure to comply.

Decisive action of this kind is the only way to forestall an eventual Ethiopian offensive against Eritrea. Ethiopia has the military strength and determination to succeed in repossessing all the territory it administered before May 1991. Public opinion would support military action. Ethiopia would face the tactical challenge of advancing into acknowledged Eritrean territory to destroy Eritrea's ability to retaliate and prolong hostilities. Initial Eritrean resistance would probably compel it to do so. Such advances would provoke cries of invasion from Eritrea. Isaias would claim that Ethiopia was trying to reconquer Eritrea.[22] There is no evidence that any significant body of opinion in Ethiopia favors conquest of Eritrea or re-amalgamation into Ethiopia. Meles Zenawi has repeatedly disavowed such intentions and expressed readiness to accept international supervision of equidistant segments of both sides of the border. Ethiopia relieved itself of a heavy political and economic burden by concurring in Eritrean independence in 1991-93.[23] There is no evidence that it wishes to assume it now.[24]

Would decisive Eritrean defeat lead to the demise of Isaias and the EPLF? Probably, though the process might take considerable time. Regimes led by dictators always look strong until they begin to collapse. Saddam Hussein and Milosevic have managed to survive heavy bombing. Nevertheless, internal cleavages in Eritrea which became evident in the 1941-1952 period and have never been completely overcome are again rising to the surface. Anti - EPLF exiles have become vocal in Europe and America and at least two groups in Eritrea, Kunamas and Afars, have announced opposition to the EPLF. Severe measures will no doubt be taken to contain them. Ethiopia has invested very little in encouraging Eritrean exiles and dissidents. They have nevertheless gained hope and momentum. Like Derg Ethiopia, however, Isaias Afewerki's authoritarian regime in Eritrea is more likely to fall to internal opposition than to exile action; it is likely to prove brittle, as Mengistu's regime turned out to be. Those who are going to suffer most are the Eritrean people, who have already endured appalling hardship and confusion during the past half century.

What will Ethiopia gain from resolution of the crisis?
It will be able to return fully to the path of emphasizing constructive economic and political development from which the Eritrean invasion has only partially caused it to deviate. Almost all of Ethiopia's basic economic indicators are promising. The government is committed to serious social and political development. Good leadership should be able to take advantage of the sense of national unity and purpose which the Eritrean invasion has generated to give its programs increased emphasis and greater resources. Ethiopia enjoys high standing in the world and is well regarded by all its neighbors in the Horn of Africa and across the Red Sea. It is feared by none. Eritrea's behavior leaves it an outcast in the region. Sadly, Isaias Afewerki has doomed Eritrea to be an international basket case for years to come. He would serve the Eritrean people best by acknowledging his misjudgments and stepping aside.

Washington, D.C.
18 January 2000

II - Does Isaias Have an Exit Strategy?

Mystery: On 16 January 1992 in the course of a wide-ranging conversation in his office in Asmara Isaias Afewerki said to me:

We have to avoid being influenced by the politics of this region. There is nothing positive in the region for us. Every country around us has mismanaged its politics. We don't want to take sides in their domestic or regional quarrels. We do want to help settle them when we can. But we will not get entangled in any of our neighbors' maneuvers against each other. We are a civilized people. We want to have a reputation for high quality in our thinking. We want to strike out on a responsible course and be an influence for economic and political good sense in the region. [25]

One can only applaud such views and intentions, as I did then. These were statesmanlike judgments. They gave hope of a bright future for independent Eritrea, though at that time it was not yet officially independent. Somehow after full independence was achieved, Isaias lost his sense of statesmanship. He quarreled with Sudan, broke relations and closed the border. He fell into a rancorous confrontation with Yemen over the barren Hanish Islands, deploying military forces and coming close to war. He threatened Djibouti. Finally, in May 1998 he sent his armies into border regions that had long been administered by Ethiopia. Such behavior was in total contradiction to the principles he stated in 1992. Why did he raise every issue with neighbors to the level of a military confrontation? What did he assume when he attacked Ethiopia?

We cannot read his mind. He has not explained his intentions. We can only guess them from what followed. He seems to have assumed that Ethiopia would not react. If it did, he thought it was weak and could not push back Eritrean forces. He considered the EPRDF government shaky and believed it could be brought to the point of collapse.

These assumptions were illusions. Ethiopia reacted strongly but it refrained from mounting a counter-offensive for the better part of a year while it prepared carefully. Isaias had plenty of time to shed his illusions and recognize reality. But even after defeat at Badme in February 1999, he failed to do so. Now, almost two years after the initial attack, he has wasted thousands of young Eritreans' lives. He is wasting the money Eritreans in the diaspora send home. He has brought the Eritrean economy close to collapse. He has caused Eritrea far more damage than he has done to Ethiopia.

Eritrea's War has already had two irreversible negative results for Isaias:

- Far from being weakened, Ethiopia's national unity has been reinforced. The domestic political scene is more constructive and the country is more unified than it has been for decades. The EPRDF is preparing for parliamentary elections with the participation of numerous political parties, many of which formerly refused to participate in the political process. All ethnic groups in Ethiopia have supported resistance to Eritrean aggression. Eritrea's attempts to stir up trouble from Somalia through Oromo dissidents have failed.

- Anti-EPLF groups have been energized. The rigid unity that Isaias tried to enforce upon the Eritrean population has been shattered. Police and security forces roam the streets of Asmara looking for deserters and people reluctant to serve in Isaias' army. Children and old men are forced into military service. Soldiers who escape abroad often join ELF organizations. Eritreans opposed to the authoritarian EPLF are gaining strength and will continue to grow stronger.

These are only the most basic of the adverse consequences Isaias has brought on Eritrea. No matter how the confrontation ends, Eritrea will suffer much other long-term damage. Its economy has lost momentum; Eritrea has little appeal for serious foreign investors. The Eritrean diaspora is slowing its flow of money. The EPLF is threatening reprisals against citizens whose relatives are not sending remittances. Human rights violations in Eritrea are multiplying.

The very developments Isaias feared most are beginning to occur: ethnic and religious harmony has been disrupted. Afars, always lukewarm about EPLF rule, are resisting. Muslims are increasingly skeptical of the EPLF's intentions toward them. The hurried reconciliation with Sudan will not reassure them, for Eritreans who have been living there are reluctant to return to be forced into military service. Eritrean Catholics find their relations with Catholic brethren on the Ethiopian side of the border needlessly strained. All these trends will accelerate the longer the confrontation lasts.

But illusions persist! Isaias continues to prevaricate and maneuver to avoid committing Eritrea to honest observance of a cease-fire and mediation provisions he pretends he has accepted. He tries to pretend a desire for a cease-fire, but wants it only to be able to sit firmly on Ethiopian territory he has seized. Eritrean propaganda falls deeper and deeper into unrealism. Consider this summary of wishful thinking that appears in a recent article in the official Eritrean press:

> The TPLF regime is scared of making peace, because it cannot survive one. With peace comes accountability: taking responsibility for past actions,

policies, and practices. The regime which represents a mere six percent of the Ethiopian population has to stand before the other ninety four percent to defend why it allowed a containable minor border dispute to explode into a murderous and ultimately senseless war. This staying on the warpath is a self-preservation strategy even if that means disastrous consequences for Ethiopia, Eritrea, and the region. [26]

The article from which the excerpt above is taken argues at length for international sanctions against Ethiopia as a war-monger! Its author, Tekie Fessehatzion, has deluded himself into believing that Ethiopia is near economic collapse, kept alive only by the generosity of international donors. Obscuring the fact that it was Eritrea who attacked, while Ethiopia waited almost a year before mounting a counter-offensive, he and Eritrea's other deluded propagandists cry that Ethiopia, the victim, threatens Eritrea the aggressor, with invasion. They live in a world of fantasy.

Self-deception is a dangerous political disease. Isaias Afewerki is suffering from an extreme case of this affliction. Is it possible that an intelligent man, a man capable of the good sense that he expressed to me in January 1992, can be giving no thought to the problem of extricating himself from the predicament which he brought stet himself?

Ethiopia's exit strategy is simple and straightforward and has remained unchanged: when Eritrea stops military action and withdraws from Ethiopian-administered territories it occupies, Ethiopia will agree to international supervision of the border and accept mediation of border claims.

Eritrea gives no evidence of having an exit strategy.

While shouting about peace, its actions are directed toward prolonging the war and its propagandists are bent on deceiving the world about the situation. It recalls a saying of the ancient Greeks:

Those whom the Gods would destroy, they first make mad.

Washington, D.C.	Addis Ababa
18 February 2000	8 May 2000

III - The Denouement - Eritrean Defeat

Eritrean Intransigence: Isaias attempted to forge closer links with radical Arabs, including Libya, and traditional Arabs such as Egypt and Gulf states. He attempted to move toward reconciliation with Sudan. By these maneuvers, Ethiopians claim, he gained donations of money, arms and ammunition. Meanwhile he had his armies dig a vast network of trenches to secure their advances into Ethiopia. He had the trenches reinforced with concrete and assured his soldiers the Ethiopians could never dislodge them.

Eritrea had no regular sustainable source of revenue after the break with Ethiopia. One of Isaias' highest priorities was to keep money flowing in from the Eritrean diaspora in the Middle East, Europe and America. Eritrea is reliably reported to have been using veiled - and sometimes direct- threats against relatives at home to get Eritreans abroad to keep sending contributions. On his last trip to the United States in April 2000, Isaias had his embassy arrange a series of speeches at such prestigious locations as the National

Press Club in Washington and Princeton University. His propagandists also arranged for him to tell his story to the Africa Subcommittee of the U.S. House of Representatives. Here Chairman Benjamin Gillman did him the signal honor of comparing him to George Washington!

What was Isaias' purpose in all this? To convince his diaspora that Eritrea enjoyed American backing so that they would keep contributing money, no doubt. But also to remind American officials that since he was intransigent, the only way the confrontation could be solved would be to bring pressure on Ethiopia. Madeleine Albright appears to have been aware of this when she received Isaias at the end of his visit and pressed him to agree to go to Algiers once again and negotiate seriously to end the confrontation.

To maintain the illusion of American backing, Isaias had to accept Madeleine Albright's insistence on another try in Algiers. But he apparently calculated that he could capitalize on the Clinton Administration's desire to gain credit for brokering peace in another troubled part of the world by manipulating the situation to keep pressure on Ethiopia: Eritrea would not give an inch, devising pretexts to avoid entering into serious discussions. So a final futile six-day round of "proximity" talks in Algiers in early May again brought only stalemate. Washington panicked and declared a crisis. The crisis required a big gun: UN Ambassador Richard Holbrooke was sent to the Horn with a seven man delegation to force peace on Ethiopia and Eritrea.

Richard Holbrooke's Intervention: Holbrooke came into the situation in early May with little understanding of the nature of Isaias Afewerki's police state, the mentality of the Ethiopian leadership or the strong traditional attitudes of the Ethiopian population. Even if he had had the inclination to learn, time was too short. Shuttling between Addis Ababa and Asmara in the second week of May, he developed no arguments that could produce a resolution of the crisis. Never having developed an exit strategy and with his back against a wall, Isaias clung to the tactic of demanding a cease-fire in place to maintain his hold on Ethiopian territory. Meles Zenawi refused to abandon the straightforward position Ethiopia took when Eritrea invaded: once Eritrea withdrew from occupied territory Ethiopia would immediately agree to international supervision of the border and mediation of claims stemming from the colonial era.

Holbrooke fell victim to Isaias' guile and concentrated on trying to persuade Ethiopia to make face-saving concessions to Eritrea. Frustrated, Holbrooke resorted to bluster. It did not overawe Meles.[27] He realized the futility of continuing to depend on mediators who persisted in treating the aggressor and the victim as equals. He and his associates concluded that two years of effort to reach an accommodation with the Eritreans was enough. The threat of famine in Ethiopia's Somali region and failure of *belg* (spring) rains in north-central Ethiopia intensified the determination of Ethiopian leaders to get the confrontation with Eritrea behind them so that the country could give priority to economic development. Meles knew that the Eritreans would exploit any ambiguity about a peace arrangement to prolong the confrontation. He also knew that Ethiopia's Defence Forces were well prepared to move.

Ethiopian Military Preparations: Ethiopian Chief of Staff Tsadkan Gebre Tensae has stated that Ethiopia had fewer men under arms when Eritrea attacked in May 1998 than Eritrea. It had no significant forces along its northern border.[28] While Ethiopia had reduced its defense budget in favor of emphasis on expansion of infrastructure, education and health, Eritrea, in contrast, allocated a major share of its budget to "defense" and concentrated on developing its military forces based on conscription of all young people. Both countries fell heir to large amounts of arms and equipment from Soviet supplies to the Derg. With the exception of air power, Eritrea was proportionately better situated in terms of immediately usable arms than Ethiopia. However, the most important difference between the Eritrean and the Ethiopian military establishments lay not in equipment or manpower, but in application of doctrine and strategy.

The guerrilla army of the TPLF/EPRDF had not rested on its laurels after it overwhelmed the Derg in 1991. Its young leaders became diligent students of classic military doctrine and strategy, taking advantage of every opportunity to learn the strategic and tactical lessons of World War II, the Korean War and the Gulf War: mobility, surprise, deception, with stress on individual soldiers' initiative and self-reliance. They were admirers of the most successful American, European and Israeli experiences. They took advantage of conferences and training opportunities abroad. Their guerrilla experience had taught them the value of close relations between leaders and fighters, the importance of communication upward during operations and the value of good field intelligence. They realized that the defence forces of a large country cannot operate successfully on guerrilla principles.

The Eritreans, on the other hand, continued to organize their army according to classic Marxist principles with all orders given from the top downward. Boastful of defeating the Derg, the Eritreans became smug. They failed to make the transition from guerrilla tactics to mobile warfare. Instead they fell back on World War I notions. They dug trenches and felt secure sitting in them.

The Ethiopian Offensive: The Holbrooke delegation returned to New York on 11 May. Ethiopia unleashed its offensive against Eritrea the next day. The Eritreans were taken by surprise. They had assumed, and the Ethiopians had taken steps to lead them to believe, that if Ethiopia attacked it would be on the Central Front with the town of Zalambessa as the initial target. Isaias had concentrated 60 percent of his forces and equipment in this area behind elaborately reinforced trenches. Eritrean positions in the west were also protected by trenches. Repeating tactics that had been successful during "Operation Sunset" at Badme in 1999, Ethiopia struck first on the Western Front, sending armored spearheads through at pre-chosen points and surrounding eight Eritrean divisions in their trenches from the rear. Ethiopian forces then advanced rapidly deep into the western Eritrean lowlands. Isaias rushed troops he had been holding on the Central Front as reinforcements. By evacuating the mountainous Alitena-Aiga area to the east of Zalambessa he spared Ethiopia the necessity of fighting a major campaign to regain it. The hard-pressed Irob region was liberated. The Eritreans were plunged into so much disarray by the rapidity of the Ethiopian advance that they were never able to regroup in the west. Ethiopia captured the important town of Barentu on 18 May, advanced toward Agordat but stopped short of it to avoid over-extension, though the Eritreans evacuated it. The Ethiopian army then veered west and captured the important towns of Tessenei and Om Hager near the Sudan border. Thousands of Eritrean troops surrendered as prisoners. Other thousands fled into Sudan where they were disarmed and interned. The huge Eritrean military training center at Sawa, Isaias' pride, was first bombed and then overrun and destroyed.

UN and U.S. Actions: At news of the Ethiopian

offensive the UN Security Council convened to condemn the fighting and demand immediate cessation of hostilities, calling for return to the peace process sponsored by the Organization of African Unity (OAU) under the chairmanship of Algerian President Bouteflika. During the following days the U.S. and Great Britain proposed sanctions against Ethiopia, including the unusual provision of a prohibition of movement by Ethiopian diplomats. Africans were opposed to a measure so drastic. So were France and Russia. The proposal never came to a vote. Neither did a scheme to forbid Eritrean fund-raising in the United States while forbidding Ethiopian Airlines to land in Newark and Washington. Instead, on 15 May the Security Council approved a one-year arms embargo on both countries. A futile gesture, it had no effect on the fighting. The UNSC's actions unleashed a storm of protest among the Ethiopian public. On 15 May more than two hundred thousand people gathered in Maskal Square in Addis Ababa to condemn the American and British proposals. Large groups then marched to both countries' embassies, where stones were thrown and windows broken. Demonstrators had to be chased away by police. During the following days the Ethiopian press praised Russia for blocking punitive measures proposed by the U.S. and UK.

National Elections: National elections for members of parliament and regional councils were held in Ethiopia as previously scheduled on Sunday, 14 May, in all parts of the country except the drought-stricken Somali State. A total of 984 candidates representing forty-nine political parties competed for seats in parliament and 2,156 for seats in regional councils.[29] Over twenty million registered voters cast ballots for government – and opposition-party candidates. Voting was observed by a wide variety of local and international NGOs. With a few exceptions in the southwestern state,[30] it was completely peaceful. The fact that general elections could be held on the very weekend when the Ethiopian offensive against Eritrea was launched is evidence of the confidence of Ethiopia's leaders and a measure of the extent to which the population was united in support of action against Eritrea.

Continued Ethiopian Advances: On the Central Front, Zalambessa was occupied on 24 May and troops moved on toward Senafe and Adi Keyih, eighty kilometers south of Asmara. Meanwhile forces from the west had approached Adi Quala and Mandefera on a more western highway to the Eritrean capital. At a briefing of the Addis Ababa diplomatic corps on 22 May, Meles Zenawi expressed regret that military action had become necessary: "Our aim was to give the Eritrean Army an opportunity to withdraw from our territory by threatening their territory;" and added: "Whichever road leads to peace quickly, that will be the road that we follow." He again disavowed any designs on Eritrean territory. He concluded by denouncing the UN Security Council's approach to the crisis and recalled "the infamous decision of the League of Nations in 1936... an act where the rule of law is sacrificed at the foot of expediency." The next day the *Ethiopian Herald* featured a front-page photograph of Haile Selassie delivering his famous speech before the League of Nations in Geneva in 1936 and many private newspapers recalled European powers' acquiescence in the Italian conquest.

The War is Over: On 29 May Ethiopian Chief of Staff Lt. General Tsadkan Gebre Tinsae held a press conference at which he declared the war all but over with Eritrean forces soundly defeated, most Ethiopian territory regained, and tens of thousands of prisoners and large amounts of military material captured. He reviewed the preparations the

Ethiopian Defence Forces had made for their offensive and the reasons for their success in comparison to the performance of the Eritreans. On 31 May Meles Zenawi announced that as far as Ethiopia was concerned, the war was over as of that date: "Now that the invading army is no more in our territory we are willing to agree to a quick cessation of hostilities. We are willing to have... face-to-face talks... We are ready to redeploy to 6 May 1998 positions as soon as we have a cease-fire agreement."

Eritrean Prevarication: Ethiopia called for peace talks under OAU auspices to resume immediately in Algiers. They opened again on 31 May with the participation of the American and European Union envoys, Anthony Lake and Italian Rino Serri. To demonstrate its commitment to settlement, Ethiopia slowed its advance northward from Senafe, reduced pressure on the Bure front near Assab and began withdrawing from outlying portions of Western Eritrea. Eritrea announced willingness to return to talks in Algiers but simultaneously claimed to be mounting offensives in western and southern Eritrea. Eritrean media reports proclaimed "Ethiopian Defeat in Tessenei", "Eritrean Defense Forces Rebuffing Ethiopian Offensive on Assab Front" and claimed that Ethiopia was deliberately targeting Eritrean civilians, an allegation Ethiopia rejected. It is difficult to determine the extent to which Eritrean forces were actually attacking, though Isaias' ordering of them to do so demonstrates a willingness to sacrifice still more young Eritreans in vain. His misrepresentation of the situation convinced Ethiopia to keep its forces in place until Eritrea committed itself to a genuine cease-fire and arrangements for international supervision of the border region.

Agreement Signed: Getting Eritrea to agree to Ethiopia's simple demands for cessation of military action was not easy. It took the Algerians, OAU representatives, and Lake and Serri two and a half weeks to craft an agreement. Having lived on illusions for two full years, Isaias Afewerki ultimately had to face reality and permit his Foreign Minister, Haile Wolde Tensae, to sign a cease-fire agreement on 18 June. Ethiopia committed itself to withdraw to the 6 May 1998 border as soon as UN peacekeepers were prepared to patrol a twenty-five kilometers strip of demilitarized territory on the Eritrean side. This provision constitutes clear recognition that Eritrea had been the original aggressor. Anthony Lake commented in an interview with the *New York Times* that the two armies are "highly disciplined" and that the leaders of both nations are committed to the agreement. [31]

Peace at Last?: Impoverished Eritrea emerges from the war it started as an international basket case. It is difficult to envision how it could resume anti-Ethiopian military action of any major kind. Loss of life must affect every family in a population of less than 3.5 million. Eritrean propaganda has probably exaggerated material losses resulting from the Ethiopian offensive but Eritrea incurred serious damage to its economy and infrastructure as result of giving priority to the war during the past two years. Can the country shift to concentrate on reconstruction and reconciliation with its populous, successful southern neighbor? Can Isaias Afewerki moderate his authoritarian stubbornness and permit a more open democratic society to develop? Can he risk apologizing to the Eritrean people for the damage he has brought upon them? Can he go back to his short-lived project of persuading Eritrean businessmen, technicians and traders to turn the country into the "Singapore" of the Horn of Africa?

He has a great deal of mendacious propaganda and rhetoric to live down. The 10 June edition of *Eritrea Profile,*

37

the government's official English-language organ, announces Eritrean acceptance of the OAU peace proposal, but at the same time is filled with fallacious accounts of what has actually been happening: "Ethiopian Defeat in Tessenei". "EDF Rebuffing Ethiopian Offensive on Assab Front", "Ethiopia Targeting Civilians", "Contributions for Defense Effort Keep Momentum", "The Blitzkrieg that Never Was", "Ethiopian Children Forced into Battle." Thus the extraordinarily vicious propaganda of the past two years continues. Its primary purpose, it seems, is to mislead the Eritrean population. Are Isaias' controls strong enough to force them to believe it?

Retrospect: The original puzzle remains: What set of calculations led Isaias to attack Ethiopia in the first place? How could the man have been so irrational? How could it be to Eritrea's advantage to foment chaos in Ethiopia? Historical and cultural ties between Eritrea and Ethiopia are deep. Eritrea's ports have little purpose if they do not serve Ethiopia. The EPRDF government in Ethiopia took the risk of being criticized for permitting Eritrea to enjoy economic advantages and allowing Eritrean businessmen and professionals working in Ethiopia to send profits to Asmara. All these advantages were squandered by Eritrea's invasion. Ethiopia's leaders are not likely to be so generous again soon. Most of the military supplies and equipment paid for by the contributions of Eritreans abroad are expended or now in Ethiopian hands.

Ethiopia is bound to have cool relations with Eritrea as long as Isaias Afewerki maintains his authoritarian rule. Ethiopia has been so successful in shifting its trade through Djibouti and Berbera that it has no need of Eritrea's ports. Nor, regrettable as it may be for the individuals affected, does it need Eritrean businessmen and professionals, for the steady flow of returnees among Ethiopians who fled from the communist regime is providing Ethiopia with entrepreneurs and experienced specialists of all kinds. Whatever physical damage Ethiopia's offensive may have inflicted on Eritrea is outweighed by the damage Eritrea did in the border regions it occupied. Harm to Eritrean civilians can hardly be greater than two years of hardship inflicted on four hundred thousand persons displaced in Ethiopian border regions.

The hard-pressed Eritrean people deserve better than they have got from the leadership of Isaias Afewerki and his retinue. For the immediate future they will, in effect, become wards of the international community. There is no other way to keep them alive. They deserve to enjoy the benefits of a an open democratic society led by men of their own choice who place their people's welfare above an overwhelming preoccupation with personal power. If Eritrea had political parties, open elections and a private press, it is difficult to see how Isaias Afewerki could have made the miscalculations which have brought disaster on the country.

Were the policies and actions of the UN, the U.S. and the OAU successful in achieving a solution of Eritrea's war against Ethiopia? Consideration of these questions will be the subject of the fourth essay in this series.

Washington, D.C.
24 June 2000

IV - The American Role

The Result of U.S. Government Involvement was Counter-productive: When Eritrean military forces suddenly moved into Ethiopia's northern border regions in the first part of May 1998 and Ethiopia reacted strongly, the U.S. Government was taken by surprise. At the start of this crisis, most American officials seemed to understand the basic fact that Eritrea was committing aggression and Ethiopia was the victim of aggression.[32] Eritrea claimed the problem was conflicting border claims without explaining why debate about borders stemming from the colonial era justified precipitate military action, confiscation of Ethiopian goods in Eritrean ports, and punitive measures against Ethiopian citizens living and working in Eritrea. Nevertheless early efforts at mitigating the crisis and devising a mediation process, in which the U.S. took the lead, soon led U.S. officials into a pattern of treating both countries as if equally at fault. [33]

Eritrea as an Obstacle to Islamic Fundamentalism? The process that got under way calls to mind an earlier example of failed American diplomacy: the long years of bickering and indulging Saddam Hussein because he was an enemy of an American enemy, Iran. A few military men in Washington argued that Eritrea despite its small size and population was more valuable to America than Ethiopia because it had a long coast and possessed an outstanding fighting force. Others contended that its hostility to the anti-American regime in Khartoum made it a bulwark against the spread of Islamic fundamentalism from Sudan and a force for stability in the region. Punishing it for aggression against Ethiopia, the argument went, would be contrary to American interests. The argument that Eritrea was a force for stability in the region was negated by Eritrea's record of confrontations with all its neighbors during the previous four years.

The Case for Firm Action: Well-meaning, patient efforts

by American emissaries Susan Rice and Anthony Lake, supported by UN, OAU and EU officialdom, resulted in two years of shuttling between Asmara, Addis Ababa and Algiers that accomplished nothing. Tough talk to Isaias Afewerki in May and June 1998 and, if necessary, serious sanctions against Eritrea as an aggressor, would probably have ended the confrontation in a few weeks by forcing Eritrean withdrawal. Active military intervention would not have been needed. Tens of thousands of young Eritrean and Ethiopian lives, much human suffering and vast amounts of material damage would have been spared. If, as a result, Isaias Afewerki's dictatorship had collapsed, the Eritrean people, who have never had a chance to express themselves on their fate since the late 1940s, would have been the beneficiaries. There is no reason to believe that firm action against Eritrea would have destabilized the Red Sea region. Eritrea demonstrated repeatedly after 1994 that it was the most serious destabilizing element in the region.

U.S. Government Ineptness: American response to the war with Eritrea entailed a tragic combination of diplomatic naivete and poor judgment of where American national interests lie. In the process, the Clinton Administration ignored the key principles to which it claims to give priority in the conduct of international affairs: promotion of democracy, open society and human rights; free flow of information; and encouragement of collective security and firm action against aggression. Overlooking Eritrea's behavior had no effect on moderating it. On the contrary, Isaias' main motivation was consolidation of his hold over Eritrea by the familiar tactic of generating a quarrel with a neighbor. He developed no exit strategy from the confrontation he provoked. American negotiators' gentleness encouraged him in mindless intransigence. After all the futile palaver,

Ethiopia's well organized, decisive military action brought the confrontation to an end. President Clinton may think himself sincere in claiming that his Administration has brought peace between Eritrea and Ethiopia, but the claim is specious.

No Knowledge of History: Reporting by American and international media on the crisis was shallow and became shallower as Eritrea continued to occupy Ethiopian territory and avoid a commitment to mediation while pouring out deceptive propaganda.[34] American negotiators trying to mediate often seemed as limited in their understanding of recent history as the amateurish journalists who intermittently reported on the confrontation. None of these people made the effort to understand the mentality of the protagonists or current realities in the region.

The history of the Horn of Africa is, indeed, complex, but hardly unknowable. It is relevant. Politically and culturally Eritrea has been part of Ethiopia for as far back as history extends. Sliced off by Italy at the end of the nineteenth century it was an Italian colony for fifty years. Italy never envisioned self-government or independence — it regarded Eritrea as a base for conquering the rest of Ethiopia. Mussolini's conquest was short-lived. When British Common wealth forces overwhelmed Italian East Africa in June 1941, Eritrea became "occupied enemy territory" and after Pearl Harbor the U.S. set up bases there to support campaigns in the Middle East and man the Lend-Lease lifeline to Russia. The British were lenient administrators who gave Eritreans more freedom than they ever enjoyed before or since. Americans left a legacy of goodwill in Eritrea which is still occasionally encountered among older inhabitants today.

The U.S. and Eritrea: The U.S. took the lead in the

sequence of international decisions by which Eritrea, under UN auspices, was federated with Ethiopia in 1952. At a time when east-west tensions had led to the division of other important countries – Germany and Korea for example –it was a logical arrangement.[35] On balance, the people of Eritrea benefitted from it, though Haile Selassie was not as wise in dealing with Eritrea as he might have been. Military and diplomatic communications facilities in Eritrea served American strategic interests until the 1970s when satellites made them redundant.

The U.S. sharply condemned the brutal manner in which the Derg, with the support of the Soviet Union, kept trying to subjugate Eritrea after 1974, but in principle continued to support Ethiopia's territorial integrity until 1991. Marxism poisoned the whole area. Somalia's Marxist dictator attacked Mengistu's Marxist Ethiopia in 1977. Marxist Ethiopia had to be rescued by the Soviets and Cubans. Through the 1980s the Marxist Derg fought Marxist insurgents in Eritrea and other parts of the country. Everybody suffered. As communism in Eastern Europe and the Soviet Union withered, Isaias Afewerki finally moderated his Marxist rhetoric and sought Western support for Eritrean independence.

The End of the Derg: The U.S. had no leverage on the momentous developments in the Horn of Africa in 1990-91 except the skill of three of its diplomats who played a key role in the smooth transitions that took place in Asmara and Addis Ababa as Derg armies collapsed.[36] American diplomatic skill during this period contrasts sharply with that of the past two years. American diplomats facilitated Mengistu Haile Mariam's abdication, established constructive relations with the TPLF/EPRDF, and convinced Isaias that it would not be in Eritrea's interest to declare unilateral independence. He was persuaded to let the UN lead Eritrea to separation from Ethiopia by an orderly legal process which culminated in the referendum held in April 1993. The new government in Addis Ababa was relieved at not having to take responsibility for Eritrea. The 1993 referendum offered only a yes-or-no choice to Eritreans. It did not measure gradations of preference. But it generated enthusiasm and hope for a secure future among the Eritrean population. Like the U.S., most of the international community quickly recognized Isaias as president of the new independent country and expected he would have the good sense to lead Eritrea toward democracy, an open society and constructive participation in the affairs of the region. No one but Isaias can be blamed for the fact that things turned out otherwise.

Eritrean Belligerence: For a year and a half everything seemed to be going well. The EPRDF government in Addis Ababa led by Meles Zenawi bent over backward to help Eritrea consolidate its independence and achieve economic viability. Eritrea had a tendency to exploit Ethiopian goodwill, but frictions with Ethiopia developed slowly. Isaias turned first in other directions. In 1994 he accused Sudan of subverting Eritrean Muslims and soon broke relations, though Sudan had helped Eritrea in the fight against the Derg and was the first country to establish an embassy in Asmara on independence. Isaias eventually went so far as to turn this embassy over to Sudanese rebel groups. In late 1995 he suddenly sent Eritrean troops to occupy the Hanish islands off the coast of Yemen, up to this time also a friendly government. The crisis disturbed the region for more than a year and led to disruption of Eritrean relations with Djibouti. Isaias accused the little republic of sympathizing with Yemen and sent troops to occupy a swath of its territory.

44

Contrasting Courses: Meanwhile leaders in Ethiopia and Eritrea followed completely different domestic courses:

In Eritrea Isaias Afewerki continued the tight authoritarian control of guerrilla times. Isaias authorized only a tightly controlled official press and no independent political activity. In the mid-1990s he expelled almost all NGOs operating in Eritrea.[37] He eliminated Eritrea's historic sub-provinces and replaced them with centrally controlled geographic districts designed to divide ethnic and religious groups.

In Ethiopia Meles Zenawi headed a more collegial government. During its first month in Addis Ababa the EPRDF invited exiles from abroad as well as a wide variety of anti-Derg opposition groups to participate in creating a Transitional Government. It came into being six weeks after guerilla armies entered the capital. By the end of 1991 more than a hundred independent newspapers and magazines were on sale on the streets of the capital. Ethiopia returned to its traditional policy of favoring collective security. It supported regional organizations, and assisted the U.S. and the UN in attempting reconciliation in Somalia and Sudan. Several hundred thousand Eritrean citizens continued to work and live in Ethiopia. Thousands of Eritrean businessmen and professionals enjoyed conditions identical to those of Ethiopians.

Strains between the two Countries developed but they led to no major crises. Border problems were the least significant and were dealt with by local officials. Ethiopian traders complained that their government was too permissive of Eritreans who re-exported Ethiopian produce at a profit and provided financial support for Asmara. Isaias' continued high outlays for his military forces contrasted with Ethiopia's drastic cuts in military expenditures.

The U.S. had Good Information: All this and more was well known to the American embassies in Asmara and Addis Ababa, to USAID, Peace Corps volunteers, World Bank, IMF and EU missions, and to a myriad of U.S. and foreign NGOs. After the end of the Somali misadventure in 1993 the international press lost interest in the Horn of Africa and did little reporting. Ethiopia, however, was increasingly open to tourists, businessmen and scholars; Eritrea was more restrictive of foreigners. Reporting by both American embassies was voluminous.[38] Of course, as personnel rotated, competence varied. Nevertheless the State Department and other agencies of the U.S. Government, including the Pentagon, were well informed. There was an enormous body of professional knowledge of the region to be drawn on from the large American Ethiopianist community of scholars and specialists.

Which Country Mattered Most? By any standard that could be applied, Ethiopia was (and is) more important to the United States than Eritrea:

Ethiopia has over 60 million people compared to barely 3.5 million in Eritrea. It has enormous economic potential. Its government has encouraged evolution toward an open economy and an open society with increasingly lively political life, a steadily improving private press, and an expanding educational system. Ethiopia is a country proud of its tradition of responsible service in international crisis areas (most recently, example, in Rwanda), with no historical record of aggressive expansionism; a country with little stress on military matters as such and content with a small, professional army under civilian leadership.

Eritrea, in contrast, is a one-party police state under the control of a single man leading a single party. It has a tightly controlled economy and enforces political uniformity. Isaias permits no independent activity by religious or ethnic groups and no political parties. Eritrea has only a rigidly controlled government press. Military training is compulsory for young people of both sexes. It has established a record of strained relations with all neighboring countries.

The annual State Department human rights reports, though somewhat tempered to avoid too harsh criticism of Eritrea, confirm these contrasts. Nevertheless, it is obvious which country measures up best to American principles.

Puzzle: How, in the face of these facts and all the experience and information that was available to it, did the U.S. Government ignore its principles and fall into the position of apparently favoring Eritrea over Ethiopia? How could it let Isaias Afewerki manipulate matters to the point where he was permitted to create the impression in the mind of a leading American Congressman that Ethiopia was the obstacle to peace and himself a statesman comparable to George Washington?

A partial answer seems to be that preoccupation with other priorities among senior officials in Washington, not the least Secretary of State Madeleine Albright and National Security Advisor Samuel Berger, resulted in a situation where they let the task of dealing with Eritrea's War fall into the laps of weak subordinates who were so preoccupied with achieving "peace" that this singular notion took priority over everything else. Anthony Lake's patience and good will brought no dividends. When Richard Holbrooke was brought onto the scene, he found himself treating Ethiopia, rather than Eritrea, as the impediment to peace. He left Ethiopia, heir to a proud civilization everyone should have taken the effort to understand better, no alternative but to go to war. Holbrooke hastened the Ethiopian decision to employ the "military option". Why, asked Ethiopians, should their country accommodate to aggression any more than Margaret Thatcher did when Argentina tried to occupy the Falklands? Should the oldest independent nation in Africa be expected to respond more gently to an aggressor than Great Britain?

Eritrea's Future: Nothing said above is meant to imply that the Eritrean people should be treated harshly or blamed for the disaster into which Isaias Afewerki has led them. It is Isaias who should be held to account. Like all erstwhile oppressed peoples, Eritreans may even deserve some degree of "political affirmative action" to help them consolidate independence and develop in freedom. This kind of consideration was undoubtedly in the minds of some of the Americans who tried to effect a solution of the confrontation Eritrea provoked. But the indulgence was misplaced. It was applied to the benefit of a leader whose guerrilla organization imposed itself on a multi-ethnic and religiously varied population and numbed it into acceptance of the notion that Eritreans are not entitled to determine their own fate. It is a measure of Ethiopia's realism that so few voices there have called for retention of portions of Eritrean territory, let alone reabsorption of Eritrea in its entirety. Defeated, bankrupt Eritrea is now so unattractive that no intelligent Ethiopian should want to have it back.

It is to be hoped, nevertheless, when the Eritrean people liberate themselves from Isaias Afeworki and his EPLF/PFDJ, that the fact that they and the Ethiopian people spring from the same roots will bring both back into a mutually beneficial relationship.

The best way for the U.S. Government to begin to redeem its failure in the Horn of Africa is to resume looking at the area realistically and devise policy toward it in accordance with basic American principles and interests. Eritrean propaganda since it signed the cease-fire agreement in Algiers on 18 June continues to insist that its forces were not defeated. It continues to vilify Ethiopia. Eritrea's leaders remain in a condition of denial akin to what we see in Belgrade and Baghdad. As long as Isaias' illusions prevail, prospects for reconciliation between Ethiopia and Eritrea are poor. The United States will serve the interests of peace in this long beleaguered part of the world only if it begins to speak and act honestly.

Washington, D.C.
27 June 2000

V - Media Performance

Largest War in the World? When the Ethiopian offensive that led to the defeat of Eritrea began at the end of the second week of May 2000, journalists proclaimed it the largest war then taking place in the world. Perhaps it was at that moment. In view of the fact that the victorious Ethiopian offensive was merely the final phase of a war that Eritrea had started two years before, international reporting on it was less enlightening than on any other major international crisis in recent years. Journalists were eager to dramatize violence but made little effort to inform themselves or their readers and viewers of the factors involved in the confrontation or the historical background of the clash. Glib cliches about the two countries' history became conventional wisdom, repeated over and over again in news dispatches and editorial comment.

Eritrea set off the confrontation by moving its army into border regions under Ethiopian administration. It was a clear-cut case of aggression. Somehow this most basic fact came to be ignored in most reporting and comment.[39] So was the fact that Ethiopia was taken by surprise and had far fewer military forces in the north than Eritrea had on the other side of the border.[40] Nine months later, after Ethiopia had mobilized troops to push the Eritreans back, reporters, reflecting Eritrean propaganda, came increasingly to reflect the notion that Ethiopia had long been spoiling for a fight. The implication, reflected in editorials, was that this war was a continuation of the war that the Derg had waged against Eritrea. Therefore, both parties were labeled "foolish", but the implication was that Ethiopia was more so than Eritrea.[41] This served Eritrea's purposes, for up until this time Isaias Afewerki had stalled and blocked every attempt by the international community to get Eritrea to commit itself to the U.S./Rwandan or OAU mediation proposals. When in February 1999 Ethiopian forces mounted "Operation Sunset" and succeeded in ejecting the Eritreans from an important sector around Badme, Eritrea excused its defeat by claiming that its forces had been pushed back only because far more populous Ethiopia was willing to sacrifice waves of hastily assembled young men to overwhelm them.[42]

Eritrean Prevarication: Every effort by OAU and American and European officials concerned with the situation to get talks going during the year after the February 1999 victory at Badme was met by Eritrean prevarication and stalling. While Isaias Afewerki kept throwing his soldiers against Ethiopian positions in futile efforts to retake the territory the Ethiopians had recovered, his propagandists concentrated on elaborating favorite themes, alleging that Ethiopia:

- was squandering manpower by throwing "human waves" against Eritrean positions, and

- that Ethiopia had no desire for peace and was blocking the efforts of the international community to get a peace process under way.

Ethiopia an Obstacle to Peace? Over and over again journalists accepted these characterizations and repeated them. They continued to be repeated for the next year with little visible effort by reporters to determine whether these allegations were, in fact, true.[43] Eritrean success in spreading the notion that Ethiopia was the obstacle to peace reached its apogee when the Washington Post featured a column on its op-ed page on 3 January 2000 under the name of Congressman Benjamin Gilman, Chairman of the Africa Subcommittee of the U.S. House of Representatives, calling for pressure on Ethiopia, "Ethiopia Needs a Push Toward Peace".

The Myth of Eritrean Invincibility: Meanwhile Eritrea had expended a sizable portion of its limited resources building a network of trenches along the southern edge of the Ethiopian territory it occupied. Eritreans were concerned to maintain the reputation they had cultivated for years of being the best fighting force in Africa. From their fortified trenches they continued to probe into Ethiopia while denigrating Ethiopians' fighting ability. They found journalists ready to serve their purpose. Karl Vick in the *Washington Post* dispatch already cited above reported that Ethiopians were "sarcastically" berating Isaias as "The Mosquito" who plagues Ethiopia and characterized him as "'A God' to his People...an Enigmatic and Formidable Foe."[44]

Two historically fallacious themes became standard cliches in reporting on the conflict:

- Since Eritrea had fought a thirty-year war against Ethiopian domination, it was understandably hostile to everything Ethiopian.

- Guerrilla movements that were "brothers in arms" in the long struggle against Mengistu's Derg had fallen into a senseless fratricidal conflict.

It is difficult to find a dispatch on the conflict, or an editorial, which did not repeat, and often embroider, these misrepresentations of history. Few who repeated them seem to have realized that the two themes are contradictory. If a thirty-year struggle had resulted in widespread and visceral hatred of Ethiopia among Eritreans, how did it happen that Ethiopians and Eritrean guerrillas became "brothers in arms"? There is a rich and fascinating history here to be examined but the effort appears to have been beyond the capacity of most reporters and editorial writers. Tens of thousands of Eritreans and Ethiopians who were participants in this history were accessible for reporters to talk to. Few bothered to talk to them. There are good written sources available.[45] During most of the two-year period of the confrontation a highly informative little paperback was on sale in most of the bookshops and hotel stands in Addis Ababa: Medhanie Tadesse, *The Eritrean-Ethiopian War: Retrospect and Prospects* (Mega, Addis Ababa, 1999). It contains a wealth of information on the history of northern Ethiopia and on longstanding strains between Eritreans and Tigrayans and the often rocky relationship between the two guerrilla movements. Few journalists seem to have bought it, or if they did, to have read it. If they had dipped into this and other books cited above they would have learned that:

"Eritrea's Thirty-year Struggle" is a grossly distorted representation of reality. A clash between a group of Muslims in western Eritrea and a small Ethiopian military force in September 1961 is celebrated in EPLF mythology as the beginning of the war. It attracted little attention at the time and had no consequences except that the group declared itself part of the Eritrean Liberation Movement (later renamed Front (ELF)) formed by the Sudanese Communist Party in 1958 in Port Sudan and attracted attention from Cairo and Damascus.[46] For the better part of the next twenty years small guerrilla factions in Eritrea, supported variously by Arabs and communists (including various Soviet proxies, Cubans and Chinese), expended most of their energy fighting each other. It was only after Isaias Afewerki's EPLF emerged dominant in the early 1980s as a result of applying classic Marxist-Leninist organizational methods he and others learned in China and Cuba that a relatively unified Eritrean struggle against the Derg began. The fight with the Derg was for a long time a seesaw affair. Derg brutality eventually left the Eritrean population no choice but to side with the EPLF, but pro-

ELF as well some residual pro-Ethiopian sentiment has continued among Eritreans. Ethiopians and Eritreans share languages, religions, culture and thousands of years of history.

While Tigrayans and highland Eritreans are ethnically identical, speaking the same language (Tigrinya), the two guerrilla movements were only intermittently "Brothers in Arms" during the decade and half of the fight against the Derg. The reasons lie deep, as Medhanie Tadesse's book cited above, demonstrates. While many Tigrayans migrated to Eritrea to seek employment when it was an Italian colony and during the post-war period of British military administration, Eritreans came to consider themselves more sophisticated than Tigrayans and looked down on them as "country cousins". Such attitudes sometimes surfaced in strains among Tigrayan and Eritrean university students in Addis Ababa and other parts of Ethiopia in the late-imperial period. When the Tigrayan guerrillas-consisting almost entirely of former students - got their movement under way in 1976-77, relations with Eritrean guerrillas were mixed. There was cooperation, but there were also resentments and disagreements. The two movements developed in quite different directions. During the mid-1980s tensions developed into an open break between the EPLF and the TPLF and clashes occurred between them. Cooperation between the two was not resumed until 1988-89 when the Derg was on the verge of defeat. [47]

To those interested in political processes the history of these two movements and relations between them is a fascinating historical study. For reporters and commentators responsible for explaining events and anticipating outcomes such knowledge is essential to do a competent job. Since most writers on the crisis that extended from May 1998 through May 2000 neglected to learn much about its background, they were taken by surprise when Ethiopia administered a stunning defeat to the vaunted Eritrean forces. Thus the international journalistic fraternity deserves a failing grade for its performance. With occasional exceptions (example, Peter Biles of the BBC), TV and radio reporters displayed more shallowness and gullibility than most of the others. CNN and BBC World from Asmara served as mouthpieces of the Eritrean propaganda machine during the climax of the Ethiopian offensive at the end of May 2000. There was no comparable propaganda out of Addis Ababa because the Ethiopian government confined its information output to facts.

Shallow reporting resulted in misleading editorial comment, more often than not consisting of little more than hand-wringing over the alleged proclivity of African leaders to engage in senseless altercations while they let their people starve. It is surprising that two of the world's greatest newspapers, *The Wall Street Journal* and *The Economist,* fell victim to the shallow conventional "wisdom" about Eritrea's War that reporters purveyed. Normally these two papers deservedly pride themselves on their ability to report in depth and offer their readers solid background and carefully considered editorial judgments. In its 26 May editorial, "Africa's Lesson to History" *The Journal* at least conceded shortcomings on both sides while repeating fashionable mythology about a "thirty year war" and "friends and comrades in arms" falling out. On the other hand, *The Economist* claimed in a 3 June dispatch that the Eritreans still held "both the physical and moral high ground." Three weeks later *The Economist* bowed to reality and gave an honest assessment of the outcome of the war Eritrea forced on Ethiopia and concluded:

Will a leader defeated in battle hold on to his job? President Isaias Afewerki won the Eritreans' loyalty during the long struggle for independence. Moreover, no opposition is allowed and dissent is barely heard. Much will depend on whether Ethiopia can be magnanimous in victory. It may, but the triumphalist mood in Addis Ababa gives small sign that it will.

To this observer, the mood in Addis Ababa and throughout Ethiopia as the offensive against Eritrea came to an end seemed more one of relief than of triumph. Ethiopia's leaders did not agitate to concentrate their population's attention on the war. During the entire confrontation Ethiopia's leaders repeatedly announced that their first priority was to get on with the task of accelerating economic and social development. A good deal of development continued in Ethiopia during the confrontation-roads were built, factories opened, irrigation projects inaugurated and several new universities were established. Thus in spite of Eritrea's harassment Ethiopia continued to achieve progress in development of infrastructure, industry and education while Eritrea stagnated. National elections held the very weekend that the offensive against Eritrea got under way have been judged by foreign observers as a significant step toward consolidation of a genuine democratic political system.

Ethiopia's leaders have renounced any intention of retaining Eritrean territory and have accepted international demarcation of the border with a peace-keeping force patrolling a demilitarized strip to discourage future Eritrean provocations. As of this writing Eritrea's propaganda continues belligerent and mendacious, alleging Ethiopian atrocities and bad intentions. There has so far been not a glimmer of free expression in Eritrea while both the official and private press in Ethiopia engage in lively debate about the recent war, current developments, and future prospects. If Eritrean leaders continue their all too familiar tactic of stalling and prevarication during the internationally sponsored peace implementation talks that are now getting under way, prospects for rapid reconciliation seem poor. The choice is Eritrea's.

Washington, D.C.
6 July 2000

CHAPTER II

PRESS CONFERENCES, INTERVIEWS, AND LETTERS TO CONGRESSMEN AND NEWSPAPERS

The selected excerpts which follow are only a small portion of the statements I made during the course of the confrontation. I have included these because they sometimes contain facts and formulations that provide additional information not contained in the previous chapter. Press conferences and interviews I gave in Ethiopia during my extended visits there in 1999 and 2000 were invariably broadcast several times over radio and television in Ethiopian languages as well as English, and were published in full or in part in both government and independent newspapers.

My aim in speaking frankly on the confrontation was twofold. In the first place, I wanted to be honest in giving my judgment and applying my own knowledge of the history of the region and the mentality of current leaders. Secondly, I also aimed to counter the negative impression of American attitudes and resentment of American actions that spread among the Ethiopian public by demonstrating that an American with long experience of Ethiopia and knowledge of its history understood Ethiopian mentality and the reasons for Ethiopia's resistance to Eritrean incursions. American Embassy personnel were hampered from speaking their judgment by State Department restrictions. I had no such restrictions.

Ethiopians in modern times have had a closer relationship with the United States than any other country. In spite of continual efforts by the Derg to misrepresent the United States, Ethiopians fled by tens of thousands to America and now, as many become American citizens and more come, a substantial Ethiopian diaspora has formed in the United States. These Ethiopians too appreciated hearing a knowledgeable American sharing their own feelings and judgments. Eritrean propagandists often denounced my statements, sometimes distorting what I had said and misrepresenting my past activities. I was accused by Amare Tekle, with whom I was in close contact at the time, of falsely claiming to have been an official observer during the 1993 referendum. I was also accused of inventing interviews with Isaias Afewerki.

Personal experience of the proclivity of EPLF officials to lie reinforced my inclination to regard most of their official pronouncements with skepticism. It also encouraged me to speak out frankly and energetically on behalf of principles and truth when I was asked to do so.

**EXCERPTS FROM A PRESS CONFERENCE AT THE
ADDIS ABABA HILTON, 10 MARCH 1999
(CONDENSED FROM WALTA INFORMATION
BULLETIN, 15 MARCH 1999)**

Questions and Answers:

Q: In the beginning of the crisis between Ethiopia and
Eritrea the U.S. Government remained neutral. Why?

A: There are not many people in Washington these days
who know much about this part of the world. There
are many people in the Clinton Administration who
are not experienced in foreign affairs. They are
preoccupied with a great many other crises: Kosovo,
Iraq, North Korea, relations with China and other
problems. They have given Ethiopia and Eritrea low
priority. But let me recall a few things. The U.S. did
not support Eritrean independence until the Derg
made it impossible for Eritrea to stay with Ethiopia.
The accusation was made by some Ethiopians that
the U.S. gave Eritrea away. Eritrea never belonged to
the U.S., so it couldn't give it away. When I talked to
Meles Zenawi in Washington in 1989 he said he
wished the Eritreans would stay and progress with a
freer and more liberal Ethiopia. Isaias chose otherwise.
Nevertheless Eritrea had a great opportunity. It had
sympathy and support from the whole world when it
became independent.

Q: What do you think is the interest of the U.S. in this
part of the African continent?

A: The U.S. interest in the Horn of Africa is to have the region be peaceful and developed. That is why the U.S. gives aid to all the countries of the Horn. Most Americans can understand that Eritrea has behaved badly in attacking Ethiopia. I find no confusion in the American Embassy here in Addis Ababa. I read in some Ethiopian newspapers that the U.S. supports Isaias Afewerki and loves the dictator. That is not true, but U.S. policy is weak. If I were responsible for it I would reduce relations with Eritrea to a very low level. Not simply because Eritrea has attacked Ethiopia, but because Isaias is not following domestic policies that will lead to a prosperous, open society. But I haven't been in the U.S. Government for nearly twenty years. I don't speak for it. I have been pressuring U.S. officials to adopt a more honest policy toward the war that Eritrea started.

Q: How do you view recent UN Resolution 1227 that urges all member states to halt the sale of arms to Ethiopia, the victim of aggression, as well as to Eritrea, the aggressor?

A: I don't agree with it. It is a mistake. But it seems to make very little difference. Ethiopia has been doing well in the past two weeks. Ethiopia is making itself strong. But the Eritreans are very good propagandists. They know how to lie. Ethiopians are not so good at lying.

Q: Eritrea's leaders say they have accepted the OAU framework agreement. How do you view this?

A: Exactly as Ethiopia does. PM Meles said he had to see real commitment. Just because Eritrea says it wants to accept OAU conditions does not prove it is really going to do that.

Q: What is the logic behind the UN Security Council's actions - they called an immediate meeting after Isaias' acceptance of the OAU peace proposal but it took them months to welcome Ethiopia's acceptance.

A: [Laughing] I can't explain the logic of the UN. The UN is sometimes logical and sometimes totally illogical. The best idea for Ethiopia is to engage in strong action to protect and regain its territory.

Q: What do you think is the real cause of the conflict?

A: The desire of Isaias to have his way. There is Eritrean resentment of Ethiopia's economic and political progress. In Ethiopia religious groups, nationalities and peoples can express themselves in terms of their own interests and rights. In Eritrea no nationality can express its ambitions. Eritrea is pressed into one. The Eritrean economy is in bad shape. It has no great resources. Its major export is salt. Isaias saw what was happening in Ethiopia and thought he could disrupt it. He must be surprised by Ethiopia's strong reaction.

Q: Many people have the impression that the U.S. Government thinks that Isaias is able to protect this region from Islamic fundamentalism - what is your opinion?

A: People who think like this are irrelevant. Isaias has
been playing games with some of the worst Islamic
outlaws - Libya, perhaps even Saddam Hussein. Not
many Americans would be foolish enough to think
that Isaias could protect the African continent against
Sadam Hussein, Qaddafy and Sudan's Turabi.

EXCERPT FROM THE WALTA INFORMATION
SERVICE WEEKLY BULLETIN,
29 MARCH 1999

...Indicating that Ethiopia has all the political and
economic capacity to defeat Eritrea in the war, Mr. Henze
said Eritrea now finds itself irresponsibly plundering the
economic resources available in the Ethiopian territories it
occupied after seizing millions of dollars worth of goods in
Eritrean ports at the time it attacked. Noting that the
Eritreans are planting land mines in occupied territories, Mr.
Henze called on international human rights organizations to
condemn this brutal action. According to Mr. Henze, the
biggest mistake the Eritrean Government committed was to
consider the Ethiopian people as enemies: "This is a grave
mistake because I myself am well aware that Ethiopians
consider Eritreans brothers." During his stay in Makelle,
Mr. Henze paid a visit to the Ayder School which last June
was bombed by the Eritrean Air Force causing serious
civilian casualties. The bombing of the school, he said,
appears to have been a premeditated action aimed at hurting
civilians, for there were no military installations in the
vicinity.

RADIO ETHIOPIA, AMHARIC NEWS,
8:00 P.M., 30 MARCH 1999

American scholar Paul B. Henze has said in a public lecture that Ethiopia has behaved in a responsible fashion in trying to avert the possibility of a full-scale military conflict in the Ethio-Eritrean crisis. He indicated that Ethiopia has done its best to ensure a peaceful settlement and that Eritrea, which has not heeded peace efforts, cannot defeat Ethiopia in the event of this war between the two countries. With its commitment to international principles of peaceful coexistence, Ethiopia has once again shown the world its good image, Mr. Henze said. The bond between the government and the people of Ethiopia is as strong as ever. In spite of the war of aggression launched against it, Ethiopia remains a stable country. Isaias' invading forces have committed crimes against civilians in Ethiopia. The despotic Isaias regime has marred Eritrea's diplomatic relations with neighboring countries and the OAU. Mr. Henze's lecture on the Ethio-Eritrean conflict was given at the Convention Hall on 29 March to students of Addis Ababa University, scholars and representatives of various institutions.

ARTICLE IN *THE ETHIOPIAN HERALD*,
4 APRIL 1999

Prominent U.S. historian Paul B. Henze said the international community is duty-bound to put effective pressure on the Eritrean leadership and force it to change its war policy. Mr. Henze made the observation at a news conference he gave in Makelle, Tigray, after participating in a panel discussion held there which was attended by over two hundred fifty scholars. The American scholar said that he was saddened by the failure of the United States to take appropriate actions when the fact that Eritrea invaded Ethiopia was made clear to the international community some time ago. He also said that the resolution passed by the UN Security Council concerning the Ethio-Eritrean crisis which put the aggressor and the victim of aggression on the same footing is devoid of a sense of justice.

EXCERPTS FROM THE REPORT OF A PUBLIC LECTURE ON 29 MARCH 1999 IN *THE ETHIOPIAN HERALD*, 4 APRIL 1999, HEADLINED
"The Future Offers Extremely Great Opportunity for Ethiopia."

In the last in a series of four public lectures on the Ethio-Eritrean crisis sponsored by the African Initiative for Democratic Deliberations and Action (AIDDA) Paul Henze shed enormous light on the conflict and the future of the Horn of Africa as a whole... Henze called Eritrea's attack a serious miscalculation. He finds Ethiopia now more unified than at any time since he first came here in 1962: "Ethiopians are thinking in very responsible terms and are proud that their country is resisting aggression." For Ethiopia the future is one of greater unity and strength of purpose. The future of Eritrea, on the other hand, is one of disunity wherein its people will experience serious socio-economic and political problems. Ethiopia has waited until there is no other solution for defusing the crisis. Henze believes that Ethiopians must not be disappointed with the neglect of the international community. They must look ahead and concentrate on the opportunities that victory over Eritrea is going to open up.

Henze said that while Eritrea is the sole responsible party for the losses that are resulting from the war, it has almost nothing to pay for them. Therefore, "Except for establishing the principle, Ethiopians should not waste a great deal of time pressing for reparations from bankrupt Eritrea." Ethiopia can afford to make further progress by opening up its society and its reviving economy. Ethiopia will now also be in a position to speed up development of its democratic system.

Restoring relations with Eritrea is not going to be easy for Ethiopia, Henze declared and added, "Eritrea will experience problems restoring its ties with other countries in the Horn. It has to abandon its habit of lying and putting its energies into propaganda. Eritrea tries to tell the world that there still exists a hostile, aggressive Ethiopia keen to encroach on its independence. There is no basis for this allegation whatsoever. Ethiopia has made clear that it wants no Eritrean territory. Its interest is in peace and greater cooperation among the countries of the Horn of Africa. Ethiopia's efforts to end the problems of Somalia and the Sudan should continue. Ethiopia should be energetic in making its aims and goals clear to the world.

EXCERPTS FROM AN INTERVIEW WITH *THE REPORTER*, 7 APRIL 1999

Q: One cause for the war between Ethiopia and Eritrea is said to be economic factors. Do you have a different speculation?

A: We can only speculate because we cannot read the mind of Isaias Afewerki. Relations between the EPLF and the TPLF were often not good. From conversations with both sides, I know that it is not true that they were sister organizations. The EPLF had a much more arrogant and authoritarian militaristic approach than the TPLF. The EPLF spent much of its time in the early stages of the fight against the Derg fighting against other Eritrean movements. Once the EPRDF chased Mengistu Haile Mariam out of Ethiopia, the EPLF could finish off the Derg army in Eritrea. But without the victory of the EPRDF the EPLF by itself could never have defeated the Derg. I think they know that, but they resent it. In spite of the fact that the TPLF was quite generous in its behavior toward the EPLF [after the collapse of the Derg], the EPLF was unhappy about the way the EPRDF government developed in Ethiopia.

Q: Mr. Anthony Lake's mission as mediator from the U.S. - what is he doing and what has he accomplished?

A: I really don't know what Mr. Lake himself thinks about the situation. I suspect that he is honest in wanting to broker peace, but just exactly what he has accomplished is unclear to me. In fact, it doesn't seem to me that he has accomplished very much.

Q: Do you believe that demarcating the border between Eritrea and Ethiopia is the only solution?

A: The problem of demarcating borders is really not very serious. You can ask international organizations to make a survey and make recommendations. You can arrange for a team of specialists to survey the border and define where it is. If there are historical questions, you can go back and examine maps, treaties, and historical records. All these possibilities were open to Eritrea. And Ethiopia willingly agreed to a process like this... When the OAU was founded in 1963 it established the principle that African states should change their borders only by mutual agreement and by peaceful means. Most African states have followed this rule. Somalia, of course, did not. Eritrea is not following it.

Q: Is it true that the U.S. Embassy in Addis Ababa and the U.S. State Department in Washington do not perceive the Ethiopia-Eritrea crisis in the same way?

A: I find that everyone in the American Embassy understands the situation very clearly. But the embassy has not been able to get the State Department to understand that it should take more energetic action in labeling Eritrea as the aggressor. Throughout its history the U.S. has always opposed aggression. When I go back to America in two weeks, I hope to have some influence on the U.S. Government and on the press... One of the problems in America now is that Eritreans have been conducting very energetic propaganda. They are organizing demonstrations at the State Department and the White House.

Q: If the EPLF were completely defeated this year, what do you think would be the future of Eritrea?

A: In just six years of independence Eritrea has attacked every one of its neighbors. The key problem with

Eritrea, I believe, is that it is ruled by one man with a few people around him who don't think for themselves. Isaias thinks in military and authoritarian terms. He is sorry to find that Marxism has been discredited. He had hoped for years that somehow he could persuade the Soviet Union to stop supporting Mengistu and to begin to support him. When communism collapsed and the whole world turned toward democracy, Isaias had to make a reluctant turn toward democracy too. But he has never established a democratic system. The future of Eritrea is not very bright. Until Eritrea gets a better government it is going to be in serious difficulties. Its economy is badly damaged. I don't think its leadership is trusted by many of its people now; there is no reason why they should trust it. Eritrea is a police state and I think it will become more of a police state after its defeat.

Q: The United States provides a lot of aid to Ethiopia. Do you think the U.S. Government will continue to give Ethiopia full support?

A: There are no other countries in the world who can help Ethiopia the way America can. So Ethiopians should not think that America is not a friend. American governments come and go. Our present American government is rather confused. As an American citizen, I am not a strong supporter of my present government. I think it is a rather poor government. I don't think President Clinton has been a very good leader. I think he has been particularly weak in foreign policy. President Clinton has not understood very well what could be done in the Horn of Africa to establish basic principles. Ethiopians should not judge America simply by what President Clinton and the few people at the White House currently do. America as a country has always supported Ethiopia and will always do so. You will see that to be true in the future.

Q: Why do you think the U.S. Government is weak?

A: President Clinton has been politically very weak even though he has the capacity to talk and appear to be active. But he is only the second American president to be impeached. Polls show that most Americans feel they cannot trust him.

Q: Some people think you are a supporter of the ruling party here, the EPRDF. Would you comment on that?

A: The only government that could bring peace and progress to Ethiopia was the EPRDF. So, since I am pro-Ethiopia, I am also pro-EPRDF. I don't think it would have made much sense for me to be pro-*Moa Anbassa,* pro-OLF, or pro some other group trying to keep Ethiopia in a condition of conflict and poverty. No government is perfect. The EPRDF is certainly not perfect. As I wrote in an article for the *Journal of Democracy* last fall, the EPRDF has done a better job in Ethiopia than governments in many ex-Soviet and East European countries that have escaped from communism. If you say that much has not been done, that is always true. There is always more to do. In a country that is as backward and damaged by communism as Ethiopia, there is an enormous amount to do. But let critics tell me who would have done better than the EPRDF. Look around you — if you compare Ethiopia today with Ethiopia in 1989, you see an enormous difference.

Q: Have you ever taken the initiative to talk to opposition parties and help in organizing discussion with the ruling party?

A: I have talked to many opposition parties, but I have not been trying to bring the opposition and the EPRDF together. There have been enough people in the U.S. and Europe doing that. I don't think their efforts have been very well conceived. I don't think many opposition elements in Ethiopia understand what opposition really means. Opposition doesn't mean just being against a government in power. They have to demonstrate they could do better. Opposition means understanding what is going on in a society and offering criticism and proposals that make sense. Most opposition leaders in Ethiopia spend most of their time trying to get foreign governments to embarrass the EPRDF. That is pointless. Ethiopian politics has to be played out in Ethiopia and not in Geneva, Frankfurt, Toronto, Washington, or Los Angeles. Most opposition elements who criticize from abroad are not very responsible. I am happy, however, to see in the present crisis that most opposition groups seem to have shown a better understanding of how things are working in Ethiopia. There is a much greater sense of Ethiopian unity. I hope it continues now in a period when Ethiopia is fully victorious over Eritrea. The real problem is building the future, not arguing about the past.

71

FROM A LETTER TO THE *WASHINGTON POST*, 8 FEBRUARY 1999

In respect to your editorial of today, "A Foolish War" - it is indeed a foolish war, but who is foolish? Ethiopia which is the victim of unprovoked aggression? Or Eritrea which has committed it? Eritrean planes bombed Makelle, capital of Ethiopia's Tigray state, hitting a school and killing children. Eritrea has continued artillery shelling of people in Ethiopian towns and villages. Eritrean actions have made 300,000 people in northern Ethiopia refugees. Amnesty International shows no concern for these people. Eritrea has destroyed churches and health stations. Its treatment of the predominantly Roman Catholic Irob people of northeastern Tigray comes close to being ethnic cleansing, Balkan-style...

The UN Security Council in its resolution of 29 January 1999 strongly urged Eritrea to engage itself in OAU efforts to find a peaceful resolution of the crisis. Eritrea's answer was to launch new military operations. You rightly call on the Eritreans to accept the OAU "framework agreement". You need, however, to report in greater depth and detail on this crisis to enable your readers to understand what it really entails: an aggressive little one-party state which has quarreled with all its neighbors, defying international opinion and undertaking foolish aggression that in the end can only redound to its own disadvantage.

FROM A LETTER TO THE *NEW YORK TIMES*, 8 FEBRUARY 1999

In respect to your editorial of 7 February 1999, "Africa's Futile War", you are correct in placing the blame for the current impasse between Ethiopia and Eritrea primarily on Eritrea. You rightly underscore Eritrea's refusal to engage in any kind of mitigation process... You are wrong in your unqualified acceptance of Amnesty International's recent characterization of the deportation and human rights situation. There have been expulsions by both countries that are deplorable, but far more deplorable is the fact that three hundred thousand Ethiopians... have been made refugees by Eritrea's actions... Amnesty International needs to examine situations in depth and on the ground before jumping to conclusions... During its not quite six years of independence Eritrea has quarreled with all its neighbors: Sudan, Yemen, Djibouti. It is hard to escape the conclusion that the purpose is to keep the society mobilized behind a dictatorial leader.

FROM A LETTER TO CONGRESSMAN EDWARD ROYCE, CHAIRMAN OF THE AFRICA SUBCOMMITTEE OF THE HOUSE OF FOREIGN AFFAIRS COMMITTEE, 26 FEBRUARY 1999

... The attached article which has appeared in an Eritrean government newspaper ("U.S.-led Stampede against Small Eritrea - AGAIN" as published in *Eritrea Profile*, 6 February 1999) which is being distributed by the Eritrean Embassy in Washington is vicious in its denunciation of the United States. It wildly distorts both history and U.S. policy. This is the kind of behavior we expected from Saddam Hussein and the Serbian dictator Milosevic. It is inexcusable for a country whose independence the U.S. has supported and which has been the beneficiary of substantial official American assistance. I enclose a set of articles recounting the real history of the Eritrean-Ethiopian relationship which I and a good friend, the Israeli historian Haggai Erlich, have recently prepared... I urge you to call the Eritrean leadership to account, and press the State Department and the international community to increase pressure on the Eritreans to cease their aggression against Ethiopia and enter into a civilized process of settling border questions.

FROM A LETTER TO THE *WASHINGTON POST*, 3 JANUARY 2000

While it is encouraging to see the Horn of Africa getting some attention, Representative Gilman's column in today's *Post*, "Ethiopia Needs a Push Toward Peace", aims in the wrong direction. It is not Ethiopia that needs to be pushed toward peace, but Eritrea...

There is a natural tendency in today's world to assume that in any quarrel between a small country and a larger one, the small one must be in the right. In this case the assumption is wrong. Eritrea has quarreled with all its neighbors. The country is a police state without free press or political parties. Ethiopia, on the other hand, has been making significant progress toward a free-market economy and an open society. Dozens of political parties and hundreds of publications compete. Leaders have scheduled parliamentary elections for May of this year. In the confrontation with Eritrea Ethiopian leaders have their public behind them. The clique that rules Eritrea fears that the Ethiopian example will undermine their hold on their own population.

FROM A LETTER TO CONGRESSMAN BENJAMIN GILMAN, 4 JANUARY 2000

Your op-ed piece in the *Washington Post* of 3 January is badly off the mark. It is depressing to see you, a prominent Republican and Chairman of a major committee in a Republican Congress, abetting the Clinton Administration's unfair and unjustified stance on the Eritrean-Ethiopian confrontation... The U.S. Government strongly condemns aggression; it advocates democracy and encourages the whole world to move toward rule of law, open society and open economies. Most Americans share these objectives. But the Clinton Administration has not followed these principles in its handling of the confrontation between Ethiopia and Eritrea...

Isaias Afewerki is the same kind of leader as Saddam Hussein in Baghdad or Slobodan Milosevic in Belgrade. He permits no political parties, no free press, no open economy. Eritrea is now living off money pressed from its diaspora. Its economy is a shambles of its own making and its people are forced to sacrifice all prospect of development for the sake of Isaias' irresponsible adventurism...

The Clinton Administration is so eager to be seen as peacemaker that it pressures Ethiopia and indulges Eritrea... Eritrea has prevaricated continually pretending to want peace while spreading mendacious propaganda, continuing military preparations, drafting sixty year-olds and engaging in subversion against Ethiopia, Djibouti and Somalia...

Rather than endorse the Administration's inept and dishonest approach, the House International Relations Committee would be serving a much more constructive purpose by holding hearings on the issue and giving those of us who know the history of the region an opportunity to explain the factors involved.

FROM A LETTER TO TOM SHEEHY, CHIEF OF STAFF, HOUSE AFRICA SUBCOMMITTEE, 6 MAY 1999

Following up on our telephone conversation this morning, let me express regret that the hearings anticipated next Tuesday seem likely to be so truncated. While the Ethio-Eritrean imbroglio, which has now persisted for a year, is clearly of lesser importance than the Kosovo situation, it deserves to have the kind of light shed on it that can come from a serious Congressional hearing.

You asked me to submit a paper. I attach a statement I made in 1990 at a conference of an organization called Eritreans for Peace and Democracy in which I urged that independent Eritrea give priority to making itself the Switzerland of Africa, developing a vigorous open-market economy and open society, refraining from emphasis on military matters.[48] No neighbor, least of all Ethiopia, has been a danger to Eritrea since 1991 - nevertheless Eritrea has followed a course of extremely restricted economic and social development and has given priority to military matters. Countries which do so fall into unproductive quarrels with their neighbors, as Eritrea has done. Though Eritrean officials have been vocal in denouncing me as their enemy, no one reading this 1990 statement, or many subsequent evaluations I made of Eritrea until recently, could find that allegation credible.

Eritrea's present stance vis-a-vis Ethiopia can only lead to further hardship for the Eritrean people. The United States could mitigate this situation by pressing the Eritreans to withdraw and enter into a serious mediation process rather than putting their resources into the military and telling continually more preposterous lies about their situation.

EXCERPTS FROM AN INTERVIEW GIVEN TO
THE WALTA INFORMATION CENTER,
12 MAY 2000

Q: What do you make of the failed Algiers proximity talks?

A: ...It is clear that Isaias went to Algiers only because [U.S. Secretary of State] Madeleine Albright forced a promise to do so from him when he was in Washington. But he went determined to undermine these talks.

Q: After the failure of the proximity talks in Algiers, war seems to be inevitable any time now. Do you share that conclusion?

A: War is not inevitable if the international community and the OAU start talking tough to Isaias. If Ethiopia's leaders conclude that Isaias can be pushed back only by force, they have made clear they will take military action. They are ready to attack.

Q: A UNSC delegation was in Addis and Asmara this week. Do you think it can revive the peace process? If yes, why do you believe it can?

A: If the UNSC delegation stops pretending that Ethiopia and Eritrea are equally "guilty", it can revive the peace process. It must openly declare that Eritrea is the aggressor and Ethiopia the victim of aggression... Eritrea is clearly in violation of the entire spirit of the UN.

Q: You have written "Does Eritrea have an exit strategy?" Can you elaborate on that?

A: Eritrea pretends it wants peace. I am sure the majority of the Eritrean people do. Isaias fears the consequences of real peace because he fears he will not be able to keep control of the police state he rules. President Negaso said Monday Eritrea is a "rogue state". The OAU and the international community must recognize it as such. In war, diplomacy and in people's private lives it is necessary to have a clear idea of where actions lead. What does Eritrea want from this confrontation? Isaias has never made this clear and "proximity" talks have not produced any new evidence. Isaias' aims are negative and destructive. In the end he will destroy Eritrea. When will the Eritrean people wake up and unburden themselves of Isaias?

FROM A LETTER TO ROBERT BARTLEY, EDITOR OF THE *WALL STREET JOURNAL*, 13 JUNE 2000

I returned from Ethiopia a few days ago and delved into a month's worth of *Wall Street Journals* my wife had saved for me to catch up on the state of the world. *The Journal* does not penetrate the Horn of Africa. Just as well, perhaps, for the editorial of 26 May, "Africa's Lesson to History", which I came to today, wouldn't impress most Africans as very insightful. It is, frankly, appalling as a recitation of shallow current conventional wisdom on the conflict between Eritrea and Ethiopia. I began reading it hoping for the kind of perspective and insight *The Journal* ordinarily provides its readers. Grievous disappointment...

Journalists have parroted most of the disinformation Eritrean propagandists have put out. Meanwhile American diplomats have coddled Isaias Afewerki as assiduously as they once did Saddam Hussein, in the mistaken notion that Eritrea is a barrier to Sudanese Muslim fundamentalism. Tony Lake accomplished nothing in nearly a dozen sorties into the Horn of Africa. By equating the victim, Ethiopia, with Eritrea, the aggressor, he inadvertently encouraged Isaias to believe he could get away with his aggression. In April Holbrooke leaped onto the scene and tried to intimidate everyone into "peace". It didn't work. In effect, he hastened the Ethiopians' decision to take matters into their own hands. They see their actions as identical to Margaret Thatcher's response to Argentina's attempt to capture the Falklands. Aren't Africans entitled to defend their sovereignty and their honor in the same way Europeans and Americans do?

The Clinton Administration's policy in the Horn of Africa... has been spectacularly unsuccessful. The new administration next year will have to reverse it. Eritrea's future is bleak. Ethiopia has captured most of its weaponry and its people are destitute. Why would Ethiopia want to take over any Eritrean territory? It has been completely successful in transferring traffic from Eritrean ports to Djibouti and Berbera... The promise that Ethiopia now offers is one of the most exciting and hopeful things happening in Africa today. *The Journal* would be well advised to send one of its best reporters out to size up the situation and report accurately on what is actually happening.

FROM A LETTER TO THE *LONDON ECONOMIST*, 26 JUNE 2000

After claiming in your 3 June issue that the Eritreans held "both the physical and moral high ground", you have - thank goodness! - finally in your latest issue, (24 June) recognized reality and given an honest assessment of the outcome of the war Eritrea forced on Ethiopia two years ago...

If mendacious Eritrean propaganda against Ethiopia continues, it will be difficult for Ethiopians to be magnanimous in victory, for their country has multiple political parties and a plethora of private newspapers that permit people to express themselves. What you call "the triumphalist mood" in Addis Ababa is not the artifact of a government propaganda machine. Magnanimity will come when the peoples of Eritrea have escaped from dictatorship and can express themselves freely too.

BACKGROUND

CHAPTER III

ERITREA IN 1987

I visited Ethiopia every year from 1987 onward, usually staying several weeks.[49] I undertook several research projects for RAND (and occasionally for other organizations) during these years when the Derg was trying to whip the country into Stalinist-style communism and provoking steadily rising resistance among the population. Famine conditions which became a scandal and a worldwide concern in 1984 did not have the effect, as some Ethiopians hoped and some foreign observers expected, of causing Mengistu to moderate his "socialist" zeal or his determination to bring Eritrea to heel by military means. Guerrilla activities were growing in most of northern Ethiopia. Though no one could doubt from reading reports and articles I published in the 1980s that I took a dim view of Derg policies and actions, the Ethiopian Embassy in Washington never hesitated to give me a visa each time I applied. Derg officials in Ethiopia, many of whom were developing growing doubts about Mengistu's policies, invariably facilitated my travels and meetings with local officials. I usually enjoyed support from the American Embassy and sometimes traveled with Embassy officers.

Eritrea's War

The diary which follows records a visit to Eritrea which lasted only three days during a period when Derg armies were in control of most major towns and communications lines in this war-torn region. Workers' Party officials in Eritrea had been instructed by party headquarters in Addis Ababa to open doors to me and discuss their problems freely. I was accompanied by John Burns, the American Embassy Public Affairs Officer, and two Ethiopian officials whom I had already come to know as friends who harbored their own misgivings about Mengistu's goals for Ethiopia as well as his prospects for achieving them.

The only practical way to go to and from Eritrea even by that time was to fly, for the operations of the TPLF had already made that region insecure for the Derg. Shortage of time made it impossible for me to travel to outlying areas of Eritrea during this visit. I am not sure that such travel would have been permitted if I had requested it, for most major roads, even the highway between Asmara and Massawa, were subject to night-time attack.

I had not been in Eritrea since 1972 but I had been following the course of Ethiopian army campaigns and the growth of insurgent operations closely for many years. The situation in highland Eritrea during my visit was essentially a condition of prolonged stalemate. The EPLF had become too strong for Derg armies to aspire to do much more than hold urban areas and roads between them, but the guerrillas were still not strong enough to neutralize Ethiopian military operations except in the northern area around Nacfa and in parts of the western Eritrean lowlands. The Soviet Union kept sending massive quantities of military equipment and ammunition to the Derg. Already the guerrillas were beginning to depend more on material captured from Ethiopian forces than foreign sources, though they continued to depend on

Sudan for petroleum, food and medicine. They were also benefiting from international humanitarian relief shipments. A year after the visit recounted below, the EPLF achieved a decisive victory over Derg forces at Afabet, near Nacfa, and captured immense quantities of equipment and ammunition as well as thousands of prisoners.

The Eritrean population was caught between the Derg and the guerrillas, as the account which follows shows. It demonstrates in detail that the picture of unrelenting thirty year war during which the entire population supported the guerrillas which EPLF mythology now celebrates was in reality a highly differentiated situation. A majority of Eritreans seems to have felt no strong commitment to either side. They longed for normal conditions, peace, the opportunity to study, work, trade, raise their families and lead their lives with a reasonable degree of predictability. Young men were coming into Asmara by the tens of thousands to avoid being recruited by the EPLF. The Derg did not attempt to conscript them for its army - no doubt considering them potentially unreliable. Consequently thousands of them sought to improve themselves by studying or simply reading in libraries.

At the time of this visit lack of rain had caused severe duress in Asmara. Reservoirs were empty. Water was being supplied to a population of four hundred thousand by truck. Nevertheless hard-pressed municipal authorities were managing the situation effectively. Food supplies were adequate. Trade throughout Eritrea seemed not much affected by military operations. The unofficial economy was operating efficiently. Industries were limping along in spite of shortages of electricity and raw materials, for the Derg was desperate to earn foreign exchange from exports. Life continued in Massawa too, though the serious damage the city had suffered during the battles fought in the winter of 1977-78 was still evident and only a fraction of its original population had returned. Hope had not died for a better life, however.

During the next four years Asmara would be faced with far greater hardship than it was experiencing in the spring of 1987. And when the Derg's air force attacked the historic old city after the EPLF captured it in early 1990, Massawa would suffer far greater damage than I saw three years before. The insanity and futility of Mengistu's ceaseless drive to conquer Eritrea left the Eritrean population no choice but to welcome the victory of the EPLF in 1991. Today EPLF propagandists will contest this judgment and claim that the picture I give of the heart of Eritrea in 1987 is an invention designed to whitewash Derg actions and intentions, denigrate Eritrean resistance to the Derg, and resuscitate Ethiopian claims on behalf of the EPRDF - led government in Addis Ababa. I doubt if many of those who read the account which follows with an open mind will agree with such allegations. The purpose of this account is to give an honest picture of what I saw, felt, and was told during an extraordinarily busy visit during a time of comparative lull in the Eritrean struggle.

Entire populations, anywhere in the world, seldom remain gripped by permanent ideological fervor for long unless they are forced into it by an authoritarian system. The majority of human beings have always had a capacity to adjust to the circumstances in which they find themselves and make the best of their predicament. Lies, no matter how often repeated, cannot obliterate the truth. That is what I witnessed in my brief stay in Eritrea thirteen years ago. I also saw officials who put up a good front, but behind the front they were beset with doubts about the policies they were trying to carry out and their chances for success. I deliberately reinforced their doubts by questioning them about fundamentals and prospects, as my account of the meeting with Worker's Party Secretary Teferra Wonde demonstrates.

I came back to Eritrea several times after 1991. It was a more hopeful country then, especially at the time of the 1993 referendum, as my diary of that experience will demonstrate. But by 1996, when I last came to Asmara, Eritrea was in the midst of a rancorous confrontation with Yemen which its leaders had provoked by sending troops to occupy a disputed island off the Yemeni coast. Relations with Sudan remained ruptured. His authoritarian approach to statecraft next led Isaias Afewerki to invade Ethiopia in May 1998. This misconceived venture has ended in disaster for Eritrea's people, a population which has experienced more than its share of hardship and travail during the past thirty odd years. My impressions and discussions in 1987 seem to me to gain particular poignancy in light of this recent tragic history.

WARTIME ERITREA
Diary of a Visit in the Late Derg Era

19 March 1987 - Flight to Asmara; Asmara at night.

Departure formalities at Bole Airport took twice as long as the flight itself. It would be surprising if tight security were not maintained on flights to Eritrea. This is not a Derg innovation. When Eritrean insurgents and Marxist students began hijackings of Ethiopian Airlines flights twenty years ago, EAL was one of the first airlines outside the U.S. to adopt rigorous security procedures. I kept thinking how ironic it is that the Cubans who first started highjackings of American planes a few years ago and a few years later were supporting rebels in Eritrea are now Marxist Ethiopia's allies. Rebellion in Eritrean, then just an annoyance, has since become the single greatest challenge the Derg government has to face and enormously complicates Moscow's effort to turn Ethiopia into an African replica of the Soviet Union.

The flight to Asmara took a bit less than an hour. The service was good and the Boeing 727 absolutely full. The same team that had gone with me to Jimma last week (American Embassy Public Affairs Officer John Burns, Fisseha Zewde and Getachew Asfaw as Ethiopian escorts) - are with me on this trip. In the waiting room at Bole Fisseha introduced us to a group of his colleagues from the university, all now working for the Nationalities Institute. One, Fisseha Asfaw, sat next to us on the plane. He is a sociologist who had both studied and taught at the University of South Carolina, spending eleven years in the States in all. He returned to Ethiopia in 1980. He says he came back here with his eyes open and has them open still. He wore a party uniform but everything he had to say was more Ethiopian than Marxist. He suggested I come to visit the Nationalities Institute next week. They have many university people on their staff.

The Derg still gets the cooperation of many intellectuals, not because most of them are silly enough to believe in the peculiar synthesis of Stalinism and Maoism that the leaders of the so-called "Workers' Party of Ethiopia" have retreated into, but because they are intrigued and inspired by the process of trying to modernize and develop this beautiful, lovable old country and want to participate. This situation contains many elements of potential tragedy, for these intellectuals could end up being betrayed in far more profound a fashion than intellectuals were by Haile Selassie. The present leadership is doing damage to the country

Soon we were speeding into town on a smooth asphalt highway. We passed areas of modest new housing where I remembered countryside - quarters for military personnel? The landscape looked parched, but the eucalyptus trees lining the road were green, their graceful leaves fluttering in the evening breeze. "The city's population has grown to more than four hundred thousand", Mayor Afeworq said. "People continue to come in from the countryside. It strains the city's facilities, but we have kept all the utilities going. Mail is delivered door - to - door in Asmara. There is ample electricity and we even have one hour less of curfew here than they do in Addis Ababa. It doesn't go into effect until midnight and is lifted at 5 A.M."

"May we walk around the city tonight?" I asked.

"You may go anywhere you wish."

We were following *Andennet* (Unity) Avenue into the center of the city. It has kept its name. It would be the last the Derg would want to change. At dusk, Asmara still appeared to be the charming Italian provincial town it has always been — compact, with houses side by side behind solid masonry walls. Asmara was built as if space were as much at a premium as it is in Italy. I could see bougainvillaea spilling over some of the walls, jacarandas blooming behind them. Passing the fifteen story Nyala Hotel, we turned into the city's grandest avenue, once named for the Italian King, Victor Emmanuel, and then for Haile Selassie. I asked the mayor what it is now called. "National Avenue." It is still lined with splendid palms on both sides. During the heavy fighting in 1977-1978, when the Derg almost lost control of all of Eritrea, I had envisioned those palms shattered by shrapnel and bombs. But they are all there: green and healthy looking, neatly trimmed, shading both the elegant avenue and the broad promenades on both sides.

which is going to be much more difficult to repair than that which the old Lion of Judah allegedly did.

The evening air was crystal clear and the sun on the verge of setting when we landed at Yohannes IV Airport. To the east a wall of white cloud billowing up from the edge of the escarpment caught the final rays of the sun. The rainy season in the Red Sea lowlands has apparently not quite ended for cloud of this kind marks a sharp break in Eritrean weather from December into March when the plateau is at its driest. The attractive airport terminal looked unchanged from pre-revolutionary times but a great many additional buildings have been put up.

As I came down the steps from the plane, the Mayor of Asmara, Guad (Comrade) Afeworq Berhane, came up to greet me: "Welcome to Asmara. We are delighted to have you here." I told him I was happy to have the opportunity to visit his city, especially when it was having such beautiful weather. "It has its bad side," he said. "We are suffering a severe water shortage, for the little rains have not yet begun in the Eritrean highlands. Our biggest reservoir is empty, so we have turned off the city water system and are trucking in water from springs and wells. We are also urgently drilling new wells. We are keeping everyone supplied but they have to be very careful how they use water."

He moved on to greet other arriving passengers, including the Nationalities Institute team, then returned to escort our party to a white Mercedes waiting beside the terminal. "You know Asmara?" the mayor asked. I said I had visited it perhaps twenty times between 1968 and 1972 and often spent several days at a time here but had not seen the city for almost fifteen years. "You will not see much that has changed," he observed. "Has there been no destruction here?" I asked with a bit of skepticism. "Almost none," he replied.

To our left were the grounds of the Governor's Palace built by the Italians, like most of Asmara's large buildings. I recalled first entering it in 1969 to meet Ras Asrate Kassa, Haile Selassie's Enderassie[50] in Eritrea from 1964 until 1970. He was replaced by a general, it was said, because the Emperor had given up hope for compromise with the separatists and wanted the fight against them pursued with more vigor. I forgot to ask the mayor what the palace is now used for, for we turned into a side street lined with stately old Italian villas set in gardens, passed the Hamasien Hotel and pulled up into the curved driveway of what was called the Imperial Hotel when I last stayed in it in 1972. It was newly opened then, the city's finest. It has been renamed the Ambasoara, after Eritrea's highest mountain, but still maintains international standards. There is a military guardpost in front and everyone coming in and out is checked. It serves as a social center for officialdom and the military here. Mayor Afeworq saw us checked into our rooms, then said good evening and invited us to come to his office tomorrow at 8 A.M. for a formal briefing on life in the city.

After dinner, we set out for a walk through the city. The sky was filled with stars and the air cool, scented every now and then by flowering trees and shrubbery. Occasionally, there was a whiff of sewer gas. Streets were not as animated as I remembered them, but there were a good many people about. We walked the full length of National Avenue. The impression I had driving into the city from the airport this evening was confirmed. The palms are intact. The paving tiles are all in place. Both the roadway and the sidewalks look swept. Buildings are well maintained. The enormous red brick Catholic cathedral and its auxiliary buildings, seat of the Catholic hierarchy in Eritrea, rise imposingly behind their wall. Shops have had commercial signs removed but some of their windows had displays of shoes and leather goods, jewelry, men and women's clothing, furniture, handicraft items. What is missing is electric appliances and electronic goods, watches, Far Eastern imports of the kind one sees in Diredawa or Djibouti. I saw no bookshops but there were many little eating and drinking places.

We saw no white faces during our stroll. I was reminded how much in evidence Americans used to be here when Kagnew Station had a complement of three or four thousand American soldiers and their dependents. There were always tourists from other parts of Africa and the Middle East too. In the 1960s foreigners working in stifling places such as Khartoum and Jeddah came to enjoy a few days of coolness and good eating and drinking in Asmara. American diplomatic and military wives came here to have babies at the Kagnew Station hospital. There was a good dental clinic and the PX was the best in Africa. Ethiopian officers used the Kagnew Officers' Club and the royal family and high officials were allowed to shop at the PX. Social life was lively and everybody mixed. Americans married Eritrean wives. It is hard to believe that the Russians do any comparable socializing or provide any amenities. If there are Russians here, they do not go out on the streets at night.

All side streets have lines of water barrels which trucks fill daily. People come to get their water in plastic jugs and buckets. Insurgency has left no visible scars on downtown Asmara. The mayor was right - little has changed. We saw few political signs and slogans, with one exception. At the inner end of National Avenue a big red arch forms the entrance to a new "Revolution Square". At the top of the arch red light bulbs frame a portrait of Mengistu. They are stationary for a minute, then blink and rotate clockwise, like an old-fashioned movie marquee. Red neon slogans in

Amharic and English glow on each side of the portrait. Only the first three letters of the Amharic were working tonight. John and I laughed at the tawdriness of the whole thing. Getachew and Fisseha were visibly embarrassed but said nothing. Beyond this monumental entrance, Revolution Square was dark and utterly empty.

20 March 1987 - Morning of Briefings in Asmara; Lunch beside Derg Army Generals.

I woke at dawn, had a good shower-hot and cold flowed normally until 7 A.M. sharp, then stopped —and climbed up to the top story of the hotel to see the city greet the sunrise. Since the Ambasoara is almost in the center of Asmara, its roof offers views over tan and yellow buildings in all directions. In between are dots of greenery, clusters of red and orange bougainvillaea and bright purple jacaranda rising from gardens. Roosters were crowing. People keep chickens in backyards. There were almost no sounds of traffic. The scene was all peace and order. War-torn Eritrea is not supposed to look this way! It would not be a good newspaper story, especially in these times when the image of Ethiopia TV has left in the minds of the Western public is a barren desert blasted by war and populated by skeletons.

Our party gathered in the Ambasoara dining room for a good breakfast, Fisseha last because he had stayed up until 3 A.M. talking to friends and acquaintances. Abraha Mebratu, representative of the Ministry of Foreign Trade who seems to double as public relations man for the Eritrean Government (there is not much foreign trade), was waiting with cars. I thought he looked familiar. He told me he had been Foreign Ministry representative here before the Revolution. John Burns and I were driven in a white

Mercedes to the *Municipio* where Mayor Afeworq was waiting. The former city hall has been taken over as Party Headquarters for Eritrea. The present *Municipio*, nearby, is another of those solid, functional Fascist-era Italian structures. The mayor served excellent coffee as we sat down at his conference table for an hour-long briefing.

Afeworq, a native of Asmara, has been mayor for four years and knows his city well. He used no socialist jargon, made no effort to deny the fact that running the city is a demanding job. I took notes as he described the situation: "The population is over four hundred thousand and keeps increasing. We are not forbidding people to come into the city. A major component of the increase is young men from the countryside. They do not relish being recruited by the secessionists. (This term is consistently used here for what otherwise in Ethiopia are variously called separatists, rebels, *shifta* or bandits, depending on the degree of negativism implied.) They are non-ideological. They come looking for work or education or both. They represent an enormous challenge for the city."

"The city is divided into 107 *kebeles* grouped into nine higher *kebeles*. There is a one hundred fifty member city council with an executive committee of seven members. The mayor serves as chairman of the executive committee. The city administration has a permanent staff of about thirteen hundred. City employees have increased substantially since the Revolution. The greatest difference between the past and the present is that the city administration used to be only concerned with municipal services. These continue to be important, of course, but the municipality now has political and economic responsibilities as well."

"Our number one problem is water. There has been a deficit for several years. We are trying to reconstruct a dam fifteen kilometers from Asmara, also to dig more wells. This will take time. Meanwhile trucks are the only solution. The population cooperates well, but it is very difficult, also for industry."

"Problem number two is housing. The city is building cooperative housing but building materials are short. We don't expect to solve the housing problem soon because more people keep coming in."

"Problem number three is unemployment. Eritrea has one third of Ethiopia's industry. Most industries are working, but not on a full scale. Even if they were, there would not be enough jobs for the steadily increasing population. We compensate for it by giving young people as much opportunity for schooling as we can. We have more than one hundred thousand students in schools in the city. Several new schools were built last year. The government's policy is to put as much of the responsibility for schools on the cities as possible. There is a teacher-training institute here, a nursing institute, a technical training school and, of course, Asmara University. There is an Italian secondary school. 7,602 students sat for the Ethiopian School Leaving Certificate Examination (ESLCE) here this past week. one hundred sixty thousand have taken it in all Ethiopia.[51] Students are eager for university education. Asmara University is already overstrained. We must do more to satisfy young people and give them greater opportunities to study."

"We are very concerned about our industry, not only in Asmara but in all of Eritrea. There has been some progress in expanding and renewing it. Italy has made new investment of 12 million birr in cotton manufacturing and 17.5 million birr for a new mill in addition to Red Sea General Mills. We are trying to get the population to think of creating new industry according to the theory of competitive advantage. There are unexploited resources in Eritrea. Fishing, for example, is underdeveloped. The Red Sea is rich in fish. We are thinking too of expanding export-oriented industry. We are doing some exporting now: textiles and leather goods. We would like to revive tourism. To lay the basis for all this, we need to expand electricity production. We are investing 70 million birr in new electric generating capacity. This is the largest single investment in Eritrea."

I asked about the health situation: "The health of the population of Asmara is good. We can give the population adequate health care. Garbage is collected door-to-door by the municipality." What about food? "Food is now abundant. Fruit and vegetables are available in large quantities. *Kebele* bakeries are having difficulty selling their bread because they are undersold by private bakeries. Wheat comes in from abroad and is currently selling at 50 birr per quintal. *Teff* here is much more expensive. The current price is 210 birr per quintal. Relief assistance from abroad has helped restore the market."

I was skeptical of the mayor's assurances on food supply and said I would like to have the opportunity to visit public markets. He said he was sure time would be found for that. Saturday, when they were at their busiest, would be best. John Burns asked about the information situation: "We do radio broadcasting in Amharic, Tigrinya and Tigre. There is news, music and entertainment. We also have educational broadcasts in Amharic and Tigrinya. There is a daily newspaper in Tigrinya: *Hibret.*"

What about security? "The situation is stable and conditions within the city basically good." When were curfew hours shortened? "Imposition of curfew was advanced from 9 P.M. in the evening to 11 P.M. about four years ago. Two years ago we extended it to midnight."

What is the situation in respect to religion? "The majority in the city is Christian. 90 percent of the Christians are Orthodox. There are about forty Christian churches and about twenty mosques in the city. They all operate according to their own rules. Christians and Muslims in Eritrea have known how to get along with each other for a long time. There is no tension between them."

An hour had passed. Mayor Afeworq suggested we go out to see life in the city. What did we most want to see? I said I would like to see some operating industry. John said he would like to visit the former American library. We both said we wanted to visit the university. We were also eager to see markets, churches, schools, daily life and water distribution in various sections of the city. It could all be worked in, Afeworq said, and began telephoning to make arrangements. He asked whether he could take us to see one of his own favorite projects: a new public library. We drove a few blocks to a large building painted apple green that looked as if it might originally have been a factory or warehouse. Several bicycles were parked in front and over the door was a sign in the national colors (green, red, yellow): *Yehizb Bet Metshafoch* - Public Library.

We walked into a large, attractively arranged reading room-everything newly painted, sunlight streaming through lightly curtained windows. A couple of dozen long tables with straightback chairs took up most of the open space but there were also smaller tables and clusters of chairs in corners. Bookcases filled all wall space without windows and were also arranged as dividers cutting the large room into smaller areas. There were racks for newspapers and magazines, a bank of card catalogues. In atmosphere this library matched good city and suburban libraries in the United States. The place was full of readers and, notably, they were almost all young men; there were perhaps a dozen young women. Almost no older people at all! I walked among the tables. Most of these men were reading serious books, taking notes from history and economics books, diligently going through encyclopedias, copying mathematics formulas. It was a good practical illustration of what Afeworq had told us about young men coming into the city and occupying themselves in furthering their education.

When had the library been opened? Only last year, the mayor said. Getting a building was much easier than getting books. A Canadian foundation donated the books. We examined the shelves. Fully two-thirds of the volumes were published in the U.S. in the past five to ten years. The rest were British and Canadian and equally up-to-date. All were in English. Every book was numbered and all were wrapped in transparent plastic. If there was any ideological bias, it was markedly pro-Western - recent books on U.S. and European history and politics; international affairs, with a great deal on the Third World; much current literature; handbooks of all kinds; almanacs and yearbooks; full sets of several encyclopedias; books on archaeology and travel (I even noticed a copy of George Bean's classic *Turkey Beyond the Maeander*); great numbers of books on economics, science, electronics, computer technology, agriculture, all neatly arranged according to category. There were multiple copies of many.

Can users take books home? "Yes, they can sign them out for two weeks." Do many keep them? "Very few disappear, for there is too much appreciation of their value and these young people respect others' desire to use them too. Besides, if a person takes a book out and does not return it, he loses his borrowing privilege."

If there had been censorship and elimination of certain kinds of books, it was not obvious. What was most interesting was the absence of anything Russian or Russian-supplied. I did not even see the ritualistic shelf of classics of Marxism-Leninism that the libraries in Jimma had had and forgot to ask if there was one, I was so interested in the positive side of this library. There were no political slogans. On one wall there was a portrait of Mengistu flanked by the national and party flags. Otherwise someone who dropped into this library from the outer world might think he was in Atlanta or New Orleans.

The mayor told us that libraries in Asmara are kept open on evenings and weekends and are often busiest on Saturdays, Sundays and holidays. The mayor said he was preparing a building for another library in a different section of the city that would be a duplicate of this one but had not yet been able to get promises of enough books to stock it. John Burns caught the hint and immediately volunteered to help get books for it.

John and I parted ways for the next phase of the morning's visits. John went to the former USIS library, nationalized in April 1977 when the Derg expelled the U.S. Consulate-General here, closed everything that remained at Kagnew Station and confiscated the USIS library. The chief librarian, Kaffele, who was put on the payroll of the municipality, had recently visited John at the embassy in Addis Ababa. He came by the hotel last night to be sure John did not fail to come to see his library today. This institution, which goes back to the earliest period of American presence in Asmara (i.e. the early 1940s), is a remarkable example of how superficial some changes in Ethiopia have been. Though nationalized by the Derg with a great deal of political fanfare in 1977, the library was left intact and has remained open and in continuous use ever since. There was no culling of books. It had been well stocked but until recently no new books or magazines had been added. Until the mayor's new library was opened, it was Asmara's main public library. The city has continued to finance it and Kaffele, the devoted librarian, has kept it in very good condition. USIS has, in effect, got continual return from its original investment with no expense whatsoever. When John met me an hour later at the university, he was elated at what he found and determined to find means of sending more books and supplying magazines on a regular basis.

Meanwhile, I spent an hour at the Asmara Textile Kombinat, the former Italian-owned Cotonificio Barattolo, which was producing high quality cotton goods before the Revolution. (My family still has several of its T-shirts bought at EXPO' 72).[52] Our drivers still referred to the place by its former name. As we drove through the triumphal arch over the gate to the factory compound, we were treated to a vast array of communist sloganry and paintings celebrating the triumph of the proletarian revolution. The Derg has decked it out the same way the Soviets do their factories.

We parked in a large courtyard decorated with giant, freshly painted portraits of the Communist Trinity and Mengistu Haile Mariam. Banners with proletarian slogans hung from all the buildings. The impression of booming socialist industrialism all this was supposed to convey was thin indeed. The rest of the establishment looked as if it were under occupation by a rather inept army trying to make things work against obstacles of its own making.

I was directed to the wood-paneled office of the director but he was absent. I had a few moments to examine the charts on the wall. They showed that the factory has regularly failed to meet its quotas for either production or sales, usually falling one-third to one-half below quota level. This must indicate that quotas are set too high. The production manager appeared and took me on a tour. A rather bedraggled looking, no longer young, soldier in uniform with an old carbine slung over his shoulder also tagged along. We moved systematically through the various stages of the production process from the point where bales of cotton come in through carding and spinning to weaving, sizing, and preparation for sale. In the main section of the factory the pre-revolutionary machinery was only about one-third operative and the halls where it is installed look dismal—fiber all over the floors, the air heavy with lint. Such an installation would be closed down as a health hazard in any country in the non-communist world. If government inspectors did not take the initiative itself, labor unions would. What about AETU here? [53] Not present.

The production manager told me proudly that the factory now operates entirely on Eritrean cotton which comes from the Gash-Setit region along the Sudan border. It provides employment for three thousand two hundred workers, 70 percent of whom are women. This was quite evident as we walked through the production halls — very few men. The production manager's showplace was the hall where they have installed new Italian machines for producing cotton knitwear. Here, almost all the looms were working, the air was reasonably clean and the hall less cluttered with debris and trash. We went from the weaving hall to rooms where T-shirts were being sewn and packaged for shipment. The production manager said the new machinery had cost $6 million and they hoped this year to be able to buy $15 million more. They need it.

The T-shirt fabrication operation was efficient and colorful, so I raised my camera to photograph some of the attractive women at work and experienced a good example of the idiocy of socialist authoritarianism. The military man jumped in front of me. "Photographing *kilkil naw!*" [54] I told the production manager I wanted to have a few photographs to demonstrate that industry in Asmara was operating and women were provided employment. I did not add that they could be thankful I had not had the bad taste to try to photograph the Dickensian conditions in other parts of the factory. He made a few half-hearted gestures toward the man in uniform who seemed an unusually thick-headed type. To no avail. It was clear that the word of the military goes unchallenged in the Asmara Textile Kombinat, at least at the level of the production manager. I wonder whether things would have been different if the factory director himself had been present. He finally caught up with us a few minutes later as we were touring the shipping room. He apologized for his lateness—he had been out of the office when the mayor called and was contacted only a few minutes previously.

We moved out into the decorated courtyard again while the director reviewed the factory's operations. He stressed that they were producing mainly for export, said they are sending T-shirts to both Italy and Germany and hope to expand their sales in Europe further. If they can earn more foreign exchange, they hope to be able to invest some of it in further modernization and expansion.

We were due at the university at 11 A.M. As we drove back cross the city, it occurred to me that I had just witnessed in microcosm an example of the total bind Ethiopia's military Marxists have got themselves into with their economy. They are squeezing this nationalized factory as hard as they can to get some production out of it. It may belong to the "proletariat" but working conditions, except where recent Italian generosity has made a difference, are worse than anything proletarians in the capitalist world have tolerated in the past century. Under its original Italian ownership this was a textile enterprise that functioned up to international standards. It was taken over in name of "the people". The slogans and the gaudy portraits do not obscure the fact that it is a shadow of what it once was.

Everybody has lost as a result. Who has lost most? The Barattolo family has lost its investment, but it was compensated by the Italian government and this same government has turned around and provided new machinery for the factory. So Italy's taxpayers have paid double for nationalization. (Italians are still working off their guilt for the brutalities of the Fascist invasion.) The real losers are "the people" who are supposed to have been the beneficiaries of nationalization. More workers would be employed, working under better conditions and earning more, if this factory had gone on as it was. For the Ethiopian consumer it now produces coarse blue and white cloth, ticking, not much finer than canvas. Priority is given to production of T-shirts for sale to the officially scorned capitalist world. What does the foreign exchange earned go for? Weaponry? Probably not, for the Soviets still keep pouring that in. Investment in state farms or other socialist enterprises? Perhaps. Public works? Maybe. Whatever the foreign exchange is used for, priorities are not set by the people or intended to benefit them but by bureaucrats whose interests are very different from those in whose name they claim to exercise power.

Would the EPLF be doing any better than the Derg if it had succeeded in taking over Asmara in the winter of 1977-78? They might have changed, but their party program is still as dogmatic about nationalizing industry as the Derg has been. Conclusion: nationalization has cost heavily and set this valuable Eritrean industry back by a couple of decades. Only foreign – Western – generosity and know-how can get it moving again.

Neither Fisseha nor Getachew accompanied me on the factory visit, but we all joined together on the steps of the huge main university building and marched up to the office of Dr. Tewolde Berhan Wolde Mariam, its rector, a scientist by profession. He was educated in Wales and even speaks English with a trace of Welsh accent. He was suffering from a bad cold, but even functioning at less than his best, he was an impressive and appealing personality. I felt I was face to face with an honest and serious man who was simply concentrating on the responsibilities given to him. He told us he had had no administrative experience when he was appointed to head the university in 1979 contrary to his personal desires.

At that time the university had sunk to the point where it had only 300 students and a handful of instructors. He has built it up to 1,600 regular students and 1,800 night and part-time students. The regulars come from all over Ethiopia, assigned on the basis of the annual competitive ESLCE. As a result, the majority of the regular student body are from Shoa. The part-time students are naturally almost entirely from Eritrea. They must pay some of the cost of their education; those assigned through the ESLCE, in keeping with the principle that was also operative in the Emperor's time, get totally free education. The pressure on the university is enormous. It could take in several times the numbers of part-time and night students it now serves if it had staff and room to handle them.

Dr. Tewolde Berhan confirmed everything Mayor Afeworq told us about the lust to learn in Asmara. Young people come from the countryside and beg at the university's gates to be let in. But the Ministry of Education is reluctant to assign more regular students to the university because employment opportunities for graduates are so limited. I recalled my conversation only yesterday morning with Guad Dinder at the Central Planning Commission in Addis Ababa. Everything I heard here in Asmara confirmed the fact that basic problems in Ethiopian higher education remain much the same as they were in Haile Selassie's time: too many young people pushing to get into already overtaxed educational institutions. There are two important differences of degree, however. One, before the Revolution students had much more freedom to express themselves and did; and the government and university authorities tried to listen to them. Marxist agitators made that difficult, however. And two, there were more openings for employment of university graduates then because the country was developing faster and there were opportunities for private as well as government employment.

Asmara University has plans to create a full-scale engineering faculty and to set up branches in Ghinda for practical work in agriculture and in Massawa to develop marine biological research. I thought how useful it would be for them to have the help of the Israelis in this latter endeavor, given the common interest of both countries in the Red Sea. I asked Tewolde Berhan how much foreign help they were getting. Not a great deal. He mentioned East German instructors with no great warmth. English is the basic language of instruction at the university, he noted, and foreigners who know English well are best: Americans, Britons and British Commonwealth people. He said they hoped to attract some Canadians. Could we do anything to arrange for a few American Fulbrighters to come? he asked, adding that they would be assured of a good welcome.

Given the Derg's new nationalities policy and the fact that Tigrinya is spoken by at least a plurality of the people of Eritrea, I asked whether there was any teaching done in it. None, Dr. Tewolde Berhan said, and continued: "Amharic is the second language of the university and the native language of most of the regular students. The local students, of course, all speak Tigrinya, but they have no interest in being educated in it. There are no textbooks and the language does not lend itself to university use. The students all want to get a good command of English. This is why we need more instructors who can teach in native English."

I was reminded of something I have so often seen theoretical social scientists ignore or forget: that practicality and political symbolism are very different things in language use. The same seemed to be true in the new village we visited a week ago near Chitu in south Shoa where the village "reading house" had nothing in either Orominya or Guraginya. For practical purposes people use Amharic and those who do not grow up speaking it want to learn it because, having been the national language of Ethiopia for hundreds of years, it is simply part of life here. If you have greater ambition, you want to learn English, for it is truly the second language of Ethiopia and is likely to remain so indefinitely. If Mengistu or any of his fanatic friends ever toyed with the notion of getting Ethiopians to learn Russian, they had to give up on it long ago.

Everything I have observed in Ethiopia in recent years indicates that Amharic is firmly established as the national language with English firmly in second place. Other native languages serve primarily local and regional purposes. What this goes to prove is that the imperial regime could have safely afforded to be much more open-minded about language questions than it was.

Back in the Ambasoara lobby at lunchtime, we found ourselves surrounded by military uniforms. Fisseha introduced me to the new Defense Minister, Major General Haile Giorgis, to the new Eritrean commander, General Ragassa Jimma, and the general commanding in Tigray, a gray-haired man who had flown up from Makelle this morning and was wearing civilian clothes. It was a poor occasion for serious conversation, however, for they were not clear who I was and apprehensive, I suspect, that I might be a journalist. Fisseha explained I was doing research on the Ethiopian economy but had long been interested in the country. I said I appreciated the opportunity to visit Eritrea for the first time in almost fifteen years. General Ragassa has been here for years and speaks both Tigrinya and Tigre,[55] though he is an Oromo. The defense minister said they were making progress in overcoming the "secessionists" and expected to make more, but then he was called aside to greet another general who had just arrived and that was the end of the conversational opportunity, for we had to go up to get our bags to be ready to set out for Massawa as soon as we finished lunch.

During lunch in the main dining room we sat a stone's throw away from the generals. About a dozen were seated on both sides of a long table with the defense minister at the head. Relations between them seemed to be easy. As they ate, they all participated in the conversation which was lively, though occasionally everybody stopped to listen to the defense minister. They were a tough looking lot. Several of them looked easily ten years' Mengistu's senior. I studied their faces during lunch as often as I could without appearing too obvious. I kept wondering how battle-hardened men such as these could take orders from the likes of Sergeant Legesse Asfaw and other Derg types and keep their self-respect. Most officers of this age group must have had training in the U.S. and extensive contact with American and Israeli military aid officers in earlier years. For years they have been pushing conscripts to fight in Eritrea and pursue guerrillas in Tigray. They have had to face tough situations over and over again on Ethiopia's battlefronts. They have had to accept humiliation from Cubans and Russians with whom it must be very difficult for them to establish rapport. How does all this look to them? Do they intend to go on like this forever? Isn't there some other alternative? I would like to have gone over, sat down and asked them —but that was beyond the bounds of possibility under the circumstances.

Rumors here are that former Defense Minister Tesfaye Gebre Kidan came back from Moscow with a promise of $900 million in new small arms from the Soviets over a period of several years with the proviso that Ethiopia must provide transportation for them itself. Peculiar. No other support is to be given. That sounds as if the Soviets may be putting the squeeze on Mengistu – trying to discourage another Eritrean offensive and push and prod the Ethiopians into compromising with the EPLF. It would not be an illogical position for Gorbachev to take, but it contrasts sharply with the course he is following in Angola and Afghanistan.

20 March 1987 - Drive Down the Eritrean Escarpment

Between 1:45 P.M. and 4:25 P.M. this afternoon we made our way down the Eritrean escarpment to Massawa. The governor of the Red Sea Awraja (Qay Bahr, as it is now called officially, formerly Samhar) came to the hotel after lunch to accompany us. He bears the distinguished Ethiopian name of Yekuno Amlak Belay [56] and is a native Eritrean born in Akele Guzay. A professional civil servant, he has served as governor of four of the nine Eritrean sub-provinces. Almost totally bald, he is a light-skinned, stocky fellow. He gave the impression of being pleased with our visit and delighted to be able to play host, but I learned this evening that he had expected to stay in Asmara for several days and had been ordered by party headquarters to return to

Massawa with us and see that all goes well. So far we have placed no demands upon him.

The military are visible everywhere along the escarpment highway but they do not interfere with traffic, which was heavy-busses, trucks, Toyota Carryalls and other four-wheel-drive vehicles, as well as smaller private vehicles. The highway is in excellent condition. It is a great monument to Italian skill in road-building. Along the upper escarpment there was little sign of fighting or destruction. Most of this region was terraced years ago. Construction of terraces began during the Italian period and was still being continued in the early 1970s with the support of the USAID food-for-work program. Eucalyptus trees planted then to hold back erosion have grown and formed good stands on some of the steeper slopes. Groups of houses perched picturesquely on knolls and curves in the landscape looked charming from a distance but life in them looked rather lean when one got a closer view. Fields were being plowed with animals but the upper escarpment was dry as Asmara itself and will need good rain to produce much this year.

I had hoped for good views of Debra Bizen, above Nefasit, where the highway from Decamere comes in, but a small patch of fluffy cloud hovered along the crest of the mountain where the famous old monastery is situated and blocked our view of it. It is said to be going about its business normally. We had splendid panoramas both to the north and the south as we descended into Nefasit. Its Italian-style church, with a tall bell tower, and its Turkish-style mosque not far away, symbolize key features of Eritrean history: the two religions, side by side. Nefasit, a strongpoint on the escarpment route, has extensive military installations. From here all the way through Ghinda we saw large numbers of troops. From their faces it was evident that they are not from northern Ethiopia.

As we descended, rounding curve after curve with continually changing views over a landscape as spectacular as the lower slopes of the Himalayas, we experienced a complete change of climate. Within the space of a few miles we entered a green world of flowing water and fields lush with green and ripening crops. The road was edged with white and yellow wildflowers. Toward Ghinda we passed through orchards and a landscape which, even when not cultivated, carries a good growth of brush and trees. A dramatic church with a high tower rises on a hill on the edge of Embatcala. Now and then we saw a roofless building or one with holes blasted in its walls along the roadside, but the towns were intact and lively with market activity. There were large quantities of fruits and vegetables for sale. The middle escarpment gets generous rainfall from December to March. It has a Mediterranean climate and atmosphere. Cattle and horses looked healthy. Everywhere people were working in the fields.

In Ghinda we stopped at a restaurant that offered espresso hissing out of a shiny Italian machine as well as Fanta, Sprite and Coca-Cola. The place was decorated with old advertising signs. We sat under a mirror promoting Marlboro cigarettes. Governor Yekuno Amlak told us that this area supplies a considerable portion of Asmara's food and enjoys a fair degree of prosperity as a result. Relations between the military and the local population are good, he said, but people do not move about much after dark. The "secessionists" are seldom able to penetrate to the main highway and usually suffer severely if they do, so life is reasonably secure and local people cooperate with the government. This is the official version and the governor articulated it convincingly. The EPLF would doubtless just as convincingly claim the local people are all cooperating with them. The truth, no doubt, is right in the middle — people here look out for their own interests and try their best to avoid cooperating with either side enthusiastically enough to draw the wrath of the other upon them.

We drove on past Dongollo and looked down over a broad green valley with the lake of Sabarguma in the distance. The springs there continue to supply Eritrea with effervescent mineral water. By this time, we were down to about 300 meters above sea level. Visions of cool mineral water helped stave off discomfort as the temperature rose and humidity increased. Curves and more curves with views of the Samhar and in the distance a blue haze covered over the Red Sea. The true desert forms only a narrow strip a few miles back from the sea. The coastal lowlands consist first of a tangle of hills and gullies which carry a good growth of brush and acacia and provide pasture for goats and camels as well as a source of firewood. The highway twists and turns through these with as many curves as on the escarpment but gradually the greenery thins to the point where there is little left but doum palms in dry watercourses.

We saw more shot-up roadside buildings in this region, the scene of skirmishes between rebels and government forces at some point during the last ten or fifteen years, but there are no villages and little evidence of current human habitation at all. The most dramatic sign of former fighting was the electric line, built in the 1960s with tall concrete poles. The wires were cut over and over again in the 1970s and still dangle from the poles. The poles themselves, with their crosspieces, have become nesting places for storks. Long lines of poles with huge nests resembling small brush piles stretch oddly across the barren terrain. The rebels could cut the electric line but the solid old steel-reinforced concrete bridges built by the Italians still stand and give good service.

Shortly after crossing one pockmarked with shrapnel, we caught sight of the new Dogali monument, erected only two months ago — a large red star on a knoll dominating a featureless plain. When I traveled through here in 1968, there was nothing to indicate that this was the famous battlefield where Ras Alula, the ruler of Hamasien,[57] dealt the Italians a resounding defeat in January 1887 when they first tried to advance from the coast into the highlands. Haile Selassie felt no need to erect a monument here. The Derg found the hundredth anniversary of Ethiopia's first victory over the Italians, a full nine years before the Battle of Adwa, a convenient occasion to celebrate. They have not only put up this somewhat incongruous monument and issued special stamps, but they also held several commemorative events early this year, including a seminar with foreign scholars from Italy, England and Israel. It was not abstract love of history that prompted this effort but the specific aim of underscoring Ethiopia's historic presence in this region and its determination to defend it against "secessionists".

As we approached the coast, we passed caravans of camels along the roadside. They were being driven by lanky men with headcloths blowing in the wind, a reminder that this is also the edge of the Middle East. Some camels carried wood, others bundles; some had no loads. The temperature was over ninety degrees Fahrenheit. All cloud had disappeared. Three or four months from now the afternoon temperature in this region will reach one hundred twenty five. It is a raw and nasty region for rebels to contest or government forces to defend.

20 March 1987 - Evening in Massawa.

The outskirts of Massawa reminded me of Sinai towns after the 1967 Egyptian-Israeli War — piles of rubble among

The author (second from left) with Red Sea regional governor
Yekuno Amlak (far right) in Ghinda, 1987.

The author meeting with Isaias Afewerki in his office in Asmara
following the independence referendum, 1993.

Derelict busses on the edge of Tessenei. Western Eritrea was still littered with wreckage from the Derg period at the time of the refendum in 1993.

A Derg tank almost buried in the sand of the Barca river in 1993. New wreckage has been added to the landscape as a result of the Ethiopian defeat of Eritrean forces in 2000.

Boxes of Derg soldiers' bones still standing in the desert outside of Massawa, 1993.

Land mines buried by the Eritrean Army in Bademe, 1999.

Ethiopian soldiers in Denba Mengul, Bademe, 1999.

The Ethiopian Army at Denba Mengul, Badme, 1999.

Brigadier General Tserse Mekonnen and Colonel Aman assessing the battle field in Bure, 1999,

Armaments captured from the Eritrean army, 1999.

An Ethiopian soldier ready for the battle in Zalambessa, 1999.

The Ethiopian army training in Bure, 2000.

The Ethiopian army fighting in Bure, 2000.

ERITREA PROFILE

July 31, 1999 · July 24, 1999 · Price: 1 Nfa.

Why the Ethiopian regime is not interested in peace

by Saleh AA Younis

What does Ethiopia have to say about that? The Ethio-... takes place? Seyoum's Answer: The ... 1998." Ethiopia is also obliged to redeploy its forces from ... There is no point arguing with Mr. Seyoum that this ...

The TPLF regime continues to beat the war drum

Ethiopia's Council of Ministers issued a statement on 21 July 1999, unfortunately, is conspicuous for its inflammatory rhetoric and war mongering rather than the sobered language of peace. True, the statement contains a feeble "acceptance" of the Modalities of Implementation endorsed by the 35th OAU Summit in Algiers on July 14, 1999. But this is blighted by a distorted presentation of the peace formula and the TPLF's strident call for war. The Council's "appeal" for Ethiopia's "Defence Forces" to pursue further its war of aggression was in fact accentuated by a more strident call for continued war issued by the EPRDF - Ethiopia's ruling party - Wednesday evening (21 July 1999).

Whereas the Modalities of Implementation (MOI) provide for both sides ... ...

ERITREA PROFILE July 24, 1999

Resolution adopted by the Oromiya Liberation Council (OLC)

(Toronto, Canada, July 10-12, 1999)

Background

The current political setting and the current developments in the Horn of Africa forms significant impact on the current national struggle of the ...

Headlines and articles taken from the *Eritrea Profile*, Eritrea's government owned newspaper.

t, 1999
Page 6

CPE's statement concerning the british government's understanding of the issue of ethnic cleansing in Ethiopia

deportations with the Ethiopian Foreign Minister, who has assured our Embassy in Addis Ababa that they have ended. We are not directly aware of any children who remain abandoned in Ethiopia due to earlier deportations but we are aware of unconfirmed press reports of such incidents last December. If HHR knew of specific cases, our Embassy staff would be happy to raise them with the authorities, but before doing so will need details of the individuals involved...

victims. The climate of Assab is scorching but above 40 degrees centigrade At the Burie front-line the people walked long distances in the no-mans land and they sailed 36 hours in an open ship to the port of Massawa. On arrival in Massawa the people were exhausted. Many suffered from food poisoning and diarrhoea. One woman died of heat stroke. One man was hysterical able to bear...

possible without the wilful co-operation of the Diplomatic Community in Ethiopia.

A feature of this conflict has been the wide disparity between the views of diplomats in Addis Ababa and Asmara, as has been reflected in conflicting statements by the two countries ambassadors as well...

that Mr. G.G. Wetherill cannot report events in an even-handed manner.

In spite of all these real polisk we still believe that human rights are entitlement and claims of all humanity beings...

What part of "non-use of force to settle disputes" does Ethiopia not understand?

by Gideon Musa (Visafrik)

conflict should start off by violating these fundamental principles in the OAU Modalities for the Implementation of the Framework Agreement.

In contrast, Eritrea's acceptance speech reaffirmed the country's commitment to a peaceful resolution of the conflict. In a speech accepting the Modalities, ... Isaias Afwerki ac-

ment say where Ethiopia stands on the most important principles in the Modalities: that of non-use of force, and of hostilities and cease-fire. Instead, the Ethiopian statement focuses on the lie that Eritrea has not accepted the Modalities. It is beyond anyone's comprehension how Ethiopia can keep accusing Eritrea of not accepting the Modalities...

war is not the solution to the conflict, of the importance of a face to face meeting and of the need for an immediate cease-fire. On the other hand, every pronouncement from Ethiopia has been full of threats, saber rattling, attempts to hoodwink the international community and insults against anyone -or-ganization, group or individual- that dared to call for unconditional cease-fire and a peaceful resolution to...

all along said that the Modalities do not hold anything new to that contained in the OAU framework then why the delay in announcing its "acceptance". After all, if the Modalities are exactly the same as the Framework Agreement it approved earlier, what was there for the parliament to approve again? Could it be that the Ethiopian government was caught off guard by the Modalities reaffirming the call for a cease-fire almost ... facts. (to use Ethio-

Agordat has one of the most impressive mosques in western Eritrea.

Barentu in 1993. The attractive little town of Barentu was quickly captured by Ethiopia in May 2000.

The monks from this historic monastery in Debre Bizen, founded in the 14th century, believed it remained unscathed by the Derg because God protected it.

Senafe on the main highway between Zalambessa and Asmara lies among dramatic mountains.

Gulij, a small village and market between Tessenei and Om Hager.

The flat lands near Tessenei, not far from the Sudan border, were quickly captured by Ethiopian farmers in May 2000.

The Red Sea Hotel in Massawa, March 1987. It was later severely damaged by Derg bombing after the EPLF capture of Massawa in early 1990.

shattered mudbrick walls with roof beams and window and door frames protruding at odd angles, pieces of cupboards, old carts and rusting metal scattered around. The section of this ancient port city on the mainland shows the effects of the hard fighting of the winter of 1977-1978 when the Eritrean rebels were so confident of capturing it that they took time out to quarrel among themselves and lost their best chance to prevail over the Derg. Some of the damage was caused by Ethiopian artillery firing from the islands on which the old city stands, but soon after the Russians decided to give full backing to the Derg, they brought up naval vessels and aircraft to bombard the rebel-held mainland from the sea. The results are still gruesomely visible. People here discuss these events with frankness and as if they happened only last week. Since the scars of war are still so visible the experience is more real. No one has expressed any gratitude to the Russians in the few hours I have been here. Several local people have pointed to the destruction and commented that it was largely unnecessary but typical of the way the Russians do things and typical of the way the Derg does things too when it follows the Russian lead.

The railyards were the most depressing sight of all – a great jumble of wrecked wagons and engines good for nothing but scrap. During our descent this afternoon, we marveled at the tunnels and viaducts of the narrow-gauge escarpment railway crossing over and under the highway several times. It is a more dramatic example of Italian engineering skill than the highway itself. This railway, an easy target for guerrillas and difficult to repair, was rendered inoperable by the beginning of the 1970s. There were never any serious attempts to restore it. I doubt now whether restoring it would fit anybody's economic priorities.

If true peace could be established, the railway could become a major tourist attraction, given the fascination with trains and old railways current in the developed world. But for now the railyards will probably be one of the last parts of mainland Massawa to be cleaned up because no one is going to profit by doing so.

During the 1977-1978 fighting the rebels lacked guns that could inflict serious physical damage on the islands which form the oldest part of Massawa. Consequently the lovely old quarter on the outer island, probably the least spoiled of all the old ports on the Red Sea, shows almost no damage at all. We drove across the causeway to Taulud, the other principal island, and pulled up in front of the Red Sea Hotel. In all essentials it is unchanged since I last stayed here in the fall of 1968. It remains one of the most beautiful hotels in Africa with its graceful tall arches and floors of glazed tile. The gardens surrounding it are reasonably well maintained and a large new area is in the process of being landscaped and planted near the shore. Our first pleasure on getting into our rooms was a cool shower. Water seems to be no problem here. The air conditioning is not working, but the temperature cools to the low eighties in the evening this time of the year and we are not suffering, though the humidity is heavy. I noted some socialist inefficiency about the main desk. The gift shop which is well stocked but not open. The hotel appears to be only about a quarter occupied.

A welcome party awaited us when we came down to the lobby for drinks. It included the WPE secretary of the Red Sea Province and the *Shum* mayor of Massawa. Governor Yekuno Amlak and Abraha joined us as well. The party secretary, Guad Tekole Bekele, is a police officer from Shoa. He was born in the countryside north of Addis Ababa, graduated from the Sendafa Police Training School and has spent a total of eleven years in Eritrea out of his past fifteen years of service. The mayor, Guad Samuel, is a Catholic Bilen [58] from Keren, a bright young fellow who made a special point of telling us he had been elected to his office.

Both the party secretary and the mayor were eager to talk about their work and their problems. They must know how to use current socialist jargon and party slogans, but these were totally absent from their conversation. Both speak good English. Nothing they had to say tonight could characterize them as rabid communists. They are concerned with the practical problems of trying to get this old city back on its feet. It is far from recovered from the fighting of almost ten years ago. The city has eighteen thousand inhabitants now. It had almost fifty thousand in 1974. Essential services are restored and the port is working but, as Guad Tekole admitted frankly, "If we had more people here we would have a serious unemployment problem, because we don't have economic development going yet — that is our biggest job."

After drinks we set out on a tour of the city, including the port. Haile Selassie's statue, on a tall pedestal, still overlooks the main harbor, but it has been wrapped in burlap. I mused but did not ask whether it was to keep the people from seeing him or to keep him from seeing what has happened here since his demise. Across the harbor to the west, the domes of his winter palace are still prominent. I asked whether I could visit it and was told it would be included on our schedule tomorrow. The port was not very busy — only two ships at dock. Most ships coming in here are bringing food. Guad Tekole said traffic had been light recently but they had just sold two shiploads of salt to the Japanese at ten dollars per ton. The salt works, long an important industry in Massawa, is producing enough for

127

export and they are eager to find other foreign buyers. "How much salt did it take to make two shiploads?" I asked.

"Tweny-thousand tons," he replied.

"I wonder whether at ten dollars per ton you really made any money on it — it must have cost that much to produce it," I continued.

"That may be true," he replied,"but it was foreign exchange."

Ethiopia's import/export gap has widened ever since the revolution. Foreign currency earnings are a bright feather in the party secretary's cap. Guad Tekole pointed across the harbor to the cement works where smoke showed that work was in progress. "They are producing cement," he said, "But we have not had any success yet in arranging for exports."

We got back into our vehicles and drove across the old city. All its ornate old buildings with their graceful arches and wooden balconies are undamaged.[59] Guad Tekole promised a walking tour tomorrow. We stopped at the seaward end of Massawa island where a tall lighthouse stands. It is being renovated. Men were fishing off the wall at the base of the lighthouse and a few local citizens were taking the evening air along the shore. Even though the sun had not yet set, the air was cooling appreciably. Far out at sea we could see ships passing. Guad Tekole was interested in the fish. He enjoys deep sea fishing and goes out whenever he can find time, which is too seldom, he said: "The sea is full of fish of many kinds. They are some of the best in the world. There are lobster and shrimp too. We do a little commercial fishing now and keep Asmara supplied with fish. But Ethiopians don't eat lobster and shrimp, so these aren't used at all. We have the basis here for a big fishing industry. Fish could be frozen and flown to Europe.

We are trying to get the Italians interested in investing. We will give them very favorable terms. Fishing could supply employment for hundreds of people and bring in a good deal of foreign exchange."

Then we went back across the causeway to the mainland. The mayor pointed out a modest area of new housing that had recently been completed. We passed the salt works and drove to a beach called Gugursum to the north of the city. I recalled that Americans from Kagnew used to camp here on weekends, and there was a motel here too. "The EPLF destroyed everything on this beach when they were forced out of their positions in 1978. They deliberately wrecked the motel and restaurant, pulled down the electric lines, and tore up the highway. We have restored it all," Guad Tekole concluded, gesturing over the whole area with pride. The Eritrean trade unions are responsible for the new installations which include sleeping accommodations for sixty people, a bar and a restaurant, showers and beach facilities.

We sat around a large table in the center of the outdoor bar and drank, variously, gin and tonic, whisky, and beer through the eight o'clock TV news which Guad Tekole told me he was eager to hear because he wanted further information on the recent *shumshir* in Addis Ababa. There were no new announcements in connection with that, however. Afterward talk again turned to economic development. They described the role of the Rashaida, the principal inhabitants of the Dahlak Islands, in fishing development. They talked about other marine industries such as gathering of shells and processing mother-of-pearl. They outlined all the attractions of the area for tourism: fishing, diving, water sports.

I commented that I saw two serious problems with developing tourism: one, tourists are not going to come in any numbers until Eritrea is peaceful. There are too many other places for them to go; and two, to accommodate any real flow of tourists they will need more than the Red Sea Hotel and that will require substantial investment. Ethiopia doesn't have the resources to invest more in tourism and no foreigners are going to invest while security is so uncertain. They insisted the insurgents are not really a problem now: "We are keeping them out of the way up in the north. They will get tired of living indefinitely in the ruins of Nacfa. The young people are already tired of that. They are no longer with them. People are leaving the areas the secessionists hold now," Guad Tekole volunteered. He wanted to make clear he didn't take them too seriously and was confident they could never win.

"But how are you going to settle the problem?" I asked, sensing this might be good occasion to get more insight into how they saw it; "it doesn't look to me as if you can defeat them militarily."

"We can keep them out of the cities and expand our control of the countryside. If they weren't getting support from Arabs who have always hated Ethiopia, they couldn't keep fighting," he replied, "but even that is no longer enough to keep the young people with them." It was the same story I had heard in Asmara — they all claim the youth are deserting the secessionists.

"If you had better relations with your neighbors, you might be able to do something about Arab support," I noted. "Our government is working on that."

"That will take time, but you'd all be better off in this part of the world if you weren't fighting each other. Then you could get down to business on what you say is the most important issue: economic development," I concluded. Since they had already brought up this subject several times, I decided this was as good a time as any to get into it a little deeper. So we talked about the reasons Westerners invest in the Third World and some of the places that are attracting investment now. I described how Turkey and Pakistan have reformed their economies in recent years but still have to work hard to attract investment. Laws alone don't attract it and investors want to be convinced about a country's stability and its commitment to sensible economic policies. Investors are also increasingly interested in a good labor force, I said. Education has to keep abreast of the electronic age. They said they were aware of this problem. The mayor described their school system. They have eight elementary schools in operation in Massawa and one secondary school. They are getting ready to open a vocational school. There is a disproportionate number of young people in the population of the city. They are not encouraging more young people to come in but they want to give all those who are here as good an education as possible.

As we were speaking of young people, I realized that we were surrounded by them. A large party of local "tourists" had arrived from Asmara. They were telecommunications workers, men and women, and had been brought here in an NTO[60] bus under sponsorship of their union for a beach weekend. They gathered at tables on all sides of us. Most of them were watching local television which after news featured an American serial film. A few went out to dance on a platform between the casino and the water. Others strolled on the beach, but none went into the water. Some looked a bit ill at ease, not quite knowing what to do with themselves, unaccustomed to being on a weekend outing. Word had probably also got around that it was the party secretary, the governor and the mayor who were entertaining two visiting *ferenjis* at the long table in the center of the outdoor bar. So when it came time for a third round of drinks, John and I suggested it was time to go back to the city for dinner. Would we be able to find a restaurant with fresh fish? Guad Tekole commented it was a pity we had not asked sooner, for he had a well stocked freezer and would gladly have sent the hotel some prime fish to prepare for us, but he was sure the hotel would have fish in any case.

We drove back into the city through the warm, quiet night. Massawa's streets are deserted at 9 P.M. in the evening. The hotel served the four of us a good dinner with excellent red snapper. John Burns tells me that while we were in Jimma the Ministry of Information called his office for several more sets of my *Encounter* articles. They seem to have been sent up to Eritrea in advance of my coming.[61] This may account for the warmth of my reception there. All these fellows in their blue suits thirst for material that shows real understanding of Ethiopia, that expresses the same thoughts so many of them have.

I go to sleep with the Red Sea lapping against the shore beyond the garden. Occasionally there is the call of a seabird, but otherwise no sound at all. Up on the escarpment, I suppose, EPLF patrols may be moving through the night. If this region could be restored to economic good health, most of the guerrillas could become businessmen. Marxism is no recipe for anyone's economic health.

21 March 1987 - Morning in Massawa.

Awakened by a brilliant pink sunrise over the Red Sea, I was grateful the night was over. At some point the wind shifted and hordes of mosquitoes flew in my open window

132

from the hotel garden. I had to wrap myself in the bedsheet from head to toe to keep from being devoured by them.

Morning in Massawa was divided into two equally interesting parts. First we went to the boat works at the southern tip of the island of Taulud, a quarter of a mile beyond the hotel. Here we met a remarkable man, Ato Adefris Bellehu, who is in charge of a low-cost technology project, an excellent example of foreign aid and local initiative combined. Adefris is a Shoan who for twelve years headed the Desert Locust Control Organization of East Africa (DLCOEA), capping off a twenty-seven year career in the organization. He was a good friend of David Buxton[62] in his early years in Ethiopia and showed us a letter he had recently received from him. It had saddened Adefris, because Buxton wrote that at seventy-seven he had concluded he was too old to visit Ethiopia again.

The boat-building operation is supported by the Lutheran World Federation. How great a hand the government or party have in it I am not sure (there was little evidence of any), but Ethiopian officials in Eritrea are under so much pressure to make anything work that no matter what official stance dogmatists in Addis Ababa might take, officials on the spot welcome any help they can get and make the most of it. That was certainly the attitude of Guad Tekole, the Governor and the Mayor. Adefris seems to have warm relations with them but he is the man who calls the shots on his project. The aim of the project is to train local people to build ferroconcrete boats that can be used by fishermen to increase their catch and market it. The process is simple but requires great attention to detail. A frame is made of wire mesh. Fine concrete is then sprayed over it. The concrete is cured slowly, with frequent spraying of water. The result is a hull about an inch thick that feels like plywood. The graceful little vessel rides as smoothly in the water as if it were wood but it is, of course, not vulnerable to sea worms nor attractive to barnacles.

To date they have built six four-ton boats. After showing us two in the process of construction and the frame of a ten ton vessel that is the first of this size they are trying, Adefris took us on board the latest vessel to be completed for a cruise through the harbor area, around Green Island and back. The mayor and Getachew Asfaw accompanied John and me. Our crew consisted of two Ethiopian Navy men, both out of uniform. Adefris excitedly described the fish that teem in the sea here: grouper, snapper, tuna, palamut, mackerel as well as lobster and shrimp. The area between Massawa and the Buri Peninsula to the south, he said, is largely a shrimp bed. He pointed to the peninsul − a pale blue mountain looming over the smooth sea to the south.

It was a pleasure to be out in the fresh breeze even though the sun was hot. We learned more about Adefris, who was happy to talk about himself. He has ten children from three successive wives. He has given them all a good education. Three of them live in the States and are American citizens. Though he has extensive connections with Europe and America and dozens of good friends among foreigners who worked in Ethiopia, he has no desire to leave the country. He still follows locust control developments but says that DLCOEA has declined in effectiveness. Politics has entered into personnel management and people are favored because of their nationality, not their competence.

We had excellent views of the city, saw porpoises jumping, heard about activities in the Dahlak Islands. There are six hundred fishermen there who, with their families, make up a population of about four thousand. The boats being produced here are primarily for the Dahlak fishermen. The aim is to develop a large-scale fishing industry around them.

As we cruised, a helicopter flew over the city, heading eastward to sea. Ato Adefris chuckled. "See that Russian helicopter?" he said. "It is going out to the Dahlak islands and it is probably carrying some of our cement, for we are building a jetty for the islanders. We were having difficulty getting materials out to them so I decided to work on the Russians and finally persuaded them to haul cement. I told them they don't do any good for the people — their weapons just set everybody here against everybody and keep Eritreans fighting each other. I shamed them, I believe, into doing something for us." So the Russians are helping the Lutheran World Federation implement a project for the Dahlak islanders!

We cruised close in along the shore of Green Island. It is mostly a ledge of mangrove. A roofed shelter in an open meadow is used for picnic outings. Turning back toward the boat-building dock, we passed a spur of Taulud with a white villa visible behind walls and gardens. "Whose was that?" I asked. "It is Signora Melotti's house," Adefris explained. All the Melotti property in Eritrea was nationalized, but they were permitted to keep this house. Signora Melotti comes every year to spend part of the winter in it. I believe she is in residence now."[63] I was astonished. Marxists do have a bit of soul, I thought.

Signora Melotti was one of the *grandes dames* of Eritrean society, appreciated for her charitable activities as well as the contribution her family's business enterprises made to local life and employment. The Derg has not had many friends in Eritrea. Practical calculations probably lay behind the decision to permit the family to retain the villa. The Derg needs Italian economic aid and is getting some, as I learned on my visit to the former Barattolo textile mill yesterday. Unfortunately, we found no time to try to call on Signora Melotti.

The Party Secretary and Governor were waiting to greet us at the dock when we returned, happy to hear that we had been impressed by the boat works. Adefris invited us all into his office for drinks – choice of coffee, tea, beer or Sabarguma – and dried shark. Three wives have not dimmed Adefris' eye for interesting women. His secretary, who served us, was a tall, shapely young lady, stylishly dressed and with a spectacular braided hairdo the like of which I have never seen in Ethiopia before. I asked if she were an Eritrean displaying some local style. He laughed. She comes from Wollo!

We had more discussion of boat-building and fishing: costs of boats, possible variations in design, fishermen's earnings. Adefris had neat charts on the wall showing each working boat's catch over a period of months and the value of fish sold. There were wide variations. Everyone talked of the beauty of the Dahlaks and urged us to visit them. The party secretary said he could arrange a trip if we could stay another day. I wonder whether the Ethiopian military would permit it, given the Russian presence there. In any case, with our tight schedule, the issue was academic. The morning was fast moving toward noon, so we said good-bye to Adefris, his comely, smiling secretary and his assistants and drove off for a tour of the old city. I felt very good about this boat-building project. Not only is the Lutheran World Federation making a good practical investment but, more important, the local people are seeing an example of "appropriate technology" that works. If this kind of project could be reproduced ten or fifteen times in various fields, and if enough Adefrises could be found to operate them, Massawa might really come back to life.

Driving back across Taulud to the main island on which old Massawa was originally established perhaps a thousand years ago, we parked the vehicles at the edge of the old town and toured on foot with Guad Tekole and Shum Samuel as guides. Governor Yekuno Amlak went off on other business and rejoined us later. It seemed so natural at the time to be strolling around, photographing old buildings, looking into the courtyards of mosques, watching people go about their daily activities and dropping in at shops that I gave no thought to security, but as we were driving up the escarpment afterwards John and I, with some amazement, reflected on the fact that no policemen or soldiers accompanied us and these Derg officials were completely at ease walking around in what are supposed, for them, to be hostile surroundings. The party secretary spoke of the need for historical preservation and restoration and seemed to have developed a genuine appreciation for the architecture, calling fine examples of woodcarving to my attention, stopping to contemplate an arcaded street with overhanging balconies and pointing out that the city's oldest mosque had recently been repaired and repainted a light mint green.

Streets were comparatively lively. Boys were playing football. Women were roasting food over open grills. Men were loading and hauling things. We stopped to visit a shoemaker who was crafting leather shoes and sandals by hand. The leather was good and the shoes, both men's and women's, looked sturdy. Half the shops, however, were closed and apparently empty. The prohibition on private signs here appears not to be enforced, for a few restaurants and bars had signs and so did handicraft shops. The souvenir shop operated by the NTO had a good window display but was closed (as was the one in the hotel during our entire visit). The people in charge get the same salary whether they sell anything or not— so why inconvenience themselves by opening up? A privately run shop nearby had a great variety of things — seashells, pottery, beads, turtle shells, the awesome snouts of sawfish, doum palm nuts, old chests, Ethiopian flags. We stopped in another general-purpose shop selling everything from men's and women's clothing, soap and toiletries to flashlight batteries, candy and chewing gum. Next to the gum a tray of brightly labeled condoms was displayed. So most elementary needs seem to be satisfiable in Massawa in spite of its downtrodden condition.

The trip back up the escarpment was a repeat of all the sights of yesterday: camels in the desert, then greenery, a stop at Ghinda. It was lunchtime and the restaurant was serving spicy *wats* with and without meat. There were not many clouds today but one cluster still clung to the heights of Debra Bizen. We stopped and I got out to photograph its site above Nefasit. Soldiers at a guardpost above spotted me and came rushing out to halt us when we rounded the next hairpin bend. Our *wereketoch* (papers) convinced them that they had not apprehended a posse of capitalist spies. Traveling in Eritrea without official sponsorship would not be a comfortable experience. So much for tourism.

The escarpment highway was even busier today than it had been yesterday. Much of the traffic consisted of trucks heavily loaded with bags of grain coming up from Massawa. We must have passed as many as two hundred of them. There were also trucks coming up from Ghinda with vegetables. We saw surprisingly few military vehicles but there appears to be a good deal of passenger car traffic up and down on Saturdays now simply for pleasure. Asmara was utterly cloudless and the air clear. The city seems to generate almost no pollution. We drove past people everywhere carrying water from barrels to their houses. It was a bit after two in the afternoon when we pulled up in front of the Ambasoara.

21 March 1987-Asmara-Markets and Party Secretary.

A fellow named Abdurrahman from party headquarters was waiting to take us on an afternoon tour of markets and sections of the city we had not yet seen. During the next two hours we visited five markets: the *Edaga Kebti* (cattle market), the *Edaga Ekhli* (grain market), the *Edaga Ahmilti* (vegetable market) and the Barca Market which specializes in basketry, matting and other handicrafts. Finally we walked through the market area devoted to second-hand goods, machinery and spare parts that extends over several blocks opposite the Grand Mosque toward the huge open square in front of the Orthodox church of St. Mary. I was surprised by the amount of activity in all these markets.

This was true even of the cattle market where much of the trading takes place in the morning. Horses and mules were not being traded, but large numbers of sheep and goats were being sold. Most impressive were the oxen and other kinds of cattle accompanied by extraordinarily picturesque people. This cattle market provides a live exhibit of all the tribes and races that inhabit Eritrea. The Middle East and Africa come together here. You see it in people's faces and profiles, in their elegant posture, sculptured noses and long hands, in hair that ranges from kinky to only slightly wavy, always black or very deep brown, in skins of all shades from pinkish bronze to gray-black. Some of the people here had driven their animals all the way from Tessenei and Barentu, for prices are apparently better in Asmara.

The cattle were as fascinating as the men and boys tending them and bargaining for them. I saw every color that cattle can have and some combinations I have never seen before — hides of several colors, like tabby cats, and cream, white and gray shades with splotches and spots. Many of the beasts had splendid curved horns with a span of three or four feet. Some looked weakened by the weight of their horns and had ribs showing beneath their hides. Others looked sleek and well fed.

The cattle market covers an immense area on a gradually rising slope. From the top there is a good view of much of the city. We watched a section where plow oxen were being put through their paces for prospective buyers, turning up the dry earth and responding to commands to turn and stop. Foreigners must come to this market seldom, for we were as much an object of curiosity for the people there as they and their animals were for us. By the time we were ready to make our way from the top of the slope and back down to the entrance gate, we had collected a retinue of a couple of hundred boys. I took advantage of every opportunity to tell people we were Americans, though no one seemed to mistake us for Russians. We saw no Russians during this entire afternoon in Asmara. No one ever speaks of them. It is as if they were evil and mention of them might bring bad luck.

The grain and vegetable markets were well supplied. So much so that I wonder how they can ever dispose of all the perishable produce they have to offer. In addition to wheat, *teff*, barley and oats, there was *durra* and *dagusa* (standard millet and finger millet), a couple of dozen kinds of beans, peas, lentils and other legumes and seeds whose names I did not have time to ask. Though most of the grain sellers were men, women with the attractive Tigrean hairstyle were selling too. The block-long roofed hall of the main vegetable market was filled with great piles of produce: tomatoes, peppers, cabbage, squash, potatoes, eggplant, carrots, many kinds of onions, lettuce and other salad greens, oranges, bananas and papayas. There was too little room in the covered hall to accommodate all the sellers. Many were selling from carts or boxes in nearby streets. The spice market, exuding exotic aromas, was the most colorful of all. The assortment of spices was enormous: dozens of grinds and shades of red pepper alone, hundreds of other powders, leaves, seeds, chips and chunks. Dried fruits are sold in the spice market. Several kinds of dates were on sale.

One wall of the vegetable market hall was hung with shopping bags made of the woven nylon sacks in which emergency grain comes from abroad. The bags are made so that the legends printed on the grainsacks are readable – so the donors get continual advertising of their generosity. I bought three different examples: "FURNISHED BY THE PEOPLE OF THE UNITED STATES OF AMERICA- NOT TO BE SOLD OR EXCHANGED"; "CANADA– WHEAT – GIFT OF CANADA"; and "ETHIOPIA – GIFT OF THE EUROPEAN COMMUNITY – ACTION OF THE WORLD FOOD PROGRAM – ASSAB".

No meat was on sale in the markets this afternoon because it is Lent and Christians are all fasting. I get the impression everywhere I have been in Ethiopia on this visit that fasts for both Christians and Muslims are still strictly observed, except among Party people who, if they do observe them, cannot afford to admit it.

At the Barca market we found a more elaborate example of utilization of emergency food containers. Several tinsmiths were crafting chests of cans in which U.S. food was supplied (oil, sugar, bulgur, meal) and these too were cut so that the print on the metal was preserved and clearly visible on the inside of the chests. The inscriptions and instructions were often in several languages. Some had been printed for Turkish earthquake victims. Others had instructions in Indian and SE Asian languages. Many were in Spanish. The chests seemed to be selling briskly, for there were only three finished ones available. John and I each bought one. The Barca market has as great a selection of baskets and matting as I have ever seen in one place in Ethiopia. There is a good deal of pottery too. One narrow alleyway was occupied by leather workers. I was happy to see that the leather baby-carriers decorated with rows of cowries in the pattern of a cross are still being made and used.

Streets were crowded as we drove from one market area to another. Bicycles are popular here. Motor vehicles in the commercial sections of the city include enough old trucks, vans and wagons of various kinds to stock a museum. Except when we moved from one area to another we left our white Mercedes behind and moved around on foot. I wanted to have as little identification as possible with the Mercedes. I was surprised to see a good many shiny late-model, mostly Japanese, cars in the commercial sections of the city. "Who can afford to buy them?" I asked our young party escort, Abdurrahman. "Businessmen," he replied in a very matter-of-fact way with perhaps a slight touch of envy. "They are the ones who are making real money here now." Ever since the Italians began to develop it in the 1930s, Asmara has been a lively commercial city. Even through recent tribulations, it seems to have retained that character, though most of this "business" doubtless fails to show up in official statistics.

In the course of one of our moves from market to market, we drove up to a high point called Cherekh in the northern part of the city. It has been crowned with a new park with a circular restaurant at its center. The restaurant was designed by an architect at Addis Ababa University and the local authorities have obviously lavished a good deal of care on its surroundings. A well paved road leads up to

142

ample parking space. The slopes of the hill have been planted with cactus, eucalyptus, jacaranda and oleander and gardens along the low stone walls that circle the top contain a dozen kinds of decorative and blooming plants. With water as short as it is here, keeping all these plantings alive is a major accomplishment. Views over the city with banks of lavender jacaranda in front of us were superb. Predominant colors of the buildings are tan and gold. Since Asmara has few tall buildings, minarets and church towers dominate its skyline. A yellow Orthodox church caught the sunlight on the edge of the escarpment. Directly below, in streets at the foot of the hill, we had a less picturesque sight-long rows of more than a hundred vari-colored water barrels, a reminder of the mayor's number one problem.

While we were taking in the views, a wedding party arrived in several cars and taxis, with the bride and groom in a black limousine, for a reception at the restaurant. The bride was dressed in a fluffy white gown, carrying flowers, and the groom wore a formal black suit. A photographer posed the wedding party for pictures with first the restaurant and then the view of the city as background. They were Muslims, Abdurrahman told us, for during Lent Christians do not celebrate weddings.

The variety of things for sale in the second-hand and junk market area defies description. Items left over from the Italian colonial period and the early stages of World War II can still be found. There must be spare parts for every kind of vehicle that has ever traveled the roads of this part of the world. I have never been able to understand why sellers would keep such quantities of rusted axles, rims, flywheels and springs. If Ethiopia had an iron and steel industry such things would no doubt have been sold for scrap. Here they contribute to what is almost a museum of miscellaneous technology. Large areas are now devoted to second-hand clothing, furniture of all kinds, sewing machines and refrigerators, various kinds of agricultural machines, grinders and machine-shop equipment.

Repeating what other officials here have told us, the party secretary tonight described the influx of young men into the city they are now experiencing. It was easy to believe him after I had seen hundreds of them around the market area, especially in these second-hand sections. Some were selling odds and ends, others just passing the time. The same was true along National Avenue this evening. Before we finished our afternoon tour there at the NTO shop, we visited Asmara Mariam.

The Axumite replica structures that form the entrance to the vast open church square are beautifully maintained and parts have been newly painted. A little boy and girl dressed in traditional embroidered white *buluqo* outfits posed for me in front of a deep red door. Their parents were nowhere to be seen but the well-bred youngsters felt no apprehension about talking to foreigners. We walked across the square, past the stone bell, up to the church entrance where men and women were praying at walls and kissing the vivid rose-colored doors. This beautiful church is completely unchanged from my last pre-revolutionary visit to it.

As we drove back to the hotel John and I reflected on the absence of the hideous and silly communist banners and posters with slogans, the red flags and the shabby arches, pillars and miscellaneous monuments that deface most Ethiopian towns. We had seen none we could remember in the course of the afternoon. Without them Asmara has a much more elegant and civilized — even normal — appearance. This city nevertheless remains an ideological battlefront for the Marxist regime. Why does the Derg suppress its sloganry here? Is it because they want to avoid antagonizing Eritreans?

Or simply because they have not had time to put them up? Or because people tear them down and mutilate them?

At the hotel we learned that an early evening meeting with the Eritrean WPE Secretary, Dr. Teferra Wonde, had been confirmed. The meeting was a good climax to my Eritrean visit. Dr. Teferra's reception of me was so warm, in fact, that I feared I might in some way have been misrepresented as friendly toward the Derg rather than simply a friend of Ethiopia. If that had been the case, I corrected the illusion, I hope, in the course of the meeting.

Guad Teferra, a WPE Central Committee member, has been the senior Derg representative in Eritrea for almost four years, since Dawit Wolde-Giorgis[64] was shifted from here to the Relief and Rehabilitation Commission in Addis Ababa. His wife is also a Central Committee member, in charge of women's affairs, but has remained in Addis Ababa during the entire time he has been here. It must be an austere, hard-working life. He is a medical doctor, a specialist in parasitology with experience lecturing in both France and the U.S. I had heard very different opinions of him: hard-line communist, dedicated human being, a man over his head in a difficult job...

It was a few minutes after six when our white Mercedes was ushered through the gate of the Eritrean headquarters of the Workers' Party of Ethiopia – the former Asmara municipality – without even having to slow down. It is a grand Italian building in the most palatial Mussolini-style, with six meters ceilings on the main floor. Their pretense at being the chosen representatives of the broad masses and defenders of the interests of the poor and downtrodden never for a moment, I suspect, gives these "Workers' Party" types pause about occupying a building so monumental. The Russians like this sort of thing. The building is currently being refurbished. The polished tile halls smelled of fresh paint and varnish. I remembered that Ras Asrate Kassa's office in the former governor's palace had been much more modest.

At party headquarters long duty hours seem to be the norm. The secretary had been at work all of a Saturday afternoon. The attendant in the cavernous reception room motioned us directly into his office, a regal chamber with a large red-bordered portrait of Chairman Mengistu five meters feet up on the wall behind his chair. On his desk were Ethiopian and red flags. I did not take time to notice much else in the room except the maps of Ethiopia and Eritrea on the walls, for Guad Teferra motioned us to sit on an arrangement of chairs directly in front of the desk and we plunged immediately into conversation. Fisseha Zewde, who had not joined us on the afternoon tour, was with him when we arrived.

First, there was a lavish welcome speech — how important it was for me to visit Eritrea, how honored he was that I had time to come to see him, how good a friend of Ethiopia he knew me to be, how he had read my writings and knew that I had always supported Ethiopian territorial integrity. (But had he read the *Encounter* pieces? I asked myself and concluded that Fisseha must at least have briefed him on them.) He recalled his experiences in the U.S. lecturing at the University of Massachusetts at Amherst where he had spent two years. He obviously had fond memories of life in the U.S. — the kind of memories it is difficult to conceive any Ethiopian having of life in the Soviet Union or anywhere in Eastern Europe. But I found him a puzzling man. I suppose anyone in this Eritrean job would be. Dawit Wolde Giorgis was too.

Niceties out of the way, we got down to serious discussion and most of the remaining hour I spent with him was devoted to talk, direct and indirect, of the problem of the "secessionists". I asked him to sum up the current state of the insurgency: "The bandits are not winning. They cannot win. We have gained ground against them. The result is that they are becoming more brutal. They are on the defensive. They are trying to frighten the population into supporting them but they are only alienating them."

"What are the main changes in the situation you have observed during your four years here?"

"People are flowing back into Asmara. Not so much old people as young ones, especially young men who are anxious to avoid being pressed to join the bandits. Four years ago Asmara's schools were underattended. Now they are all overcrowded and we are hard put to find room for everybody. The recent ESLCE was taken by a record number of high school students. The pressure on the university is heavy — you have heard about that. We expect it to increase but we cannot expand enough to meet the demand. We are trying to expand vocational education. We are also trying to create more employment opportunities."

He continued: "The Eritrean people are tired of fighting and want peace. Our government has established its authority over more and more of the countryside. Farmers want to farm and get some return from it. Cultivation of cotton has increased to the point where Eritrea is now largely self-sufficient and almost all the needs of the Asmara Textile Factory are being provided from within Eritrea. In all we have forty-two industries in operation and aim to have more. We need more trade and we are trying to find more products to export so we can earn foreign exchange."

Like all the other officials to whom we had talked, Dr. Teferra showed keen concern about economic issues: "We are trying to produce as much food as possible. Eritrea now essentially feeds itself and even exports some food while

147

receiving some from the outside." The claim that the food situation in Eritrea is really solved was an exaggeration, and John Burns broke in at this point and outlined projected American food aid — twenty-eight thousand tons this year — based on current Derg estimates of needs. "These projections are based on the assumption that there will be no serious harvest failures" John stressed. "We can't really be sure until later in the year."

Dr. Teferra conceded there were still uncertainties. He also sensed the desirability of saying something about U.S. and other Western food aid: "We are still receiving American grain and it is very important to us. We appreciate this help."

I said I was persuaded as a result of this visit that they had made progress in reducing the impact of the insurgency on the most important parts of Eritrea: "Nevertheless it does not look to me as if the insurgency can ever be overcome militarily. In fact, the solution seems to me to be much more likely to be found in economic measures."

He agreed that economic measures were very important. I was eager to pursue this point so continued: "I conclude from what I have seen in both Asmara and Massawa that you still have the basis for a strong economy here. There has been less damage than I had expected. I was impressed by the large quantities of fruit and vegetables I saw in your markets this afternoon. It looks to me as if you are already producing enough of some of these things to be able to export them. But exports of any kind — especially processed food and manufactured goods such as leather and textiles — can only be successful in the framework of economic policies that make trade and foreign investment attractive." He nodded agreement.

"Realization of the importance of economic relations with the outer world seems much stronger in Eritrea," I said, "probably because this region of Ethiopia has had a close relationship with the outer world over a much longer time than the rest of the country." He agreed wholeheartedly, and like all intelligent Derg officials I have talked to, his eyes lit up at the historical reference. What history-conscious people Ethiopians are! But I did not want to drift too far back into history so went on: "It looks more and more to me as if constructive economic policies are the key to the whole Eritrean problem. That is the message the young men coming into Asmara to escape becoming guerrillas and get an education are, in effect, bringing. The whole basis of the insurgency could be removed if the province were to become a real economic success. You have tried a military solution and it has not worked. Why don't you make an all-out effort to solve the problem by economic development?"

He probably sensed I was ready to raise basic questions about Derg economic policies. This line of thought went beyond what he felt comfortable discussing and, I suppose, his authority. How many Derg officials have come to grief in the course of trying to be sensible about Eritrea! Guad Teferra does not want to suffer the same fate. So he shifted ground to discuss the historical importance of Eritrea to Ethiopia and the fact that no Ethiopian government could bargain about the country's territorial integrity. This I found a good occasion to get in a reminder of the fact that it was their models and idols in Moscow, Havana and elsewhere who had helped get them into this predicament: "You know I have always emphasized Ethiopia's territorial integrity in my writings. Nobody writing in the West makes this point more often than I do. But I am not unique among Americans. U.S. policy favored the reintegration of Eritrea into Ethiopia at the end of WWII. America has never wavered from that policy. It is the people you now claim are your friends who gave training and money and weapons to stir up Eritrean insurgency in the first place. They are the ones who built up the EPLF. I have no responsibility to speak for the American government now, but I did in the Carter Administration and we adhered to a firm position on Ethiopian territorial integrity. The Reagan Administration has followed the same policy."

This, too, was touchy ground for Dr. Teferra. He knew full well the implications of what I was saying. But this history was too recent and sensitive for him to discuss. So he nodded and talked more about the abstract issue of territorial integrity. "The bandits cannot force anyone to support their demands for independence. Ethiopia can never accept that."

I went on: "Since a military solution is impossible, you have no alternative but diplomacy and compromise. This will take time but it will be much easier if you turn the economic situation in your favor. The problem has to be depoliticized." I said Sudan seemed to me to hold part of the solution to the problem: "What do you think of the situation there? Do you see any prospect of an Ethiopian understanding with Khartoum?"

"We have no basic quarrels with Sudan. We were hopeful when the government changed. But the country seems to be in a sad state of political deterioration. It is difficult to negotiate in such a situation, but we are ready to negotiate and we keep telling that to the Sudanese." I said I thought it tragic that neither Ethiopia nor Sudan had any territorial claims on each other but remained at odds and kept doing each other harm. Both would benefit if they could find a real basis for cooperation.

He asked whether we were satisfied with what we had seen during our visit. We said we had the feeling we had worked in as much as was physically possible. I summed up impressions of Massawa and suggested they invite more foreign journalists to observe actual conditions in Eritrea to counteract the widespread impression that Asmara is a dead city and Eritrea a wrecked region.

He said he understood the need to get Americans and Europeans to understand conditions in Eritrea better. There was also a great lack of understanding of what the revolutionary government was trying to do in Ethiopia. I was not so sure of that, I said. Many Americans with a long interest in Ethiopia found the attitudes of senior people in Addis Ababa impossible to comprehend. I noted that perhaps as many as fifty thousand Americans had served in Eritrea during the more than thirty years the U.S. had a presence here and that many of these people still have warm memories of their experience. He seemed rather moved by this observation and, I suspect, had very seldom thought about this past history.

"I would like through you gentlemen to express my profound appreciation for the help the U.S. has given during the famine," Guad Teferra said with great seriousness, "and for the help the Europeans have given as well." Then, speaking slowly and shaping each phrase deliberately, he continued: "I know Ethiopia is part of Western civilization. It is part of our history and our blood. Ethiopia will never shift its orientation from America and Europe for which so many Ethiopians have such fond memories."

We had gone over more ground than I had expected to when we came. So we rose to go. Dr. Teferra noted that he would be going to Addis Ababa on the same plane as we were in the morning, for a Central Committee meeting had been summoned. He would look forward to seeing us at the airport, he said, and perhaps there would be further opportunity to talk during the flight to the capital.

Russia, Cuba, Eastern Europe, communism, Marxism-Leninism, socialism — none of the pervasive official claptrap that fills the press and official proclamations here was mentioned in this hour-long conversation. Did Guad Teferra avoid them to avoid offending us? Or because he himself sees their irrelevance to Eritrea's and Ethiopia's real problems? What the Central Committee meeting is to deal with no one is sure. Fisseha maintains it is of little importance. Others seem to expect further *shumshir* and perhaps policy changes. Hope always springs eternal in Ethiopia. Did Tesfaye Gébre Kidan bring word back from Moscow that Mengistu needs to take into account?

Evening: farewells to Abraha, who seems to have found our visit a genuine stimulus and is so excited about the Massawa boat-building operation that he wants to try to revive a fishmeal plant that existed there before the revolution. We had hoped to go to a restaurant for national food but got involved with some of the Nationalities Institute people at the hotel so ended up eating again in the hotel dining room. Our dinner group: Getachew and Fisseha and a relative of the latter whom he looked up here, Woizero Alganesh,[65] who is deputy chairwoman of the Asmara branch of the Revolutionary Ethiopian Women's Association. She was normal and agreeable, works by day for the Ethiopian Navy office here. Fisseha received permission this afternoon to accompany me to Zway and seems very excited at the prospect. He is curious about life on the islands with his genuine interest in Ethiopian history.

22 March 1987 - Farewell to Eritrea

Up at 5:15 A.M., eastern sky just beginning to show light. Water already on in bathroom. Lobby was busy with Nationalities Institute people coming down to take the same flight as us to Addis Ababa. I was warmly greeted by Dr. Kinfe Rigb-Zelleke who apologized for not having written to acknowledge publications I had sent him after the eighth International Ethiopian Studies Conference in 1984 in Addis Ababa. I couldn't remember exactly what I sent, but no matter. Anything sent to academics here encourages some thirsty mind and gives satisfaction that friends on the outside continue to be interested in Ethiopia. Fisseha, who had stayed up until 2 A.M. last night talking *shumshir* and party politics, had difficulty waking up and kept us waiting.

City streets and the airport highway were crowded with dawn joggers, most of them in Western jogging suits and running shoes. Still another example, I thought, of the Western orientation of Ethiopians —all their role models are Western; they want to be like Americans and Europeans, not like Russians. Even the party people we have been with would be grievously insulted if we told them they looked or acted like Russians.

On arrival at the terminal we were driven directly to the VIP gate and avoided all security formalities except for the baggage check through automatic machines. The sun rose and we went into the VIP lounge where the mayor and the party secretary greeted us as old friends. Dr. Teferra again assured me he would do anything I asked in Eritrea and hoped I would make another visit. Mayor Afeworq said the same. Both were going down for the Central Committee meeting. I thought to myself: How can people who are as experienced and sensible as these men, who are dealing with tough, real problems every day, put up with the naive drivel that constitutes the party line here?

In a moment we were summoned to board the plane — according to protocol. First Dr. Teferra Wonde marched out, then an army general, then John and I! How polite and how rank-conscious Ethiopians still are! At the steps Dr. Teferra waited to say goodbye and wish me a good further stay in Ethiopia. I wished him well too. But there could be no question of our sitting together during the flight; party people and the military brass all rode first class. We and the Nationalities Institute people had tourist-class tickets and rode with the broad masses.

We taxied out to the runway, the plane rose into the sunlight and we looked down on the vertical moonscape where the plateau breaks up into the escarpment. I mulled over the intense reintroduction to Eritrea I had had since landing here three nights ago. What could I conclude? Eritrea is a society neither prospering nor moving ahead. It is a society holding on. I would like to have seen some of the outer provinces, but the Derg still has stronger control of Asmara, Massawa, and the escarpment region than I had expected. "The apparatus of statehood" is being maintained. There were times a few years ago when it came close to collapsing. Officials here admit that. But the EPLF keeps bringing journalists to see the areas it controls and convinces many of them that it has created an "apparatus of statehood" superior to anything the Ethiopian central government is capable of.

Eritreans are unenthusiastic about Addis Ababa rule and even less so about Marxism-Leninism. But there is little reason to believe that many of them want EPLF Marxists to tell them what to think and do either. If they did, why would so many of them be concentrated in Asmara? Why wouldn't young men flock out to join the insurgents? They clearly prefer to avoid risking their skins. They want adequate food and they want the opportunity to improve themselves; university, schools, libraries, any temporary employment they can find or the opportunity to make a few birr in the unofficial economy.

The EPLF and what is left of the other guerrilla movements must be concerned about erosion of the support of young Eritreans. Young people the world over are not inclined to want to belong for very long to anybody. They have a natural inclination to reject any body or dogma that they are told they must accept.

I was reminded, how out of touch, I had been with world news when the stewardess brought breakfast and an Ethiopian sitting beside me asked what I thought about the Persian Gulf situation. He brought me up to date on recent news. His sympathies seemed to be more with Iran than Iraq (natural for an Ethiopian, reflecting traditional attitudes toward Arabs) but he had a good grasp of the complexities of the situation. "Where did you learn about the latest developments?" I asked. "From the Voice of America (VOA), of course," he replied in a matter-of-fact tone implying that I hardly needed to ask. "Do you listen to the Voice frequently?" I continued. His reply: "Every day." He was wearing a blue party uniform.

Time and again in conversations with people here, including government officials, I have heard references to VOA broadcasts. Everyone listens. VOA has become part of daily life in Revolutionary Ethiopia. Sometimes people mention the BBC, which has great prestige but does not broadcast in Amharic. Deutsche Welle, which does, has many listeners. But VOA is far ahead of all the rest. Ethiopians listen to their own radio too and watch local TV, but they do it the way East Europeans and Russians do. They automatically analyze what is broadcast and why but they have no illusions that they are getting complete information from regime media. Party people seem to be even more skeptical than others because they, no doubt, often know better how big a gap there is between regime claims and reality or, more often perhaps, how much is simply omitted.

155

It is not surprising that VOA has gained such listenership so quickly. Many of the people it hired for its Amharic service used to be radio and TV personalities here. The greatest permanent impression VOA broadcasts have made comes from the declarations of defectors. Their VOA programs are available on cassettes which sell for up to seventy-five birr. A more specific measure of the influence VOA has here is the quantity of mail people address to it — hundreds of letters a month. Considering the limitations on literacy and the fact that the Ethiopian postal service, though expanding, is still rudimentary, this is extraordinary. Many young people write. So do soldiers and even officers.

Back in Addis Ababa: Sunday — morning, trafficless streets, sounds of church services from all directions. There was a great crowd at Istifanos,[66] similar crowds at other churches we passed. Women's bright white dresses shone brilliantly in the sunlight. People in their Sunday best looked well nourished and happy. Illusion, in part, of course. If this country had a government that let its people develop according to their talents, skills and natural inclinations, it would soon be leaping forward in giant strides.

CHAPTER IV

ERITREA: THE ECONOMIC CHALLENGE

The essay which follows is a verbatim record of a talk, I was invited to give at a conference sponsored by an organization called Eritreans for Peace and Democracy in Baltimore, Maryland, 3-4 November 1990.[67] Earlier that year, on 10 March 1990, I had talked to a symposium organized by the same organization in Washington, D.C. I concluded that talk with an appeal to the EPLF and all concerned Eritreans for moderation, good sense, and emphasis on economic factors:

The help Eritrea will need to satisfy its peoples' needs will come only if conditions in Eritrea are attractive to investors and lenders. Eritrean society, whether the province becomes independent or remains affiliated with the Ethiopian state, must emerge from the isolation in which it has existed since the 1950s. It is a segmented and fragmented society, crisscrossed by ethnic, linguistic and religious distinctions and varied styles of life. EPLF claims that all these actual and potential cleavages have been overcome in the course of the struggle against Addis Ababa oppression are not convincing. If absolute social and political harmony prevails and continues to prevail in Eritrea, it will be an exception to all other human experience. If the EPLF frees Eritrea, it must meet the challenge of establishing a flexible, non-dogmatic political, economic and social system within which tensions can be controlled and reduced. It must ensure an acceptable degree of genuine democracy and guarantee elementary human rights for all inhabitants of Eritrea. Otherwise the EPLF will be regarded as a failure. An economically, socially and politically healthy Eritrea will have a positive effect on Ethiopia as a whole. A flourishing, successful Ethiopia is essential for peace and progress in the entire African Horn and Red Sea region. The responsibility for reaching these goals rests with the people of the region. They will receive outside help only if they demonstrate initiative, intelligence, responsibility and foresight themselves.

The message which I delivered was apparently welcomed by the group to whom I talked, for I was invited to come to talk to them again. In November 1990, I delivered essentially the same message. The message was more urgent then, for by the final weeks of 1990 it was evident that Mengistu Haile Mariam was on his last legs in Addis Ababa. In Eritrea, the Derg army held only Asmara. It had no land or sea connection to Eritrea (except Assab which had no practical connection northward) for Tigray to the south had come fully under control of the TPLF.

Now, ten years later, as I reread the advice I gave Eritreans then, I am more confident than ever that the EPLF would have been wise if it had taken it. Many of the Eritreans in the United States seemed to take this advice to heart and welcomed it, but the EPLF was equivocal. Though I urged that economic considerations be given priority in planning for Eritrea's future,[68] Isaias Afewerki did not agree and stressed political considerations. During the first months of 1991, he threatened to declare unilateral independence and paid no attention to economic realities. He was dissuaded from declaring independence by American diplomats, reluctantly abandoned this idea and accepted a two-year period for a process of legal separation from Ethiopia with UN supervision of the process.

The referendum of April 1993 offered the Eritrean population only a yes-no choice. The political and economic system which Isaias established under the Provisional Government of Eritrea, 1991-1993, continued essentially unchanged during the years which followed, though for a time there were indications that the open society and open economy I foresaw in the early 1990s might actually develop. Instead, Eritrea evolved toward a rigid authoritarian system, became a police state and fell into conflict with all its neighbors. The extent to which Eritrea's development diverged from the positive range of possibilities I described in 1990 became obvious when Isaias sent his army into Ethiopia in May 1998. Read today, the essay below sounds ironic in the extreme. Eritrea could have followed the course I outlined. It would be a success today if it had.

A VISION OF THE FUTURE ERITREA, 1990

A Changed Situation: An important chapter in Eritrean history is coming to a close. The Derg's brutal sixteen year campaign to subjugate Eritrea by military force is approaching an ignominious end. Failure in Eritrea is a critical aspect of the failure of the Derg's program for orienting Ethiopia toward the Soviet Union and locking the country into rigid communist rule. Communism has brought unmitigated disaster on Ethiopia and the Horn of Africa, as it has to all other parts of the world where it has been imposed. It is now collapsing everywhere and survives only in China, Cuba, and a few other political backwaters. The collapse of communism is not the end of the story, however. An encounter with Marxism-Leninism leaves a legacy of severe political, economic and social problems, as we see in the newly democratizing countries of Eastern Europe and in the rapidly disintegrating Soviet Empire. Though all but communist party functionaries and other direct beneficiaries of the regime welcome its demise, there can be little time for rejoicing. Everyone must go to work to repair the damage. Liberated societies face urgent new problems. If these problems are not dealt with successfully, the damage Marxism-Leninism has caused will be extended and compounded.

The revolution communists claimed to be implementing has been overtaken by a worldwide surge of commitment to democracy. In contrast to communists and advocates of other forms of authoritarianism, those who practice democracy do not claim to be able to devise perfect political and economic systems. They recognize that individuals and societies are not perfectible, only manageable and improvable. Democracy requires leaders, but it also requires that leaders be accountable to their people and be reconfirmed periodically by peaceful procedures - i.e., elections that offer real choices. Democracy is a method for accommodating diversity and coping with change. A democratic system requires interplay and competition among economic, social and intellectual forces and accommodation of ethnic and religious differences. Pluralism is an essential feature of democracy. Democracy is a system of majority rule but it provides protection for minorities. While adherence to all these basic principles is essential for real democracy, there is no single set of rules and procedures that can be applied to create and maintain a democratic political system. Every democratic system is an ongoing experiment in self-rule.

Democratic systems can fall into crisis. They need periodic adjustment, but they have a capacity for self-correction superior to all forms of authoritarianism. The greatest advantage of democracy —which the history of the twentieth century has demonstrated − is that over time democratic societies are more successful than others in generating material progress, economic modernization and constructive social change.

Everything I have to say today takes recent worldwide historical developments into account. I have not changed the judgments on the relationship of Eritrea to Ethiopia and the rest of the region which I have expressed over a period of several years in many publications, so I am not going to repeat them here.[69] Changes which have recently taken place in the world have made most of the choices which Eritreans must face even clearer, but not necessarily easier, than they were when I discussed them in a talk to this group eight months ago.[70]

Current Realities: It is even more urgent now than it was eight months ago for Eritreans to leave arguments about the past aside and give priority to the future, for it is in their hands. Ethiopia's experience with communist militarism has been so devastating and disillusioning that the country will have to be reconstituted as a federal state to be able to survive at all. If the Derg's armies which have benefited from more than $12 billion dollars' worth of Soviet arms cannot subjugate Eritrea (or Tigray, or other parts of the country that have escaped Derg control), no foreseeable government in Addis Ababa is going to be able to impose its will on the country by military force. No foreign power is likely to be interested in intervening in the region. The Eritrea of the future will not need to protect itself against dangers that no longer exist. Ethiopia (and all Horn countries) will have to be governed in the future by consensus based on compromise. If no foreign power supplies weapons, there can be no possibility of imposing central government authority by force. Eritrea's autonomy — its right to self-determination in the sense of self-rule is — thus no longer at issue. The future is in the hands of the leaders of the Eritrean struggle and Eritrea's people. They can manage it well or badly. It is their responsibility. If an open, democratic society can be created in Eritrea, Eritreans stand a fair chance of developing a flourishing economy that will benefit the entire region.

Not so many years ago insurgent leaders appeared to be offering Eritreans only two choices: one, to join the Arab world or two, to become an Albania on the Red Sea. Both were so unpalatable to many Eritreans that the Derg seemed a lesser evil. People who championed Eritrean aspirations gave no priority to economics. Nevertheless, many Eritreans, natural traders from ancient times, ignored dogma

162

and made the best of a bad situation. Some moved abroad and sent money home. The majority who remained in Eritrea created an underground economy that serves elementary needs of the people and maintains links with the entire region. The Derg never felt strong enough to attempt to impose its total economic design on Eritrea. An endless flow of Soviet weaponry was supposed to solve all problems. Gradually, insurgent leaders evolved in their own perceptions of the world. Life was maintained in Eritrea in spite of severe handicaps. Starvation was averted by local exertions and food from abroad. With all this, however, Eritrea has only been existing, not prospering, for more than two decades. With the end of the struggle for self-determination, Eritreans' expectations for rapid improvement in their situation will rise rapidly.

Urgent Tasks: Economic challenges are more urgent than political issues, though there is a direct relationship between the two. Urgent economic tasks include:

- Feeding the population and providing elementary needs: water, fuel, clothing, medical supplies, etc.

- Bringing the underground economy to the surface: restoring trade, crafts, and basic services.

- Extending and restoring utilities and transport.

- Activating industries which are capable of producing consumer goods, and, as soon as possible, exports.

- Restoring banking facilities and maintaining dependable financial arrangements.

- Implementation of a revenue system to support local and regional government services.

Eritreans will be eager to help themselves but need assurance that their efforts will be rewarded. To be encouraged to produce maximally, farmers need to be able to sell freely and at a profit. Markets need to be free and open. Farmers need to feel secure in use of their tools, animals and land so they will invest and raise productivity. State farms create inefficiency and waste. Most should be turned over to other forms of ownership. Commercial agriculture has a proven potential in Eritrea. Rapid restoration of confiscated agricultural estates to their owners will have a beneficial effect on the entire economy and will encourage new foreign investment. Enterprising Eritreans should be encouraged to expand commercial agriculture.

Unemployment will be a major problem in a peaceful Eritrea. People in both rural areas and towns will need opportunities to work and earn. Hindrances to trade and practice of crafts should be removed. Eritrea still possesses one-third of Ethiopia's industrial base. It should be put to work as soon as possible and arrangements for privatization of ownership or, at a minimum, privatization of management, should be specified and implemented. While it may be desirable for some industries and services to continue under government ownership and management, the entire issue should be approached pragmatically with maximal efficiency and profitability and potential for contribution to economic recovery and growth the prime considerations. An autonomous Eritrean administration should avoid proliferation of government bureaucracy and government-sponsored employment schemes. The less administrative interference in the economy, the more rapidly it will flourish.

Economic Principles and Policies: The new Eritrean administration will be wise to give economics priority over politics, for future political arrangements are likely to be sounder if they are grounded in economic realism. No easy assumptions about the availability of foreign aid and investment are justified. Eritrea is in competition with the rest of Ethiopia, the rest of the Horn, the rest of Africa, the entire Third World, and all former and reforming communist countries for aid and investment. Governments, international lending institutions, and private investors have a broader variety of opportunities open to them than ever before, worldwide. Funds for aid and capital for investment will not be sufficient to fill all needs and opportunities. Needs are so great that many economists forecast an increasing shortage of investment capital during the next two decades. Most aid-givers and investors base their decisions on realistic review of prospects for success of the undertakings they support, not sentiment. Eritrea has better infrastructure, more talented people, and a more favorable geographic position than many African and Third World competitors, but these advantages alone will not ensure a flow of aid and investment. Good prospects for economic and social stability, clear legal and financial provisions, and realistic policies and political predictability are the most important considerations.

The openness of an economy is also a critical factor. Closed economic systems are unattractive to investors. Autarky is incongruous for Eritrea, for it has been a cultural and commercial crossroads since ancient times with historic links to the Mediterranean, Africa, Persia, India and the whole Muslim world. By itself, Eritrea's varied population is too small to be significant as a market for major manufacturers or distributors. On the other hand, the hundred million people who live in the Red Sea region constitute a major market that will attract investors interested in manufacturing and distribution. Eritreans already know these areas. The Gulf, Egypt, Israel, and Europe offer further economic opportunities for Eritrea. Eritrea has open economic access to the fifty millon people of Ethiopia. Poverty stricken as they may be today, they represent an enormous economic potential once the country has a more popular and constructive government. Ethiopia's existing relationships to European, African and Middle Eastern economic development and trade groupings are advantages Eritrea can ill afford to lose. The continued strength of the Ethiopian birr and Ethiopia's high international credit ratings represent benefits which a peaceful Eritrea would be unwise to jettison. The same is true of the services provided by long-established transport and communications facilities which Ethiopian Airlines and the Ethiopian Telecommunications Authority, both of which owe part of their dependable performance to Eritrean talent. These services will be far more valuable to a peaceful and economically resurgent Eritrea than they have seemed to be in the recent past.

Haste, dogma and emotionalism in dealing with fundamental economic issues such as these can cost Eritrea dearly and adversely affect economic and social progress – and therefore political stability – for decades to come.

Eritreans Abroad: More than a million Eritreans are living outside Eritrea. There are half a million in Sudan and at least half a million in the rest of Ethiopia. There are, at a minimum, tens of thousands in the Middle East, in Europe and in America. Like those of you here today, many are highly educated and skilled professionals. Eritreans do not easily forget their origin. Large numbers of Eritreans send money to relatives at home. Monetary contributions from Eritreans abroad have helped maintain the struggle against the Derg. The huge Eritrean diaspora can be beneficial to a peaceful Eritrea in numerous ways, or the potential it represents can be squandered and lost. How many Eritreans will return from the Middle East, Europe and America? Under present circumstances, calculation is difficult. Some returnees may be motivated by idealism to apply their energy and experience to the rejuvenation of a peaceful Eritrea. Idealism cannot be relied upon for long as a motivating factor, however. More often than not, the decision to return – and to remain – is likely to be made on the basis of professional, financial or family considerations. And for those accustomed to life in open societies the decision to remain is likely to be heavily influenced by the degree of openness, freedom and opportunity that will prevail in the future Eritrea.

Many Eritreans in exile have accumulated capital to invest. This can be a valuable asset for Eritrea. Even some of those who choose not to return – and those who decide to keep a foot on both sides of the water – may be prepared to invest in undertakings in Eritrea. Those who invest will expect their investments to be well used. Talented and skilled returnees are likely to expect to have a voice in economic decision-making and opportunities to apply the experience they have gained abroad.

Eritrea is not overpopulated. Once the economy becomes reinvigorated, labor shortages may develop. Returnees from Sudan can supplement both the agricultural and industrial labor force. Many will be concerned about restoration of property rights. So will many Eritreans now living and working in other regions of Ethiopia. Eritreans continue to hold important positions in the professions, in the economy, and in public service in many parts of Ethiopia. The broad spectrum of relationships between Eritreans and Ethiopia will generate both problems and opportunities for all parties concerned. If opportunities for mutually beneficial interchange and contact not only remain open but are extended, everyone will benefit.

Expanded Economic Development in Eritrea: With restoration of peace, many sectors of the economy which have been marking time or entirely stagnant will gain new life. The Eritrean railway has not operated since the late 1960s. The cost and gains of refurbishing it need to be calculated. The construction industry will be among the first to face opportunities for expansion. There will be high demand for construction materials. The textile and leather industries appear to offer immediate opportunities for rejuvenation and expansion, and will set in motion demand for raw materials to supply their needs. Food processing of both elementary and sophisticated products is a field with almost unlimited opportunities, both to satisfy local needs and reactivate exports.

Two fields which were only beginning to be developed in the 1960s and have remained stagnant ever since offer promising possibilities for rapid expansion and good returns in foreign exchange: one, fishing and seafood processing, and two, tourism. Both require relatively modest investment in infrastructure to be reactivated. They are fields well suited to private initiative. Both are likely to be attractive to foreign partners. Both can generate broad employment opportunities.

Eritrea as the Hub of its Region: From the viewpoint of geography, culture, history and experience, the most logical region for Eritreans to relate to economically is the rest of Ethiopia. Tigray is a natural reservoir of labor for Eritrea. Ethiopian regions farther to the south are a natural source of raw materials for Eritrean industries. The rest of Ethiopia constitutes a vast market into which Eritrean industry and commercial enterprises can expand. Eritrea is a natural outlet to the sea for the rest of Ethiopia. For Tigray, Gondar and Wollo there is no practical substitute.

I have often compared Eritrea of the past two decades to Lebanon in its present deteriorated condition.[71] There are many basic similarities between the two territories and they are not all negative. Until a quarter century ago, Lebanon was the economic and cultural focal point of the Arab and Eastern Mediterranean world. Beirut was a financial and trading center equalled by no other in the region. Wealth flowed in from many directions. Banks and multi-national companies maintained regional headquarters there. Students flocked to Beirut for higher education. Arabs from a dozen countries, Iranians, Armenians, Greeks and Turks concluded business deals in its restaurants and night clubs and maintained summer residences in the mountains above the city.

Eritrea has many of the same characteristics and advantages in the Horn/Red Sea region that Lebanon used to have in the Levant and Arab world. It is physically attractive and its population represents a mixture of religions, cultures, languages, foreign influences and links and different ways of life. Eritreans have commendable habits of tolerance when times are good. I have already emphasized their aptitude for enterprise and trade. A peaceful Eritrea, with an efficient administration that does not intrude into every aspect of citizens' lives but lets them develop their talents and skills and benefit from them has the same potential to become a focal point for its entire region that Lebanon once had – and may at some future time regain.

Politics and Economics: A peaceful Eritrea will not remain peaceful if it becomes a police state, if leaders attempt to impose dogma on a population that is fed up with ideology. On the other hand, if economics takes priority over politics, if political decisions are made with beneficial economic impact as the priority, the energies of the population will be absorbed in useful work and people will look forward to the future. Political and social tensions will be reduced. The outer world will judge Eritrea primarily by one, the success of Eritreans in reducing communal antagonism, and two, the degree of economic momentum its leaders and people are able to sustain. Help and support will be provided in response to evidence that it will be effectively used. A system moving toward democracy is a necessary requirement for generating real economic momentum. A genuinely democratic Eritrea will have a positive impact on the entire region of which Eritrea forms a part — indeed, of which Eritrea is the hub.

CHAPTER V

THE ERITREAN INDEPENDENCE
REFERENDUM
APRIL 1993

I spent all of April 1993 in Ethiopia, having come first to Addis Ababa along with Professor Samuel Huntington of Harvard to consult with the Constitutional Commission that was then sitting under the chairmanship of the distinguished diplomat and former Foreign Minister, Kifle Wodajo. Following those consultations, I spent a week in Tigray to observe progress toward economic recovery and visit historic sites and then traveled overland to Eritrea, where I had been invited to serve as an observer for the independence referendum.

Several months earlier, when I submitted my application to serve as an observer, I asked to be assigned to a location in western Eritrea. I had traveled extensively in Eritrea in the pre-revolutionary period but during the Derg era, I visited Eritrea only once. (A record of that visit is included in this book as Chapter Three). I had never traveled farther west than Keren. I also wanted to experience an area that is largely Muslim to gain impressions of Christian-Muslim relations. My request was taken seriously and I was assigned as far westward as it is possible to go — to Om Hager on the Sudan border. Traveling to and from there offered the opportunity to visit Agordat, Barentu, Tessenei and numerous smaller towns and villages in between and to have contact with the varied ethnic groups that live in the region, including Kunama and Beni Amer.

Though I have omitted and/or condensed portions of my daily notes that relate only to incidental or personal matters, I have included all impressions and information relating to the referendum process as well as a wide variety of observations on life, attitudes and activities in Asmara, Massawa, Keren and western Eritrea. I have included a number of vignettes that provide insight into the moods and attitudes of Eritreans at that time as well as impressions of the great variety of foreigners who served as observers. Two years had passed since the collapse of the Derg. This was a happy period in Eritrea and a time of great confidence about the future. Rains were good and agriculture was recovering. Eritrea had, in effect, been independent during this time under the Provisional Government (PGE) organized by the victorious EPLF guerrilla army in May 1991. The Transitional Government of Ethiopia (TGE) made no effort to exercise authority over Eritrea during this time.

When I returned to Asmara from Om Hager, I was invited to come for a long conversation with Isaias Afewerki. I recorded that meeting practically verbatim, for I considered it historic. Little did I realize then how puzzlingly historic it would prove to be, for in a year or two Isaias began to take actions and express judgments totally different from those he stated to me during our conversation on the eve of formal independence. To the reader most of these contradictions will be obvious in light of the course of history since. I discuss their implications in the final chapter of this book.

DIARY OF AN OFFICIAL OBSERVER [72]
16 - 28 April 1993

16 April 1993 - Makelle to Asmara.

We were delayed leaving Makelle this morning. I called on the governor, Gebru Asrat, and his deputy, Woizero Aregash, an impressive lady. We talked about development priorities, the need for more understanding abroad of Tigray's problems: education, tourism, road-building. I then picked up Araya Zerihun[73] at the office of the Tigray Development Association (TDA). We had to wait while our driver obtained gasoline and a good spare tire. At 10:30 A.M. we were finally on the road. We stopped to see the colorful church with pre-Axumite foundations south of Edaga Hamus-Nequal Emni Mariam Tehot. In Adigrat we stopped for a light *som* lunch at the Africa *megeb bet*. I talked to Araya about TDA priorities and plans. His dedication is impressive. He returned from a good job in the States to run TDA. He was born in Adwa, grew up and went to school in Asmara where his family moved when he was two. Like so many Ethiopians of his generation, he has family scattered in the U.S., in Tigray and in Eritrea. His mother, who maintained a beautiful house in Asmara all through the period of troubles, died only six months ago.

Crossing into Eritrea from Tigray at Zalambessa was simpler than I had expected. At the border post the Eritrean official checking documents said he had been told I was coming, stamped my visa and stamped Araya's paper and we were on our way through the spectacular landscape around Senafe. Back toward the southwest we had a fine view of Debre Damo. The weather was good and the landscape fascinating. We passed many trucks coming from Tigray and more distant parts of Ethiopia; otherwise there was little traffic. After Adi Caieh storms began to gather. We made our way over the raw, broken terrain through rain and hail to Saganeiti, then through fog as we approached Decamere. Through the curious area strewn with huge boulders the highway climbed up to the plateau again. The sun came out and accompanied us into Asmara through a landscape filled with bronze aloes at their best now. Recent rains have produced a good deal of greenness in the landscape. Prospects for agriculture this year seem good.

We arrived in Asmara at six and went directly to Araya's mother's house — a beautifully furnished place, lovingly maintained with good furniture, art on the walls, good china and crystal. Members of his family, including a sister who works for Ethiopian Airlines, had prepared a Good Friday supper — excellent fasting food including some dishes I have never had before in Ethiopia such as *halbut*. We drank a bottle of good Dukam. Another sister had just returned from the States and greeted me as an old friend because she had attended my talks in Washington, last year.

After dinner, we went to [Referendum Commissioner] Amare Tekle's house to hear about referendum planning. Andreas Eshete and a Professor Nzongola from Howard University were there. Nzongola arrived here this morning from Addis Ababa, having left Washington on Wednesday. We heard that Massawa was hit today by an unprecedentedly violent hurricane which knocked together cranes in the port and, according to Amare, blew away many of his polling stations which were constructed of poles and matting. From what Amare told us I get the impression that preparations for the referendum are still a bit confused, but briefings for observers are to start at 9 A.M. tomorrow. I already sense that this observer adventure will require a good deal of flexibility.

As of 9:20 P.M. this evening I am in the Ambasoira Hotel where I have been put up temporarily and told that I will be moved tomorrow, but then again, since many expected observers have not yet arrived, they tell me I may stay here for the next two or three days. The Ambasoira still charges Derg-era prices and requires hard currency for payment.

17 April 1993 - Asmara

Rain during the night. Rainy skies this morning. I started the day with the luxury of a soaking bath!

The first briefing session for observers was held in a large auditorium at the Chamber of Commerce — freshly painted, bookcases filled with brochures, comfortable chairs. The briefing was opened by a welcome from Amare Tekle. Then Tekie Fissehatsion from Baltimore gave a long talk on the history of the Eritrean movement — a more palatable serving of mythology than the usual EPLF line. He showed respect to Haile Selassie for his cleverness in managing the Eritrean situation after WWII. John Spencer was Tekie's *bete noir*. He conveniently coasted over the whole period between 1978 and 1988, and avoided saying anything significant about the strains between guerrilla factions in the 1970s. Answering a number of questions (many of the observers seem to know nothing of the political background of this region), Tekie delivered a fascinating final comment about the necessity for Eritrea and Ethiopia to work together and harmonize their policies in all respects. This kind of talk would have been unthinkable two years ago. Two years have encouraged some realism among many of these EPLF supporters.

I met Gerard Prunier at the end of the briefing. We walked into the center of the city for coffee and then had a good fish lunch at the Ambassador Hotel. Gerard ascribes greater importance to Ethiopian dissidents abroad than I would be inclined to give, is more critical of the EPRDF. He makes a good point about the need for the EPRDF to reach out and broaden their political base, which they do not seem to be doing. Gerard has been following Somalia closely and explained the situation there at length. He recounted the muddled situation in Djibouti. It would take an Evelyn Waugh to do all this intriguing justice.

Heavy rain again this afternoon. The afternoon briefing session featured a talk by Tekle Woldemichael, a soft-spoken fellow who lives in the U.S., on "the ethnic and social basis of the Eritrean nation." His talk was remarkably honest and objective. He even discussed the tension and civil war that developed between guerrilla movements in the 1970s and continued into the 1980s. He made no effort to deny the ethnic and religious cleavages that exist in Eritrea or the potential for strife between ethnic and religious groups. The audience sensed the sensitivity of these topics so few questions were asked. Afterwards some of us walked around the rainy city to observe preparations for Easter. Two men came up to me at one point to ask whether I was Paul Henze. Like Araya's sister they had attended some of my talks in Washington and were pleased to see me here. I stopped in a bookstore where the owner recognized me from my picture on the jacket of *Ethiopian Journeys*, which he pulled from a shelf. He sold many of them when the book first came out, he said, but has only this copy left. He rents it out for payment by the day.[74] I told him I would try to find another copy to send him.

Amare Tekle hosted a big party for referendum observers tonight at the Ambasoira. There were food and drink in great quantities (no need for dinner) and a good opportunity to meet a lot of people who I knew must be here, example Steve Morrison, Hagos Gebre Hiwot, Amde Berhan [Asmara University President], Siegfried Pausewang from Norway, Kathrina Eikenberg from Hamburg, and many people from the African-American Institute and UN groups. I find I am the only one who arrived here overland, all the others flew in via Addis Ababa. Berhane Wolde Haymanot of the observer staff told me I will be going to Om Hager – - exactly what I requested. I suggested to Gerard Prunier that he go too and we take two days to get there, seeing a good deal of western Eritrea on the way. Meanwhile, Steve Morrison may be taking a trip to Massawa and suggested I come along. Hagos tells me he has been instructed to set up meetings for me with the tourism people and several other officials and also a session with Isaias who has asked to see me. They told me that my arrival was announced last night on the radio.

18 April 1993 - Asmara.

Easter Sunday. Night-long services were coming to an end at dawn. I was awakened by the sound of bells from all sides of the city. This morning's briefing session did not begin until 10 A.M. so I had time for a good walk around Asmara in half-sunny weather. Coffee bars are all open this morning but not many other shops. Displays in windows, however, indicate a considerable quantity of goods for sale. Progress is visible everywhere. I passed men sweeping the streets and shop owners cleaning the sidewalks in front of their shops. People, especially children, were out everywhere in their Easter finery — little boys in new blue jeans and jackets and ties, little girls in ruffled dresses with ribbons in their hair. I was asked for money only once. Young men do not follow you around here. If this kind of pride could only be instilled in people in Addis Ababa! Doors were closed at the great Orthodox church, Asmara Mariam, but there were still people lingering around and coming up to kiss the doors.

The briefing session was devoted to voting procedures. There were dozens of questions after the formal presentation. Many of them seemed endlessly refined for the likelihood of fraud in this referendum seems to me to be slight. There is not that much at stake, as there would be in a combative multi-party election. Problems are most likely to arise from confusion or arbitrary actions on the part of officials. Only people with registration cards are to be allowed to vote. They say there were no problems whatsoever during the registration process, which was overseen by the UN. Only eight hundred thousand people were registered, which they say represents one-fourth of the population over eighteen. The truth, I suspect, is that a lot of people have not registered. Many who are registered may not vote. They are concerned about that for even with a yes vote but low participation the outcome will not look impressive. So one of the things to watch for will be officials herding people to the polls, especially in the western regions.

Coming back to the hotel after the morning session I met two Irish nuns who operate a health center at Edaga Hamus in Tigray, Sister Mary Malone and Sister Teresa Maher. They were enjoying a beer. Happy, talkative types, they were eager to hear what I had seen in my travels Tigray and ready to tell me about their work, which consists mostly of trying to teach people sanitation and disease prevention at a very elementary level. These ladies come up to Asmara every six months to buy supplies and enjoy a bit of cosmopolitan life. They have their own Landrover and are quite familiar with their area, having recently visited the church of Arbatu

Insesa. I urged them to go to Enda Medhane Alem. One of them was here for three years during the Derg period when they were not permitted to go more than a mile from their village. Now they are free to travel as they like, as are the Tigrayans.

After lunch at the Ambasoira I met Joe O'Neill (Charge d'Affaires at the U.S. Consulate in Asmara) in the lobby and went with him to his residence for a half-hour chat on life and issues here. He says Isaias is very worried about Islamic extremism and feels the West is not measuring up to the challenge. He also fears short-sighted Israeli influence on the Clinton Administration. He would like to stay here as ambassador after independence but considers his chances poor. I learned from Steve Morrison that Bob Houdek is in line for this ambassadorship if he wants it.

Afternoon session at the Chamber of Commerce building: Amare Tekle on the referendum process. Long question session, then off with Gerard Prunier and a lady *Le Monde* correspondent to the city park outdoor cafe for talk about the situation here over guava juice. Back to the Capital Theater for evening panel: Tekie Fissehatsion, Prof. Nzongola, Andreas Eshete and myself with Steve Morrison as moderator. The huge Capital Cinema was half filled by the time the discussion got well under way. We all talked about democracy and complemented each other rather well. Questions ranged from speeches that were not questions (one fellow maintained all Eritreans hated Africans and hated the OAU because they didn't support independence) to the serious and sensible – problems of political parties, constitution-writing, and voting procedures. I turned the discussion toward economics at every opportunity. Steve adjourned the panel about 8:15 P.M. Amare told us he was delighted with it. It is the first kind of public discussion of political issues that has taken place here since the EPLF victory.

Berhane told me this afternoon that everything is set for me, Gerard Prunier and Tekle Woldemichael to go as the referendum observer team to Om Hager, leaving early Tuesday morning. This will give us plenty of time on the road and time to settle in there before the voting begins. Meanwhile I have arranged with Steve Morrison to go to Massawa tomorrow, so time is being well used.

19 April 1993 - To Massawa and back to Asmara.

I was awakened this morning by a cacophony of religious sounds: a muezzin calling while church bells were ringing and sounds of chanting coming from the nearby Orthodox church. Can the EPLF forge unity from all this? If they try too hard they will not succeed. If they are tolerant and light-handed they may. The biggest challenge is fully integrating the Muslims into Eritrean society. I know of little evidence that Eritrean Muslims are naturally extremist or fanatic. They are accustomed to living in a crossroads region where everyone has to show a certain amount of respect to everyone else. The main problem is disruptive outside influences. If the EPLF succeeds in generating steady economic progress while at the same time steadily opening up the political system, but maintaining firm and well understood rules of the political game, then it can bring the Muslims along. These subjects formed most of the breakfast conversation this morning when I joined Steve Morrison, Terry Lyon and Leah Leatherby in the Ambasoira dining room. Terry is going to be observing in Assab and Leah in Massawa.

I took a taxi to the U.S. Consulate, recognizable as its old self though they have not entirely got the place arranged yet and there are packing boxes, new equipment and furniture everywhere. I met Congressional Staffer Gil Kapen there. He, Steve and I made up the party for Massawa today. We departed at 10:30 A.M. in a consulate vehicle with an experienced driver, Haile Mariam.

The upper section of the escarpment highway was in thick cloud, so we saw little until after Nefasit. From there on everything was vividly green. Cattle, sheep and goats are unable to consume all the forage. Corn in the fields around Embatcala seems to be growing as you look at it. In Ghinda everyone seemed to be selling tomatoes, no bananas or oranges. We had tea at one of the many little eating houses. As we came onto the Samhar at Mai Atal the road surface changed for the better. This trip was just the opposite of the one I made in January 1992, for the repair they first did on the first half of this highway has worn out and the upper section is full of potholes and breaks. The final section of this road is still edged with tanks and wrecked vehicles, though considerable additional debris has been hauled into the collecting areas on the edge of the city. The tree with boxes of Derg soldiers' bones is still there, unchanged, on the left. We walked over to it. Someone had set up a row of skulls along the top of the boxes - gruesome. A mosque on the outskirts has been repaired and as we crossed onto the island of Taulud I was surprised to see St. Mary's church completely renovated, all the cracks filled and the building painted a bright cream-white. At the Red Sea Hotel, however, nothing has happened. It was wrecked by Derg bombing in 1990 and has remained a wreck since. They should give it to some entrepreneur for a token price in return for a guarantee that it will be repaired.

Reports of the damage the hurricane did to Massawa proved to be exaggerated. Except for the shanty town behind the railroad tracks on the mainland we saw little new damage. People in this area were already rebuilding their shacks. Some NGO has provided camping tents which are pitched among them. There has been some cleaning up around the imperial palace, but Mme. Melotti's villa looks unchanged except that the garden has dried up. Everywhere we saw evidence of the heavy rain that fell last Friday. We could see little damage in the port area. Two ships were being unloaded. Piles of grain under tarps seem to have got wet in places, but the loss did not appear to be great. Here and there in the old city we saw signs of repairs and smelled paint, but not a great deal. Since we were in Massawa only between 2 and 4:30 P.M., we did not see much commercial life. Massawa follows Red Sea hours with a long afternoon break. There were referendum signs everywhere and two groups of dancers were performing in the streets at the time we left. Their music was as if for a wedding. We had a cool Melotti and bread rolls at the Luna Hotel. The Dahlak Hotel where I stayed in January 1992 is close to being renovated.

We set out at 4:30 P.M. on the return trip and were back in Asmara at seven, having enjoyed spectacular evening scenes along the upper escarpment. At dinner tonight Colin Legum came up to greet me and I joined him at a table of Brits afterward. They are all eager to see how Eritrea is actually developing, hopeful that the EPLF will permit a more open society here after independence, but not entirely sure. Observers were issued light sleeping bags today, but everything else is our own responsibility. Our little team is ready for departure at six tomorrow morning.

20 April 1993 - Asmara to Keren.

A very good day. The early morning drive past Adi Teklesan and through the gaunt countryside to the north gave us an opportunity to get acquainted with our driver, Bereket. He was born in a village in this region, moved with his parents to Addis Ababa when he was nine. He grew up there but during the Derg years he spent five years in Sudan and five in Saudi Arabia. He returned to Eritrea in 1991. He speaks four languages and has a grasp of the way life works in many places. He drives for a Norwegian NGO. He thought we were going to be a batch of tenderfoot *ferenjis* who knew nothing about this part of the world. He was happy to learn otherwise.

We bought a generous supply of bread, cookies and bananas at an Asmara grocery store on the way out this morning and were given the better part of a bushel of oranges at Elaberet, so there is no danger of starving. Our stop at Elaberet [76] was a surprise to both my traveling companions, for they did not know of it. The estate has been largely rehabilitated. The most noteworthy change since my visit last year is the newly planted vineyards. They are flourishing. They told us that Elaberet wines will be back on the market in two or three years. The cattle and pig herds have multiplied steadily. The cattle are fed on fresh-cut corn. The pigs were remarkably clean. Silt has been removed from the reservoirs and they have been filled by heavy rains. The tomato paste factory is working. In the workers' village, four polling stations had been set up and people were "practice voting". The operation was going off smoothly amid much good humor. We were greeted with ululations and chants of welcome when we came to watch the process.

The condition of the road from Asmara to Keren was worse than I had expected. On the descent down the escarpment a thorough rebuilding job is under way. The roadbed is being widened to three times its original width. But at the rate they are going it will take a long time for this road to be finished. A World Bank infrastructure allocation could make a big difference. Among other people on the way we met a young German from Stuttgart today who works for a Catholic relief agency. He and a friend have been biking around Tigray and Eritrea for three weeks and plan another couple of weeks of bike travel before going home. He says there are sixty thousand Eritrean refugees in Germany. He described projects the Germans are going to undertake to help as many as possible resettle here: a German school in Asmara, a credit program, a grant program for those who come back to set themselves up in business. If the Eritreans can draw on this kind of help from several sources, they cannot fail to make progress.

On arriving in Keren we took rooms in the Hotel Eritrea at five Birr per bed per night, sharing two rooms with a total of five beds. Our mid-afternoon sight-seeing started with the fort that rises high above the town. It is a mess of wreckage. Then we went to the Italian and British cemeteries where soldiers from the campaigns of the 1930s and 1940s are buried. We stopped at a remarkable little church, Mariam Darit, built around a huge baobab tree in pleasant gardens along a riverbed. Finally we walked through the market at the end of the afternoon. It was very busy, very picturesque and little changed from my first visit in 1968. Shops are well stocked with elementary foods, spices, soap and household items. Tailors are busy; textiles for sale included *banas* from Manz. The handicraft section had great quantities of good traditional *jabanas*, gaudy tourist souvenir pottery painted in bright colors, every conceivable kind of utensil made of tin cans.

People took little notice of us in the market but one man greeted us in Italian and asked if we were Italians. When we said no, he said, it didn't matter, it was good to have white men back.

Keren is a lively place tonight. From late afternoon until well into the evening the center of the city was the scene of marches and demonstrations, many of them by school children, celebrating the referendum. All came past the Keren Hotel, not accidental I am sure, for the UN has established its observer headquarters here today and the town is crawling with UN cars and observers — all in all not a highly impressive lot. A French member of the UN Group told Gerard that they were warned by their Scandinavian supervisors to have no contact and share no information with other observers. There is plentiful Melotti here, so we settled for drinks on the porch of this hotel after the market and watched the parades converge toward the main square. Here a great crowd assembled with music and singing from a makeshift grandstand. Marching groups came in with flaming torches as dusk settled in. It is evident that there has been organization behind this display of enthusiasm, but everybody seems to be having a good time. There is little reason to doubt that the vote here will be overwhelmingly in favor of independence. Farther west there is said to be some reason for doubt, for in the Barca region the ELF is strong. But why would the ELF vote against independence? That is not their complaint. It is the domination of the government by the EPLF.

Gil Kapen and Steve Morrison walked onto the terrace of the Keren Hotel shortly after 9 P.M. They had left Asmara at 4:30 P.M., delayed in departure because Hagos arranged for Gil to meet Isaias. He says Isaias looked thin but healthy. He is concerned with Islamic extremists and fears the U.S. does not understand the danger they represent to the area. He has recently sent his ambassador back to Saudi Arabia in an effort to get relations with the Saudis back on track. He is positive about relations with Israel.

21 April 1993 - Keren via Agordat to Barentu.

We drove through barren, dry country ravaged for ages by the herds of spry little white and brown goats we saw everywhere bouncing over the rocks and nibbling at the dry grasses and bushes. We had a flat tire between Agordat and Barentu which, with a faulty jack, required some lifting and several flat rocks to change. From what I saw along the road today, I am left puzzled why this region could be seen as of great value to anybody. But with rains the landscape doubtlessly turns green and fields are planted. The villages look poor and are few and far between. The only large expanse of green we saw was the Barca river. The riverbed was edged with doum palms and was broad and sandy with no water on the surface. A bridge over it was in good condition. Approaches to it were being rebuilt.

Agordat was a rather empty feeling town. Polling booths made with mats have been set up in the central square not far from the large mosque. Barentu in contrast is much more compact but not much more than a large village sitting at the foot of an outcropping on which the governor's house and his guesthouse are located. We arrived here about 2 P.M., spent the next hour and a half in a half-finished compound at the edge of the town called "the club". They had warm Melotti, Fanta and food: goat *tibs* and *caporetto* (goat boiled in tomato and pepper sauce) with heavy dark *injera.* Then we drove up to the Asmara Hotel. Before taking a room with four beds for twenty birr, we checked out the governor's guesthouse but found the UN had taken it over completely. We called on the governor, a local man, Germano Noti, and had a good talk. He told us about problems with Muslims and insists they are a minority, for Gash-Setit, he says, has a Christian majority. He talked about Eritreans returning from Sudan (all informally) and trade across the Sudan border which is not subject to much control in either direction. He said that the towns along the border are largely dependent on supplies from Sudan.

We went out for an early evening walk around the town as sunset turned into a rich pink dusk. The main street was busy and in the market there was a great deal of grain for sale. We stopped for coffee and met a man who had returned here two years ago from thirty years as a teacher in Kassala. He is currently a representative of the referendum commission. He led us through picturesque back streets. Houses have no electricity, little light but hearth fires and occasionally lanterns. Good odors of food roasting and cooking. Peaceful atmosphere. The evening air began to cool.

Back at the Asmara Hotel, we reflected on the fact that we had seen little referendum enthusiasm in the towns and through the country we traversed today. But the vote will probably nevertheless go strongly in favor of independence. We sleep on the open terrace on rope beds with just a sheet. The wind blows steadily. It keeps off flies and other insects.

22 April 1993 - From Barentu via Tessenei to Om Hager.

We took a walk through the town and market and then left Barentu this morning before 8:30 A.M. We first drove through an area dotted with baobab trees, said to be populated by Muslim Kunama who are called Nara. We crossed the Gash River in muddy flood from a recent storm. After Aikota, where racing UN vehicles overtook us, the road to Tessenei was rough and often dull, relieved occasionally by spectacular scenery – great hulks of mountain rising sheer from the plain. The temperature was over hundred. Like yesterday, we passed countless reminders of the fighting that had ravaged this region for more than twenty years: hulks of trucks and tanks in ditches, guns sunk in the sand of streambeds, mine craters in the roadbed, countless piles of spent shellcases and other military debris, including boots, uniforms and gear of Ethiopian soldiers who failed to make it across the Sudan border in the final days of Derg collapse and were said to be buried by the thousands in nearby shallow graves. Road repairs were under way in several places. We saw occasional construction in towns, but for the most part the region lags behind highland Eritrea in level of recovery.

In Tessenei the freshly painted mosques and churches were among the first buildings to be repaired, but large sections of the town remain in ruins. There is trade with Sudan, however, with many Sudanese products in shops, so the western border region gives the impression of livelier commercial activity than the area between Agordat and Barentu. After lunch at Tessenei (young, tender *caporetto* in tasty sauce with *injera* of *mashila*), we drove out to see the Ali Gedir (former Barattolo) cotton plantation, badly wrecked but being put in shape to produce again with irrigation. We returned to the Nacfa Hotel for an elaborate coffee ceremony. A girl in a rose-colored dress with a gold front tooth named Fereweyni prepared the coffee. It was served in classic Tigrayan style: first, two cups (called *awal*), then a third cup *(kalaiti)*; and a final cup *(baraka)*, four cups in all. After coffee came chilled guava juice. We noticed that all the girls at the hotel had a single gold front tooth, a beauty mark in this region.

It was almost 3:30 P.M. by the time we were back on the road again. We were told that we would be in Om Hager in only an hour and a half. It took three hours. The highway from Tessenei to Om Hager is being rebuilt. The first forty kilometers. or so are deceptively good; then the route reverts to an old Italian track, badly rutted and cratered by mines. Here, for the first time, we encountered an armed EPLF patrol, two young men and a girl. The road turned into a mere track over a grassy plain that would be impassable in wet weather. The country was vacant – no plowing or planting, though it was evident that large stretches of land had been planted during the past crop year. Last year was very good for durra in Sudan, so large amounts have been brought into Eritrea. (Quantities were being unloaded in Barentu this morning.) The three of us passed the time in discussion along this slow-going stretch: ethnicity, history, politics, science versus history, religion.

"Welcome Referendum! Welcome Referendum!" the tumultuous crowd chanted as our dust-covered Land Cruiser finally pulled into the main square of Om Hager at sundown. We were surrounded by young men singing, leaping and pounding drums, children cheering, women ululating as if their lungs would burst. They hardly left us space to crawl out of the vehicle and make our way into the administration building, one of the few intact structures in this sprawling town that is mostly piles of ruins and rubble interspersed with thatched tukuls, makeshift shops and *buna bets*. On all sides people crowded in to shake hands, touch us, smile and shout "Welcome!" over and over again. They seemed to regard us as the embodiment of the referendum itself.

Once inside the tin-roofed, lattice-walled administrative structure, we were officially welcomed by half a dozen young men and women, referendum officials, who offered us hot spiced tea and began to explain how the voting, starting the next morning, was going to proceed. But the singing and dancing outside built up to such a crescendo we could barely hear each other. Cheers, songs, great surges of "Welcome Referendum!" reverberated from the walls. We all decided it would be better to find a place to stay and get together later in the evening to talk about referendum procedure and the next days' schedule.

In spite of our hectic welcome, we found that we were not the first observers to reach Om Hager. The UN group that had overtaken us on the way to Tessenei had separated and an Englishman, Michael Askwith, head of UNDP in Asmara and a Norwegian lady, Astrid Suhrker, were assigned here. They were already established at what seems to be Om Hager's only hotel, the Red Sea, when we booked the last four of its seven beds: two of them, three of us, two drivers...

The local administrator, Abu Bakr, a man in his late 40s, joined us for a long, leisurely spaghetti dinner in the hotel courtyard. He had been an ELF fighter and had spent time in Sudan. There was now no serious tension between the ELF and the EPLF, he said. He described Om Hager's population: mixed, with Christians probably outnumbering Muslims, fifty-five to forty-five. Refugees were returning gradually from Sudan: families send a member or two to size up conditions and the state of their former homes, then decide when to come. He expects no great sudden influx, but most Eritreans did not want to remain in Sudan. As soon as the economy begins to develop again, most will return. Eritrean Muslims are moderate Khatmiya adherents, he says, like himself. They are not sympathetic to the Islamic Brothers. People went back and forth all the time during the Derg era. Eritreans will come from Sudan to vote here but their votes will be counted separately. When the two UN people joined us we talked about UNDP efforts to get a program under way in Eritrea, privatization, refugees, prospects for economic development. All these seem formidable tasks from the vantage point of this destroyed frontier town.

23 April 1993 - Om Hager.

Singing and dancing throughout the town had never stopped, even when electricity went off at ten and we went to sleep in the hotel courtyard under a black, star - studded sky. I awoke several times and looked up at the stars. No mosquitos. We were awakened well before dawn by trucks arriving from Sudan with cheering voters. After a breakfast of bananas, cookies and a glass of hot tea we made our way to the polling area at the northern edge of the town and were cheered with shouts of "Welcome referendum!". Voting was to begin at 7 A.M. The sun rose over a vast carnival scene. The red-blue-green banners of the EPLF with the yellow star and blue olive-wreath Eritrean flags fluttered everywhere. In front of Polling Station no.153, two long lines had formed: one was headed by priests bearing crosses and deacons with lighted candles; the other was led by Muslim clerics with religious banners. Leaders of both religious groups recited prayers and blessings before leading the voters behind them to the registration desk. A few hundred feet away, at Polling Station no.152, a similar process took place. Lines of voters formed throughout the area, some formed mostly of women, some of men from

Sudan, some of particular ethnic groups. Tigrinya-speaking highlanders wore classic white garb, women in beautifully embroidered gowns; many carried large round bread loaves etched with maps of Eritrea and freedom slogans. Beni Amer women were a sea of color. A group of Beni Amer swordsmen performed a lively war dance to the throbbing of drums. Children waved flags.

Slowly day dawned as the sun struck puffy tan clouds above patches of blue sky. High wind. UN officials came with forms to be filled out and voting began. The empty ballot box was shown to everyone and then sealed. We watched an old gray-haired man cast a negative vote, the only one we observed in the first twenty-five or thirty. A gray-haired Tigrayan woman cast her yes vote and kissed the ballot box. People trucked in from Sudan came to vote in groups. The men shouted *"Allah Akbar!"* as they joined the line. Some carried banners with Arabic slogans. Conscientious young officials in blue and tan caps ran to and fro with huge registration sheets flapping in the wind as they searched for names and had voters put their fingerprints on the page beside their names. People kept cheering. The voting process actually went rather slowly. Goats and donkeys were wandering around through the crowd.

We observed for a couple of hours. The UN people went off to other polling stations. Our group is assigned only to no.152 and no.153. Everything was orderly. At 10 A.M. we went back to the hotel where beds had all been stacked and water was being thrown around the courtyard to settle the dust. Bereket had already cast his vote but reported that our Land Cruiser had a broken spring leaf —could it be repaired here? Doubtful, but he would try. We sit and talk. Gerard has washed the T-shirt he has worn for the past several days. Tekle is going to wait until tomorrow to vote. He tells us of places where he has taught in the U.S.: Hamilton College Black Studies program — sounds incongruous, and apparently was. He did not like it. He liked Connecticut better. In California at Irvine now he is happier. He likes having Asians in his classes. He is an American citizen. He says he may return to Eritrea but I doubt he has any real intention to do so. The man heading the local referendum commission returned from Sudan two years ago, having spent seven years there. Originally from a village near Asmara, he is now a merchant here. At 10:30 A.M. Joe O'Neill arrived. He first asked for a glass of water, then "for some decent conversation." He drove all the way from Asmara to Tessenei in a day and stayed overnight at the Nacfa Hotel in Tessenei, told us about a good place in Agordat kept by a Greek who serves Greek food. Joe loves this part of the world; is deeply disappointed that he is not going to be named ambassador — says he has just had a message to that effect.

This afternoon we drove in Joe's car to the Ethiopian border along the Setit River, flowing muddy into Sudan. Humera is on the other side, looking a bit more prosperous than Om Hager. We took the governor, Abu Bakr, along to tell us about places where fighting had occurred. The bridge across the Setit is said to have been built by the Russians. It is a solid Bailey-bridge type but its wooden planks are badly deteriorated. Then back in Om Hager we visit the partly wrecked mosque, the hospital (a few sick people in appallingly sparse circumstances), the school (surrounded by wrecked vehicles, meager furniture and instruction material) and then back to the polling stations. Everything was going smoothly and the voting process had speeded up. We saw no one voting negatively. After cokes at our hotel, Joe took off, plans to spend the night back in Tessenei after driving north to see how polling is going in that region. He will return to Keren tomorrow and then up to Asmara Monday morning.

A man turned up with four large papayas as a gift for us at the hotel this afternoon. He would take no pay for them but wanted to be photographed with them. Then another came to present us three ears of very ripe corn and three long stalks of durra and also wanted to be photographed giving them to us! The hospitality of the local people is touching. We spent the latter part of the afternoon talking local politics and religion with the governor, Abu Bakr, an intelligent and perceptive man. We were joined by a young man named Asmarom who had been a medical technician in Sudan. Both made sensible observations on all the issues on which people pontificate from a distance and oversimplify. No UN people returned here. We did not envy them spending the day driving from one hot dusty village to another and filling out their forms in polling places. At least, they give the local people a thrill, for to have *ferenjis* come to see the polling activity has a special legitimizing character.

The day came to an end with a feeling of accomplishment and satisfaction. When we came to the polling stations shortly before seven, we found the young men and women manning it very pleased with their day. Their count of voting showed almost two thousand voters had passed through the two polling stations, 80 percent of the total registered. So there will not be much polling left to be done tomorrow. They went through the ceremony of taping the slits of the ballot boxes before our eyes to show how honest the procedure has been. Then they burned the contents of the discard boxes. Finally they gathered in front of Polling Station no.153 to be photographed. The sunset turned the western sky a vivid apricot pink. In the huts around people were going about their evening routine — baking *injera* made of reddish purple *mashila*, stirring up malted barley on griddles preparatory to brewing *sua* for Sunday's celebrations. Bereket spent the day getting the spring of our vehicle remade and told us in the evening that the task had been accomplished.

24 April 1993 - Om Hager to Tessenei

Distant sounds of dancing, light drumming last night as I fell asleep, but the commotion and exuberance of yesterday morning is gone. No truckloads of people from Sudan today. Breakfast: bananas, papayas, Sudanese cookies. While we ate we discussed Om Hager's future. It should be promising, for it is in the midst of a potentially rich agricultural area. We recalled the vegetable gardens we had seen along the Setit River — good crops irrigated from the river, an example of what can be done if only a few more people had the ambition to do it. But with road conditions as they are, almost nothing can be profitably transported to market, so people have little incentive to grow perishable crops. There are said to be plans for planting of sesame this year in considerable quantity. Pre-1974 this region used to produce enough that two million birr in revenue was collected from the Om Hager district. There were eighty tractors here on private commercial farms. The Derg nationalized everything, most of the entrepreneurs fled to Sudan. Everything has gone downhill here since. So the area has a long way to go to recover. Perhaps in ten years the town will have been rebuilt but for the present development here is well behind Tigray. There is much more construction in Tigray. This is not what one is told to expect in Eritrea, where everybody is said to be on the go...

We left here a few minutes before eight, stopping at the polling stations to check proceedings and say goodbye. People were sorry we were leaving, as was Governor Abu Bakr. Great crowds assembled to see us off. Bereket's Land Cruiser sailed smoothly over the rough, winding tracks, spring repaired, and we saw a bit of wildlife on the way to Tessenei. A young gazelle stared at us from the brush along the roadside, guinea fowl flew up repeatedly, a rabbit ran across the track, birds everywhere. We stopped to look at a field where a bumper crop of sesame had been harvested last year. A friend of Bereket's grew one thousand quintals and sold it all at a good profit. He plans to plant again this season. But we saw no preparations for planting yet, no plowing. They will have to work energetically to get ahead of the rains which are creeping northward from Tigray. But the first effect of light drizzle is to raise dust.

At Gulij the young official at the polling station gave us his figures for yesterday—79 percent of registered voters had voted. A half dozen men were lined up to vote this morning. As the registers were shown us, I could see that the columns with blue fingerprints were almost full. At the Gulij well a group of brightly dressed Beni Amer women were taking turns leaping up and down to work the long handle of the pump producing a steady flow of clear water, filling all sorts of shabby plastic pails and jugs. The women still do the hard work. We watched a couple depart: the wife carried two large metal buckets on a shoulder yoke, the husband carried the baby.

We did not aim to come farther than Tessenei today. The day has been by far the hottest we have yet experienced. We were welcomed back to the Nacfa Hotel before noon by the same crew of friendly girls who entertained us two days ago. They all had new T-shirts and wanted their pictures taken. Soon after we settled in, Joe O'Neill arrived, having got up at 6:00 A.M. this morning and driven to several polling stations in the countryside north of here. Everywhere it was the same story we experienced at Om Hager and at Gulij this morning: about 80 percent of registered voters cast ballots yesterday, only a few are trickling through today. In regions close to the Sudan border, large numbers of people were trucked across. Their votes are counted separately. Everywhere the young election officials appear to have done a conscientious job. But the carnival atmosphere has dissipated quickly and now the long, hard task of giving the people some real satisfaction from independence begins. In these wrecked towns where people seem for the most part to be squatting among the ruins, that is not going to be a simple undertaking.

The side street next to the hotel is blocked by the skeletons of two large tan busses and a jeep sitting on top of a pile of rubble. Not much effort seems to have been made yet to clean up the debris of war. In the countryside wrecked tanks and trucks have to be left where they are – the effort of trying to collect them would be too great. But in towns here it is surprising that there has not been some rebirth of civic pride. They have had two years to start cleaning up. Perhaps the mythology of thirty years of relentless war needs reinforcing, so they keep all the destruction around them. This hotel is a wreck itself. Showers don't work. We take water from pails in the courtyard.

By the time we arrived here, Tekle was a bit indisposed, so he took a long rest. I was not indisposed, merely dusty and consumed by thirst, so after lunch of *caporetto*, tomato salad and *durra injera*, a Coke, two glasses of water, four cups of coffee, and three mugs of whipped papaya, I too took a rest. In the heat there was nothing else to do. High wind came up at 4:30 P.M. and then rain. The UN team arrived back after a day of certifying procedures at nine polling stations. We all gathered around a table in the courtyard and talked into the evening. Joe O'Neill contributed a bottle of Johnnie Walker Red Label. Discussion centered on economic development in Eritrea. Michael Askwith is trying to work out a coherent program for UNDP. I gave him a copy of my "Economic Challenge" paper. Topics discussed: how much pressure should the international community put on the EPLF to avoid keeping too much under government control? Are too many of the old entrepreneurs gone to support a major program of privatization? Will commercial agriculture be encouraged again? Is there any other way to get a dependable food supply? Why has the TPLF generated so much more economic momentum in Tigray? Why aren't Eritreans as committed as Tigrayans to community development effort? Does the extremely mixed population here inhibit it? How important is education in rural areas? How can they make rapid progress on expanding infrastructure —highways, electricity? Is there much serious thinking about development at the top levels of the EPLF?

The Norwegian lady revealed herself to be a bundle of contradictory *bien pensant* and "politically correct" attitudes! Though outspokenly critical of almost everything she has seen here, at the same time she stoutly defends the EPLF's approach in a general way: "We must not try to push them, they must go their own way!" She reminded me of characters in Waugh's *Black Mischief*. I could not judge the degree to which UNDP or any of the NGOs and donor countries has productive dialogue with the EPLF on all these issues. It is needed.

25 April 1993 - From Tessenei to Keren.

Curious night. Almost everyone in the hotel slept on rope beds called *angarebs* in the huge open courtyard. A storm passed over about 3:30 A.M. and rain came down heavily for ten minutes or so. Most people moved their beds up to the porches, some even into stuffy rooms. Since mine was under a section of thatch, I decided I would not mind getting a bit wet and stayed where I was until the first signs of daylight. I tuned in BBC – talk of the referendum in Russia today. In contrast to the ritual that has just taken place here in Eritrea, this Russian referendum can have worldwide importance. But no one I have met among observers here seems to have any interest in what is happening in Russia, Eastern Europe, or Asia. They are either preoccupied with procedure –most of the UN types –or are so enveloped in parochial African concerns that they are oblivious to the world outside. Tom Killian from Bowdoin is concerned about being taken on as a Fulbrighter at Asmara University next term. He teaches history, but Amde Berhan, the university president to whom I talked at last Saturday's party, says he does not want to use up Fulbright slots on historians; he wants scientists. It is too early for a *ferenji* to be trying to help historians rewrite their history here. Killian is a great enthusiast of everything that has happened in Eritrea, but given the narrow intellectual world he lives in, I doubt he can do the Eritreans much good.

We drove out to Ali Gedir past huge stacks of Sudanese durra, some of it leaking from broken bags. We were told the piles contained three thousand tons. Who it belonged to and why it was not better protected from the weather was not clear. We heard more about plans for producing cotton and then we set out on the road back to Barentu. We raised numerous guinea hens, passed three gazelles. There was evidence of overnight rain in many places, puddles in the road. We met the UN team at Aikota, they are content that everything went well. We stopped in Agordat mid-afternoon for lunch. Then on to Keren. Storms on all sides, dramatic scenery as we climbed up to twelve thousand meters. We stretched our legs at Hagaz, a prosperous-looking village on the way, arrived in Keren at seven. The owner of the Eritrea Hotel was so happy to see us that he provided dinner free, but first we took bucket showers.

We walked to the central square to observe the celebrations under a new moon and then on to the Keren Hotel, found Nzongola and talked about Zaire. Referendum observers we met there all reported smooth voting and very few no votes. Singing and drumming continued into late hours but on the whole celebrating was less boisterous than it was last Tuesday.

26 April 1993 - From Keren to Asmara

A heavy rainstorm cooled the night, good sleeping. BBC Morning news: Yeltsin well ahead. We left for Asmara at 7:15 A.M. The road: continuous puddles, some of them pools. The Anseba River was tumbling through its bed as a river of mud. Trees looked fresh and some were coming into bloom. The bougainvillea at Elaberet, all freshly washed, shone brightly. We stopped for tea in Adi Teklesan. As we neared the plateau, Bereket suggested we turn off to see an area called Semenawi Bahri. A good road led over utterly gaunt, treeless, anciently terraced countryside—all cultivated with scattered hilltop villages. The most striking feature of these is the church which always rises at the highest point, always newly painted now. We passed through a large one called Afdeyu and then another called Wokie, which is Bereket's birthplace and where he still has a good many relatives. A short distance beyond we came to the edge of the escarpment, an area still dotted with cedars. The first views were down long valleys to distant green mountains.

The farther down we went the more spectacular the terrain became – great chunks of escarpment merged into the sea of puffy cloud that overlay the Samhar. I recall hearing of this area but none of the descriptions did it justice. It seems to have been interlaced with narrow roads since Italian times. It was the scene of much back-and-forth and some heavy fighting both immediately before the Derg period and during it. A back route to Massawa is possible through this region. On the heights the dominant trees are cedars, some of them well preserved, but lower down they give way to wild olive and large acacias. Here and there terraces have been built up for a bit of agriculture, but for the most part the region is lightly populated. We saw goats being herded and women gathering firewood, but the area as a whole is said to be reasonably well protected. We hiked through the tangles of trails where gun positions had been set up, past huge heaps of twenty millimeter. Cartridge shells, ration cans and odd pieces of military clothing and equipment. There were splendid scenes over blooming orange aloes and yellow cactus, and occasionally other flowers. As we descended over a complex series of twists and turns, we passed trees hanging thick with Spanish moss – evidence of extended damp weather during a substantial part of the year, for the region attracts rain from the lowlands in the December-April period and gets spillover from highland rains from April through September. It deserves to be set aside as a nature preserve and would be an ideal location for a simple hostel, or series of hostels which could be linked to existing trails and provide a paradise for trekkers and vacationers. No doubt there is some wild life. With less disturbance, more will return.

We drove back up and Bereket took us into his village to the house of an aunt next to the ruins of the house in which he was born. For a rather rough-cut character he showed a high degree of sentimentality about being back in his native place, showed us the dusty slopes on which he played as a child, the school where he began studies. Several relatives came by to greet him as the aunt prepared coffee for us. It was preceded by *sua,* a fresh kind not yet entirely fermented and with a semi-sweet malt taste. With the coffee we were served a local whole-wheat flatbread called *Qicha*. They had a good crop this year, the aunt said, and are making bread of their own grain which is better than the foreign grain they got as food aid.

The aunt's house was classic Eritrean village style, probably of a type that predates Axum. One of the most interesting features inside was the wall of square niches for storing things directly above a three-part "stove" — holes in a clay surface with a fire chamber underneath.

On the way into Asmara we agreed that we were all highlanders at heart. There would be little to be said for this part of the world if the best parts of it did not consist of highlands. Lowland Africa has not produced much in the way of civilization, Egypt excepted. Back at the Ambasoira at 3 P.M. to indulge in satisfying little pleasures: warm bath, fresh clothes, a toilet that can be sat on and does not smell, electric light during the day, telephone. The hotel is full of observers who have returned from the bush and are exchanging stories of their experiences — rugged travel and rough life in outlying areas. On the map our trip to Om Hager looks as adventuresome as any. A walk at dusk with a pale orange sunset lingering over the city for almost an hour. I dropped in at the Nyala Hotel but found no one I knew. Asmara still has a holiday air, people are strolling in the streets, seem to be wearing their best dress. Colored lights decorate intersections. Grocery shops are open, little else except bars.

27 April 1993 - Asmara

A telephone call to Hagos Gebre Hiwot before eight o'clock this morning brought a return call from him while I was having breakfast — an appointment with Isaias Afewerki at 10:00 A.M. The car was in front of the hotel to pick me up at five to ten. The session lasted more than an hour and a half. Three or four times in the course of it Isaias commented that I was very important to them and that my judgments could have impact on their situation.

We talked first about my impressions of the referendum at Om Hager and what I had seen traveling through the west. I said I had been pleasantly surprised to find so little evidence of Christian-Muslim strain and so little reason to believe that Eritreans returning from Sudan were bringing religious extremism along with them. Contrary to what I have heard from others about Isaias' current concerns, he expressed very confident views on religion. The Islamist government in Khartoum has tried to recruit a few Eritreans to spread its line here, he said, but has had very little success. "They can be counted in tens only — when they come back here, they discover that Eritrean priorities are most important". He favors free movement across the border and believes that all the refugees who want to return can be accommodated as economic development accelerates. I expressed confidence that Eritreans will see their interest in maximum development of the country, both economically and politically, and not in being easily drawn into political or religious adventurism. The outcome of the referendum has confirmed this feeling.

The conversation turned quickly to discussion of ethnicity, political parties, democratization, and Ethiopia. Isaias remains deeply disturbed by the course political development in Ethiopia is taking. He believes the EPRDF must moderate its preoccupation with ethnic structuralism and ethnic politics. He spoke quite disdainfully of last year's rush to elections, said the EPRDF had naively assumed that they would win Western approval. He characterized parties based on ethnic groups as harmful to democracy. He says he wants political parties in Eritrea that are required to have political programs that reflect various views of national interests. Religion and ethnicity are out as bases for party organization. People have to be prepared for voting: "We have not had elections in two of our regions – Asmara and Dancalia – because they are not yet prepared for them. We want to build political participation from the ground up. We are working on a party law that will be part of our constitution." I said I thought it important that the constitutional process not be hurried. I told him I had urged Meles to avoid setting a rigid timetable for the Ethiopian constitution and to give careful consideration to the application of ethnic principles in administration. Looking backward Isaias said, the EPRDF had miscalculated on the importance of the OLF. It was clear that the OLF lacked first-class leadership and strong support among the people.

Isaias sees Ethiopia's domestic political and economic problems as well as its international situation as quite parallel to those of Eritrea. He expressed concern that the U.S. is pulling out of Somalia too fast. I reminded him that continued large-scale involvement there would leave no American resources for African countries that were trying to make something of themselves. He said he considered it important for Ethiopia to be involved in Somalia — Ethiopia could push Somalis into creating some kind of order. I commented that at least one problem has been settled — Somali irredentism is no longer a worry for anyone in the Horn. Somalis in Ethiopia are happy to be there and insulated from troubles across the border.

He was interested in Afars. It is wise of the Ethiopians to have made Habib Ali Mirah head of the Afar region, he said, because "the fellow is a moderate who understands where the best interests of the Afars lie, while Ali Mirah himself is a confused man who still has visions of himself as a grand sultan to whom all Afars owe allegiance. The Afars who are happiest today are those in Dancalia, for their interests and those of Eritrea coincide." Isaias described the Afar problem as the result of Mengistu's arming of the Afars who then fled into Djibouti territory and stirred up trouble there, He thinks the French could have asserted more authority and prevented this: "The Afars are at best only 40 percent of the population of Djibouti and are less developed than the Issas in every respect. They cannot gain dominance. But they have little respect for life, are a wild people, and can be led into fanaticism that serves no one's interests. Our problem is to draw them into development and this will take time." Isaias considers it a distinct advantage that Habib was educated at the University of Asmara and understands Eritrea.

Isaias considers Yemen an integral part of the Horn. He believes the Saudis treated the Yemenis badly. He is encouraging maximum trade with Yemen in both directions and is confident that over time the Yemenis will make a success of the unified country. Saudi Arabia, on the other hand, he considers a time bomb: "an explosion waiting to happen." He continued:"Money cannot buy stability. No country can develop on the basis of foreign labor that has no stake in the country's development. We will not let the Saudis play with us — we insist on following our own interests. They must learn to live with that."

He spoke very positively of Israel: "Israel has a great deal to offer us and is being very helpful. We are not going to let anyone tell us we cannot manage our relations with Israel as we wish."

We came back to discuss ethnicity and politics two or three times — both in respect to Ethiopia and in respect to developments in Eritrea. Isaias cited the American approach to ethnicity as the kind of model he wants to follow: "People should be free to express their unique interests in ways that do not undermine the national interest and national development goals. Most Eritrean Muslims are Khatmia—they are naturally moderate and sensible. Neither ethnicity nor religion are priorities with them. They want peace and a better life and the task of the independent government that is now being created is to gain those objectives for the Eritrean people." Isaias is eager for foreign investment, especially from the United States. He wants rapid reconstruction of roads, irrigation facilities, and says the World Bank will be giving Eritrea generous support for road development.

I gave Isaias a brief summary of my impressions from visits to the ex-Soviet Union in the past year.

Near the end of the meeting I mentioned our stop in Semenawi Bahri yesterday and our delight at the beauty of the area. He commented that they are going to turn it into a national park and develop it for tourism.

All in all, I had the impression that Isaias had given considerable thought to what he wanted to say to me. The series of statements he made about his policies and Eritrea's present state of development were very carefully formulated.

He repeated several times how important it was for Eritrea to have a constructive relationship with the U.S. He glowed when I suggested he come to the States later this year. There were a couple of times when he impressed me as tired, but on the whole he displayed considerable energy, laughed several times, was delighted to have our picture taken together "so that you can prove to people in the States that I am neither dead nor disabled." He was dressed very casually — light shirt and sweater, sandals. Hagos had on blue jeans and a nylon jacket. There is still very little formality about the Eritrean government. Tewolde took meticulous notes during the entire conversation and commented to me as we went out to the car that he had enjoyed the discussion of issues very much.

Back at the Ambasoira I encountered the American Embassy Public Affairs Officer from Addis Ababa and two USIA officers here from Washington who are looking into setting up an office here. They say they have been assured that the local authorities will welcome it. It will be the first since Mengistu expelled USIA in 1977. Hagos says they will seek a new building for their embassy in Washington and will now conduct themselves as a regular diplomatic mission.

Isaias held a press conference in the palace (now officially called the museum) this afternoon to announce the official results of the referendum — 99.8 percent in favor of independence. It was a festive occasion. The palace grounds have been beautifully groomed — flowers everywhere. The affair was so overwhelmed by TV cameramen and journalists that observers and officials attending could see little of what was going on in front of the hall. Isaias read a short speech in Tigrinya; it was then read again in Arabic. There were many familiar people there. I found Tesfai Ghirmazien

[Minister of Agriculture] sitting in front of me so I had a brief talk with him. Tea and cookies were served afterwards. I talked to Jennifer Parmilee and Terry Lyon who came back yesterday from observing the referendum in Assab; they report little celebration, great heat and good lobster and fish. The yes vote in Assab seems to have been as high as everywhere else in Eritrea. Joe O'Neill told me he was going to the Foreign Ministry to recognize independence officially even though he had no instructions from Washington. Several other countries' representatives have done the same. Sudan was the first.

Official independence day will be 24 May, according to Isaias' announcement, to recognize that *de facto* Eritrea has been independent ever since the EPLF moved into Asmara and accepted the surrender of Derg forces on 24 May 1991. If Eritrea had gone off on the kind of petulant course Isaias had to be talked out of in the spring of 1991, this would be a sad day portending trouble for the entire region. But an enormous sense of responsibility and perspective has come over the EPLF leadership since that time.

I have had repeated expressions of personal warm feelings from people I have encountered in the course of the day. On my way back to the hotel this evening two men recognized and greeted me on the street. An old gentleman commented to me after the press conference that he hoped Isaias and his friends would take my paper, "*Eritrea - the Economic Challenge*", seriously. I told him I saw good signs that, that is exactly what they are doing. The town is ringing with sounds of horns, cheers, drumming, and dancing tonight. These people worked harder for independence than most of the rest of Africa. They could make more of it. One can only wish them well.

I walked from the hotel down to Avenida Vittore Emmanuele-HSI, Avenue-National, and Avenue-Freedom

Street at 7:00 P.M. tonight to Isaias' reception at the Municipio where I had last been received, under tight security, by Teferra Wonde, WPE First Secretary of Eritrea in 1987. There was no checking of invitation cards at the gate. Following a line of men and women on the bright red carpet that led up the stairs to the huge reception hall, one of the first persons I met was Isaias. He was not actually in the receiving line, which was manned by two lesser officials, but in a corner of the room that seemed to be dominated by fighters. He looked very trim and happy in a conservative dark suit. We had a brief chat and I passed on to the drinks and the food and to an endless series of conversations about equally divided between Eritreans and *ferenjis* – many of the observers I had encountered on the road, others who went to other parts of the country such as Siegfried Pausewang who went to a highland region along the Tigrean border. Some of the Norwegians got caught in flash floods. Everyone who went to Dancalia found it too hot.

I learned from Amare Tekle that the Ethiopian observer delegation, led by Negaso Gidada, had made an eloquent statement at this morning's session at the Referendum Commission which I had intended to attend but missed because I was meeting with Isaias. It seems that nothing untoward happened in Addis Ababa over the weekend – no violence by opponents of Eritrean independence, so the worst is past. People are citing Goshu Wolde claiming that there is serious tension between ELF and EPLF with amusement. At the same time most of the Eritreans are talking of the need for reconciliation and cooperation between Eritrea and Ethiopia. All of the hate talk against Ethiopia, so eagerly embraced by the American and European guerrilla groupies who championed the EPLF in its Marxist heyday, is absent now. The semi-official position now seems to be that the Eritrean and Ethiopian people were never at odds – it was only the leaders.

There must have been one thousand people at this evening's reception. When the crowd had thinned to half after nine, I decided it was time to leave. The main avenue was filled with revellers: singers, drummers, women still waving bouquets and sprigs of leaves, young men dancing and leaping – almost Oromo-style. The mood has much African spirit in it but there is an element of higher civilization too. Most of the faces are more Caucasian than Negroid. It would be hard to imagine a people so genuinely good-looking, with such a large percentage of handsome young men and women and attractive children. Old people here age with dignity and character. It took me half an hour of steady plodding step by small step with a good many sidesteps, to make my way through the crowd up to the side street that leads to the Ambasoira. Now, at 10 P.M. in the evening, horns are blaring over the city and sounds of singing, cheering, ululating rise up from every side. If all this enthusiasm can be harnessed for the good of all, this will indeed become a nation.

But I will be glad to be flying back to Addis Ababa tomorrow. The mood will be different there, perhaps almost indifferent. So far I have achieved all my aims on this visit. The last four days in Addis Ababa will doubtless be busy as the final days of a visit always are and I will want to make the most of them. My first period in Addis now seems far away in time, but it will be useful to meet with the Constitutional Commission again and do what I can to steer their thinking along constructive lines. I hope to be able to meet Meles and talk more frankly and less formally than I did the first week I was here. Tigray now seems even farther back than Addis but my visit there was a splendid experience. I will need to contact Alemseged and Teshome to bring them up to date on the rest of my Tigrayan visit and to hear their reflections on the part of the visit during which they were present. I am curious about the conference on ethnicity that was going to be held at the university in June. With Tadesse Beyene dismissed, I would think that this conference might not now take place. A good idea basically, but it had nevertheless become inopportune.

28 April 1993 - Asmara to Addis Ababa

Celebrations continued through the night and seems to have cleared the air over Asmara, for the sky was utterly cloudless this morning and the air still. Hardly any traffic. The population was exhausted. The Ambasoira Hotel staff was exhausted too, for the main desk was not manned and breakfast, served in a room behind the bar, was minimal. Breakfasts declined steadily over the past ten days. When I first arrived there was cheese and meat in the morning, pastries and rolls, a bowl of fruit. Today there was only orange and papaya juice and bread; the coffee was weak and there was little of it. This hotel needs the kind of shake - up good private management could provide and is unlikely to be able to compete as other hotels here improve. With economic resurgence Asmara will be attractive to international hotel chains. If Americans or Europeans do not want to come in, Indians may.

The USIA driver, who remembered me from year ago, was ready to take me along to the airport this morning, but that lively German-Californian Eritrean, Meg Kidane, came by with a pickup and I went out with her. The airport was well organized and efficient. Observers were given a bit of special treatment but still had to pay the B25 departure tax and some had to go through baggage check. Waiting to get into the end of the line, Siegfried Pausewang and I and a couple of the Norwegians were taken by Amare Tekle through the VIP exit and thus avoided all processing. Joe O'Neill was waiting outside the VIP lounge and wanted to hear about my conversation with Isaias yesterday. I told him that one of my strongest impressions was Isaias' concern for the stability and integrity of Ethiopia. That concern, Joe feels, needs to be better understood in Washington than it is. He wants me to emphasize this to Bob Houdek.[77]

The flight to Addis Ababa started half an hour late. It was smooth but after we landed the captain told us he had lost one engine in the course of the flight. The Boeing 727 had given no sign of losing power. The countryside over which we flew was red in Eritrea with tiny patches of green around hilltop villages. Over Tigray we saw streams flowing with muddy water and more green. Finally over Shoa, everything was green and even the littlest streams were sparkling in the sunlight.

CHAPTER VI

WHO "LOST" ERITREA?

This essay was written shortly after my return from serving as a referendum observer in Eritrea. At that time Eritrea, though confirmed as independent, was "lost" only in the judgment of diehard opponents of independence in Ethiopia. I wrote this essay to discourage further agitation by those in Ethiopia who had unrealistically called for "action" to prevent Eritrea's independence. The agitation receded quickly in the weeks following the referendum and the subsequent official declaration of independence on 24 May 1993. It was never clear that any "action" at all could have been taken.

I was optimistic at the time I wrote this essay. My optimism was reinforced by the meeting I had had with Isaias Afewerki, at his request, when I returned to Asmara in late April 1993. The conversation during this meeting is reproduced practically verbatim in Chapter Five of this book. The judgments and policy intentions Isaias expressed during this conversation proved to be completely at variance with his subsequent policies and actions.

"WHAT HAS BEEN "LOST"?

Grotesquely, Ethiopian centrists bemoaning the consequences of the Eritrean independence referendum keep on blaming the United States for their "loss" and berating Herman Cohen for allegedly "giving away" Eritrea in London in May 1991. For a history-conscious people, such Ethiopians display a peculiar blindness to historical evidence, both recent and more distant. They overlook the fact that the United States Government maintained a firm commitment to Ethiopia's territorial integrity until the Derg's disastrous war against Eritrea had run its course and Ethiopia's "territorial integrity", as far as Eritrea was concerned, was no longer at issue. Except for a small group of EPLF enthusiasts, most of whom had little grounding in the history or politics of the Horn, the great majority of Americans specializing in Ethiopian matters continued to support the concept of Eritrea remaining a part of, or in close association with, the Ethiopian state until it became irrelevant.[78] If the "loss" of Eritrea can be laid at the doorstep of any single individual or group, no rational reading of recent history could identify any other culprit than Mengistu Haile Mariam and his Derg associates.

The process has a longer past, however, and rests on a sequence of clearly established historical events. Eritrea has only been on the map for one hundred three years. Italy, by a combination of military effort and political intrigue, carved off a segment of the northern Ethiopian borderlands and set up a Red Sea Colony — *Colonia Eritrea* — in 1890. It was the first phase of an effort to establish hegemony over Ethiopia. Emperor Menelik's defeat of the Italian invaders at Adwa in March 1896 gave him an opportunity to regain

Eritrea. He chose instead to compromise —let Italy retain its colony in return for a peaceful stance toward Ethiopia, securing a stable northern frontier while he concentrated on rounding out Ethiopia's borders in the south. Menelik thus confirmed Eritrea's "loss" to Ethiopia. Some Tigrayans have never forgiven him. The if's of history are incalculable, but Menelik's decision was not casual or irrational. He was a pragmatist. If he had devoted his energies to expanding Ethiopia's ill-defined frontiers in the north, he might never have been able to stabilize the south and consolidate control over the empire. Ethiopia might then have fallen victim to European colonialism from all sides.

Italy made no pretense of building a separate nation in Eritrea. During the half century of Italian rule, highland Eritreans never lost their consciousness of belonging to Ethiopian civilization. By the late 1920s Italian imperialists were again planning to use Eritrea as a base area from which all of Ethiopia could be conquered and made part of a new Fascist Roman Empire. Events far beyond Italy and Ethiopia made this venture short-lived, and "liberated" Eritrea emerged as a problem to be addressed by the international community.

By consistent, dogged effort Haile Selassie worked to re-unite Eritrea with Ethiopia during the decade 1942-1952. For a long time the task looked unpromising. Eritrean highlanders were inclined toward Ethiopia, but from the official Allied viewpoint Eritrea was conquered enemy territory and became one of the new United Nations organization's first "disposal" problems. If Eritrea had come onto the international agenda ten or fifteen years later than it did, it would in all likelihood have been set on a straightforward path to independence, as all other African colonial territories eventually were. But independence was not yet fashionable at the beginning of the 1950s. Britain's desire to disengage from Eritrea, mounting American strategic needs, and Haile Selassie's ambition to regain old Ethiopian lands as well as a seacoast coincided to make some form of association with Ethiopia seem logical. The UN oversaw the crafting of the federation arrangement that came into effect in 1952. It was a carefully crafted undertaking.

The mechanics and fine points of federation were irrelevant for Ethiopian nationalists who regarded Eritrea as regained for Ethiopia after more than six decades of separation. In retrospect, it is clear that the concept of federation represented an opening which could have been exploited, over time, to reconstruct the entire Ethiopian state on a more modern, viable, federal basis. But neither the Emperor nor the Ethiopian political elite had reached a stage where they could comprehend this possibility. Instead, the federation evolved in the opposite direction. It was never fully implemented on the Ethiopian side and the framework for a multi-party, democratic system with which Eritrea had been provided was progressively eroded.[79] Haile Selassie's fear of Nasserite expansion and rising Arab militarism contributed to termination of the federation in 1962. Had at least the formal structure of federation been retained, it is possible that the Eritrean problem which gradually became more serious as the 1960s advanced, might have been more amenable to peaceful solution. Many factors, both internal and external, contributed to its exacerbation.

It is unfair to blame the old Lion of Judah for the Eritrean tragedy, for in his prime he was always capable of creative initiative and compromise. At the end of his long reign his capacity for adroit statesmanship failed him. His demise was hastened by the inability of the Ethiopian political elite to meet the challenges of transition from paternalistic rule to accelerated modernization. The

Ethiopian political establishment collapsed in confusion in 1974 and let an ill-assorted and inexperienced military junta take power. There was still a window of opportunity for a few months when bold initiatives might have settled the Eritrean conflict. Rivalry between Eritrean rebel factions complicated matters but the opportunity was irretrievably lost as Mengistu gained ascendancy, killed General Aman, and committed the Derg to a military "solution" in Eritrea. In the decade and a half which followed, even with $12 billion worth of Soviet arms, Ethiopia was incapable of subjugating Eritrea. On the other hand, until Eritreans, Tigrayans, and other Ethiopians joined in a determined effort to defeat Mengistu, they were unable to win. Mengistu's blind stubbornness both prolonged the final agony and made the outcome inevitable: the establishment of separate governments in Asmara and Addis Ababa in May 1991.[80]

The role of the United States in this historic denouement was constructive but tangential. Nothing could have prevented the EPRDF and the EPLF from taking power — they won it on the battlefield — but the process could have been prolonged, bloody and destructive and the aftermath confused. Ethiopia could have turned into a Somalia. U.S. mediation helped minimize random violence and helped make the transition comparatively peaceful and orderly in both Eritrea and most of Ethiopia. The independence referendum which took place among Eritreans in the last week of April 1993 and the declaration of independence which followed were the culmination of a process which began in late 1974, when Mengistu opted to resort to ever mounting military force to dominate Eritrea.

A country must pay a price for a brutal, totalitarian dictatorship. Germany had only twelve years of Hitler, but paid a far higher price than Ethiopia is paying for seventeen years of Mengistu.[81]

On balance, how great a "loss" does Eritrea really represent? It can be argued, it seems to me, that by insisting on independence, Eritreans are sparing Ethiopia a major portion of the costs of Mengistu's destructive misrule. Let us consider a few basic facts.

No part of Ethiopia's territory was more damaged by war than Eritrea. This is immediately apparent to anyone who travels through the Eritrean countryside which is likely to continue to be littered with military debris for many years to come. Or to any visitor to Massawa or the towns of the north and west. Deplorable as the losses and damage in other parts of Ethiopia were, it is arguable that the cost in lives, physical destruction, and environmental degradation was greater in the Eritrean region than in all other parts of Ethiopia combined. Eritreans have demanded no reparations and, in insisting on independence, are taking responsibility for repair of all this damage onto themselves. If Eritrea were to remain part of Ethiopia, much of the cost of rehabilitation and reconstruction would have to come from Ethiopia's budget in competition with the needs of all other Ethiopian regions. Eritrean independence relieves Ethiopia of this burden.[82]

Whether Eritrean independence represents a serious economic loss for Ethiopia in the broader sense, and over time, depends on current and future judgments, decisions, and actions by both governments and both peoples. The degree to which economic interdependence has already been recognized on a pragmatic basis is encouraging. Ethiopia has lost its seacoast. Since maritime resources were poorly exploited, this is more a potential than an actual loss. Ethiopia no longer has jurisdiction over the two major Red Sea ports. The real issue is not, however, legal jurisdiction, but economic utilization. Massawa and Assab cannot operate profitably if their service only narrow Eritrean needs. By serving a steadily expanding Ethiopian economy they can prosper. This fact has already been recognized in interim agreements between the Provisional Government of Eritrea and the Transitional Government of Ethiopia.

Eritrea's comparatively substantial industrial base was severely damaged by Derg mismanagement, neglect, and military operations. Rebuilding it (and attracting foreign investment for it) makes sense only if it is to operate in a broader economic context than Eritrea by itself can provide. Eritrea's population of three million is too small to provide raw materials and markets for Eritrean industrial and commercial capacity. While there is potential for expansion of Eritrea's economic relations with Sudan, the Arabian Peninsula, and more distant countries, Ethiopia, with a rapidly growing population of more than fifty million, is Eritrea's most logical and natural economic partner. Fortunately, Eritrean leaders appear fully aware that notions of autarky make no economic sense. Neither Ethiopia nor Eritrea can afford to indulge in petty economic thinking or practice without undermining their own viability and reducing prospects for improving the living standards of their peoples. In a broader sense this principle is true of the entire Horn of Africa region, but the best prospects for economic integration of the Horn/Red Sea region lie in enhanced Eritrean-Ethiopian relations, building on the experience and framework created during the past fifty years.[83] Geography, cultural affinities, and economic logic all argue for the closest cooperation between Ethiopia and Eritrea — for neither can lose; both can gain.

The same is equally true of considerations of politics and international relations. It is clearly in the interest of both Ethiopia and Eritrea that the other enjoy internal political stability, freedom from social, religious, and ethnic strain, and the advantages of an open social system and a free flow of information. Long-established habits and patterns of professional, educational, and cultural interchange should be maintained to the advantage of all. The leaders of both governments have committed themselves to creation of working democracy. Democracy must be a continuing experiment in self-administration and tolerance. Each can profit from the other's ongoing experience.

It is difficult to envision how Ethiopia and Eritrea could develop widely divergent perceptions in the field of foreign relations. They share the same neighbors and the same attitudes toward them. They share the same interests in political, economic, and cultural relations with developed countries and international organizations. Both will gain from these relationships if they cooperate, lose if they attempt to disadvantage each other or compete. It is difficult to envision an issue on which Eritrea could rationally take a position sharply different from Ethiopia in the United Nations or in the Organization of African Unity. An independent Eritrea, in fact, constitutes a natural partner for Ethiopia in such bodies and, in effect, doubles its voting impact.

If Ethiopians contemplate the formal political separation of Eritrea from Ethiopia with dispassion and perspective, rather than with an attitude of petulant nostalgia, it is difficult to define a serious "loss". In what would it consist? Imperial pride? That should have passed with the passing of empire itself. Security? How does an independent Eritrea endanger Ethiopia? Precedent for further fragmentation? Only if Ethiopian leaders fail to meet the aspirations of a majority of their own people for secure existence and improving living standards.

The 1952 federation arrangement envisioned a high degree of autonomy for Eritrea within which Eritrean society could continue to develop and modernize with a substantial political freedom. Ethiopia's political system was still too backward, and evolving too slowly, to make these aims realizable. From the 1960s onward a combination of internal and external circumstances propelled Ethiopia and Eritrea into a downward spiral of deterioration which led to tragedy for both. The deterioration stopped with the fall of the Derg. The consequences can prove irretrievably harmful only if shortsightedness on all sides fuels tension and vindictiveness. Ethiopians and Eritreans can afford to go on nursing the grievances of the past only at the expense of jeopardizing their future and squandering their prospects for economic development and international respectability.

Washington, D.C.
May 1993

CHAPTER VII

A SHORT HISTORY OF ERITREA

Introduction

The name Eritrea came onto the map of Africa only at the end of the nineteenth century. Until then "Eritrean History", as far back as it extends, was Ethiopian history. During the 1980s when it fought the Derg, Isaias Afewerki's Marxist Eritrean Popular Liberation Front (EPLF) encouraged the notion that Eritrea had always been a separate polity with little connection with Ethiopia. This idea has been spread by EPLF propagandists ever since. It has gained wide acceptance abroad among journalists and others with scant knowledge of the history of the Horn of Africa and has become dogma among many Eritreans in the diaspora. It is mythology. The real history of the region begins four thousand years ago, but much remains still to be discovered by archaeological research.

Ancient Times

The first records of the region that today includes Eritrea come from four thousand year-old Egyptian inscriptions that recount trading voyages to the Land of Punt. Punt was a general Egyptian term for the entire southern Red Sea region. The first visitors to the Dahlak Islands and the nearby coast where the port of Adulis developed were probably Egyptian sailors. From the natives they bought incense, gold, ivory, and skins of exotic animals. As commerce increased, they brought live animals – zebras, giraffes, and even elephants –back to Egypt. Some of these are pictured, along with the boats they came on, in paintings in Egyptian tombs. Later, Greek voyagers made regular trips into the Red Sea and the Indian Ocean beyond. Some of their sailing handbooks have survived. They provide extensive information about ports, peoples, and products of the region. One of the most famous is the *Periplus of the Erythrean Sea* written by an unknown Greek author in the First Century AD. It has been translated, studied by scholars, and published in several editions.[84]

Adulis, a port on the Bay of the same name south of Massawa, became a busy trading station frequented by ships from Egypt and South Arabia.[85] Gold, ivory, incense and other tropical products flowed in quantity to the Mediterranean world. In time Adulis developed to become the principal port of the Aksumite Empire, the first Ethiopian state.

The origins of this empire, considered by the Persian prophet Mani one of the four great empires of the ancient world (the others being Rome, Persia, and China), are still being probed by archaeologists on both sides of the Red Sea. Several kingdoms arose in what is today Yemen. They developed a writing system and set up monuments with inscriptions. People from South Arabia began to cross the Red Sea to the African side perhaps as early as 1000 BC. Considerable numbers of South Arabians apparently emigrated to what is now Eritrea and northern Ethiopia and mixed with local populations. These proto-Aksumites — the best name historians have found for them — formed city — states, kingdoms and engaged in warfare and trade.

A major religious and administrative center grew up at Yeha in Tigray, not far south of the present Eritrean border, where an impressive temple still stands. Its finely cut walls of tan stone, joined without mortar, still stand to a height of seven to nine meters. They have withstood at least twenty-five hundred years of wars, storms, and earthquakes. The temple is surrounded by graves and stelae. French archaeologists dug there in the 1960s and are beginning work again at the end of the twentieth century. Much more remains to be uncovered. All over highland Eritrea, and in Tigray to the south, inscriptions in essentially the same South Arabian alphabet used on the other side of the Red Sea have been discovered and year by year more are found.

At some time around the beginning of the Christian era political power shifted from Yeha, and perhaps other centers in the region, to Aksum. Aksum is situated among low hills thirty kilometers west of Yeha. It has long been known for its skillfully carved monolithic granite obelisks, among the wonders of the ancient world. Excavations at Aksum were first undertaken by the German archaeologist Enno Littman early in the twentieth century. British, Italian, and American archaeologists resumed digging around Aksum after the fall of the Derg regime in Addis Ababa in 1991. They have already acquired new evidence about the rise of the Aksumite state, the daily life of the people, and the origins of agriculture in the Horn of Africa.

At its zenith, from the third to the seventh centuries AD, the Aksumite Empire included most of modern Eritrea and large parts of present-day Sudan. Cities flourished along the route from Aksum to Adulis, the main outlet to the sea. The remains of these can be seen at Tekonda, Cohaito, and Matara. At each of these places, as at Adulis itself, some exploration and digging has been done by archaeologists since the late nineteenth century. Much is already known about Aksum at its zenith. Emperors captured lands far to the north and campaigned deep into the west, reaching the Nile. The existence of Aksum was known in Rome and Egypt and there were diplomatic contacts. Aksumite emperors struck coins in bronze, silver, and gold. They provide a great deal of historical information. Greek was used along with the indigenous Semitic language, Ge'ez, on both coins and stone inscriptions.[86]

In the early fourth century Christianity was adopted by the Aksumite emperor Ezana. Legend attributes its arrival to two young men from the East Roman Empire, Frumentius and Aedisius, who were shipwrecked on the coast, captured, and brought to Aksum. Pious Christians, they eventually converted Ezana. The Orthodox Church has preserved colorful accounts of the process of Christianization during the next two centuries. Ezana's coins confirm his acceptance of the new religion no later than 340 AD. The symbol of the old South Arabian religion, the crescent of the moon god Alemkah, was replaced by the cross. From that time onward, the cross continued to be a major feature of the coins of Aksum. Coins are still being found all over the region and many have come to light in places as distant as India, for they were used in trade. The real task of Christianizing the population was done, according to tradition, by the Nine Syrian Saints. These were priests and monks who came as missionaries from the Byzantine Empire who translated the Old and New Testaments into Ge'ez, traveled, preached, and established monasteries.

The oldest of the monasteries is Debre Damo, on a flat - topped mountain in Tigray, within sight of the present Eritrean border. It dates from the sixth century. Several monasteries in present-day Eritrea, for example, Debra Libanos at Ham, near Senafe, are almost as early. The Ge'ez-speaking population of the highlands became fervent Orthodox Christians, and have remained so ever since. Monasteries continued to be founded during the next several centuries. The northernmost, Debre Bizen, was established by St. Philip in 1361. It is located on a twenty-four hundred ridge east of Asmara above the town of Nefasit, with a view to the sea. Its library possesses some of the oldest Orthodox manuscripts extant.

Links between peoples on both sides of the Red Sea remained close for hundreds of years after the initial migrations. There was steady trade, travel, cultural, and religious interchange. For a long time the languages and script seem to have remained mutually intelligible. On several occasions the emperors of Aksum undertook campaigns in South Arabia and conquered and ruled South Arabian kingdoms. Jewish communities were already well established in South Arabia when Christianity came. Some Jews seem to have crossed the Red Sea too. Initially Christianity spread in South Arabia in much the same way as in the Aksumite Empire. But in Arabia it was unable to outlive the rise of Islam.

In the early seventh century, the Prophet Mohammed received his revelations and began his mission. He was rejected by the men in power in Mecca, fled to Medina in 622, and his followers were persecuted. Some fled across the Red Sea, where they were welcomed and given asylum by the Aksumite Emperor. They settled at Negash in Tigray, where their tombs are still a pilgrimage site for Ethiopian

Muslims. Mohammed soon prevailed in Arabia and gradually more Muslims arrived in the Aksumite Empire, while many people along the coast were converted to Islam. Christians and Muslims lived peacefully together. Though in later centuries strife and enmity developed, the still prevailing principle of coexistence between the two religions rests on ancient foundations.

The rapid spread of Islam through Arabia to Egypt and the Near East disrupted Aksum's trade with the Mediterranean world. The period of the Empire's decline from the eighth century onward is the most obscure in the history of this region. The cities on the route to the sea faded from history. So did Adulis, to be replaced eventually by Massawa, which began as a minor Arab port on an island off the coast. The city of Aksum declined into little more than a village but remained the seat of the Orthodox church. Almost nothing is known of the later Aksumite emperors —even their names are controversial.[87] After the depredations of a mysterious warrior queen called Judith in the tenth century, the Aksumite ruling line was replaced by the non-Semitic Zagwe dynasty. These emperors established their capital far to the south at Roha in Lasta. Their most famous king, Lalibela, an enthusiastic Christian, had eleven monumental rock churches carved at Roha. After his death the town took his name.

The Middle Ages

Christianity continued dominant in the Ethiopian highlands, while the coast and the lowlands to the north and west rapidly became Islamized. Contact with South Arabia ceased. In the Eritrean highlands and Tigray to the south, Ge'ez evolved into a new language, Tigrinya,[88] and farther south Amharic developed in the same way, much as Italian,

227

French and other languages replaced Latin in the lands of the Roman Empire. The regions that today form the western and northern provinces of Eritrea alternated between control of local rulers and subjection by Sudanese kingdoms to the west. When the Zagwe dynasty was replaced by the Amharic-speaking king, Yekuno Amlak, in 1270, the traditions of the Aksumite Empire and its links to the Queen of Sheba and King Solomon were revived. The new rulers called their empire Ethiopia and claimed the lands that had belonged to Aksum all the way to the sea. When Ethiopian emperors were strong, they appointed a prince called the *Bahr Negash* — Ruler of the Sea — as the Viceroy of the northern highlands and the coast. He had his seat at Debarwa which still exists as a village south of Asmara. Ethiopian emperors never gave up their claim to Massawa.

The light of history in this region brightens at the end of the fifteenth century. The Portuguese sea captain Vasco da Gama rounded the Cape of Good Hope in 1497 and sailed on to India. There the city of Goa grew rapidly and became Portuguese headquarters for the entire Indian Ocean region. Even earlier the King of Portugal had sent explorers through the Mediterranean to the Horn of Africa to open a way to the mysterious Christian Kingdom of Prester John, the subject of curiosity and rumor in Europe for centuries. The Portuguese were motivated both by trade and missionary zeal, and the first of them reached the Ethiopian imperial court in the 1490s. A major Portuguese expedition arrived at Massawa in 1520, trekked up the escarpment into the highlands, and met their countrymen there. The mission remained six years in Ethiopia. A Jesuit priest who accompanied it, Father Francisco Alvares, kept a detailed account of their travels and impressions.[89]

During the same period, the ruler of the Muslim Kingdom of Adal (centered around Harar), Ahmad ibn Ibrahim, started planning a *jihad* (holy war) to eradicate Christianity from the Ethiopian highlands and convert the inhabitants to Islam. Starting in 1527, his armies advanced rapidly, destroying churches and monasteries, and reaching Hamasien, the area around Asmara, in the 1530s. The monks at Debre Bizen still tell visitors how God made the monastery invisible and thus saved it from being sacked by Ahmad Gragn (Ahmad the Left-Handed) as this ruler of Adal is known among Orthodox Christians.

Emperor Lebna Dengel appealed to Portugal for help, for Ahmad Gragn's army was well supplied with firearms and repeatedly defeated much larger Ethiopian forces. It took King Joao of Portugal a decade to respond to the appeal, but in 1541 a well-armed contingent of four hundred sharpshooters under Christovao da Gama landed at Massawa. Lebna Dengel had died and been succeed by his son, Galawdewos. The Portuguese proceeded up to the highlands and rescued the beleaguered new emperor. They killed Ahmad Gragn in a battle in Dembea, northeast of Lake Tana, in 1543. Ethiopia was saved. Many of the Portuguese soldiers stayed and married local women. Their descendants were gradually absorbed into the Ethiopian population.

For the better part of the next hundred years Portuguese traders and priests, usually coming and going through Massawa, played an important role in Ethiopia as imperial advisors. Jesuit missionaries became overconfident and overplayed their hand when they persuaded Emperor Susenyos to accept Roman Catholicism in the 1620s. Both the aristocracy and the common people refused to abandon Orthodoxy. They revolted and Susenyos abdicated in favor of his son, Fasilidas in 1632.

Meanwhile Massawa itself was taken over by the expanding Ottoman Empire in 1557 as the armies of

Suleiman the Magnificent advanced from Egypt down the Red Sea. The Ottomans subjugated northern Sudan and much of Arabia and Muslims acknowledged the Ottoman sultan as Caliph. From time to time Ottoman armies penetrated into the Ethiopian highlands, but for the most part – and characteristic of Ottoman practice – they persuaded local rulers to recognize their sovereignty and pay tribute, so the actual reach of their power was often vague. In keeping with Ottoman practice in Anatolia and the Balkans, Ottoman governors did not try to eradicate Christianity. They permitted Christians to administer themselves. They encouraged trade and travel with the interior through Massawa. The Turks called the area along the coast the Province of Habesh, the Arabic word from which the European form Abyssinia is derived. Ottoman rule of the coast lasted into the nineteenth century but after 1813 it was exercised through Egypt. Egypt belonged to the Ottoman Empire, but Mohammed Ali, the Albanian-origin Pasha who held power from 1805 to 1848, and his successors, were only nominally vassals of the Ottoman Sultan. Their own vassals, the Naibs of Arkiko, a town on the coast south of Massawa now called Hargigo, were the recognized rulers of the Ethiopian coast during the first three-quarters of the nineteenth century.

From the late seventeenth century onward, European interest in the Horn of Africa increased steadily. By the end of the eighteenth century, European visitors to the region were relatively frequent. Among the most famous are the Scot, James Bruce, who spent the years 1769-71 in Ethiopia and reached the source of the Blue Nile at Gish Abbay in 1770; and Lord Valentia (Viscount Annesley) who explored the Red Sea region during the years 1803-06. Valentia even named the Bay of Zula (Adulis) for himself. Bruce published eight volumes when he returned to England, Valentia three. Both are replete with fine drawings of people, artifacts, and scenes. Valentia's include some of the etchings of Henry Salt, a member of the expedition, who was sent to explore Tigray in 1804 and returned again for more travel in 1809. Many other Europeans followed and published accounts of their experiences. This vast literature is now in part available in modern reprints. In the nineteenth century Protestant and Catholic missionaries were attracted to the region. They converted local communities that still flourish in Eritrea and Tigray.

Into Modern Times

Politically, much of the territory which became independent Eritrea in 1993 was contested by several different powers during the first seven decades of the nineteenth century. Though its authority was mostly nominal, Ethiopia never abandoned its claim to the region, but it was too weak to hold it effectively. After the brilliant Gondar emperors, power in Ethiopia had dispersed during the Era of the Princes, which lasted until 1855. Then Emperor Tewodros rose from obscure beginnings and unified the country in a few years. He was too impetuous to prevail for long. By taking a group of Europeans hostage, he aroused Britain and the Napier mission was mounted from India to free the hostages. This well-equipped British military expedition landed in late 1867 near the site of Adulis and climbed up to the highlands along tracks Aksumite traders had used. They passed the ruins of Cohaito and Matara and moved on toward the southwest. On the great mountain of Magdala in Wollo they cornered Tewodros in April 1868. Defeated, the emperor shot himself.

General Napier withdrew his army over the same route he had come and left Ethiopia in confusion. The future King Menelik of Shoa had escaped from Magdala before the great battle and returned to his kingdom. Yohannes IV, a Tigrayan prince, was crowned emperor. What are now the Eritrean highlands then formed part of the northernmost Ethiopian province of Tigray. Yohannes' authority extended over the highland areas. The lowlands, however, were literally up for grabs, with Egyptians, Italians, British, French, and even Russians eager to gain a foothold on the Red Sea.

For a brief time Egypt was a major player on this scene. Its ruler, Khedive Ismail, was eager to expand into Sudan and extend Egyptian control over northern Ethiopia. To modernize his army, Ismail recruited more than forty, mostly Confederate, American officers who had fought in the Civil War. Important as these officers were for Egypt, they could not prevent Egyptian defeat in the Battles of Gundet in 1875 and Gura in 1876.[90] But in the scramble for Africa which followed, the European powers were wary of letting Egypt play a dominant role in a region where they were already competing with each other. Italy bought a base in Assab in 1869. Britain moved into Egypt in 1882 and put an end to the Khedive's adventures in the Horn. As a rival of France, Britain sympathized with the Italian aim of securing a substantial foothold in the Horn. The British made no objections to Italy's occupation of Massawa in 1885. The Italians were eager to advance into the highlands. They were in for a surprise.

As the Egyptian presence on the coast weakened, the whole region fell back under Tigrayan control. Ras Alula Ingida, born at Manawe in the central Tigrayan province of Tembien in 1847, established himself as the ruler of the northern province of Hamasien with his capital at Asmara, at that time only the site of an ancient church and a cluster of small villages. Emperor Yohannes IV was preoccupied with incursions of the Sudanese dervish armies of the Mahdi and left defense against the Italians to Ras Alula. In 1887 the Italians sent an expeditionary force from Massawa up into the highlands. At the Wadi Dogali, about twenty-five kilometers. inland, it was confronted by Ras Alula's army and dealt a stunning defeat. Ras Alula's triumph was short-lived.[91]

Emperor Yohannes IV died fighting the Sudanese at Metemma in 1889. King Menelik of Shoa succeeded him as emperor. But in northern Ethiopia, confusion spread and the Italians took advantage of it, applying lessons learned from their defeat at Dogali. In a series of well-planned operations they had advanced to the Mareb River by 1890. This was the year they proclaimed their newly conquered territory *Colonia Eritrea* – the Red Sea Colony – and chose Asmara as its capital.

Thus Eritrea came onto the map as a geographic and political entity. Expansionist Italians regarded it as merely a base for the future conquest of Ethiopia. Italian imperialists regarded *Colonia Eritrea* as the first stage in creation of a new Roman Empire. The addition of Ethiopia would follow. They were confident that Ethiopian Emperor Menelik would live to regret his defiance of them in cancelling the Treaty of Wichale. Italian emissaries and agents intrigued among Tigrayan princes, some of whom resented Yohannes' replacement by an emperor from Shoa. But they had difficulties in Eritrea. The whole north Ethiopian region had been affected by cattle disease, locusts, drought, and famine in the early 1890s. The Italians started expropriating land belonging to Eritreans to make room for the thousands of colonists they expected to arrive. Eritreans were alarmed. An originally pro-Italian Eritrean chief, Dejazmach Bahta Hagos of Akele Guzay, revolted in 1894. He claimed to have support from Tigray. An Italian force killed Bahta on 17 December and made a foray into Tigray. All this was a foretaste of the sparring that intensified during the following year and led to the Ethiopian trouncing of Italy at Adwa fifteen months later.

They had brought in more soldiers from Italy and recruited men from Eritrea as auxiliaries. It took them less than five years to be prepared to advance against Ethiopia. Not all Italians favored these plans, but imperial-minded civilians and generals dominated political decision-making in Rome. A major offensive began in 1895. Italian forces advanced deep into Tigray, capturing Adigrat and Makelle. The appetite for further advances grew rapidly. Generals were eager for glory and promotion. The Ethiopians were thought too backward to mount effective resistance. Emperor Menelik, who had refused to accept an Italian protectorate, was scorned by the ambitious Italian empire-builders. It was a serious misjudgment.[92]

Menelik mobilized his Shoan forces and moved them north. Regional kings and princes from all parts of Ethiopia responded to his appeal to join in defending the country's independence. Menelik assembled his armies around Adwa, a short distance south of historic Aksum. He set up his headquarters at the ancient Monastery of Abba Gerima, founded by one of the Nine Syrian Saints. Other Ethiopian leaders placed their troops at strategic locations among the spectacular volcanic mountains which extend eastward from Aksum and Adwa for forty kilometers – the direction from which the Italians were known to be advancing. Menelik had hundred thousand men under his command.

With less than a fifth of that number, almost half of them Eritrean auxiliaries of doubtful loyalty, the Italians rushed to attack the Ethiopians. Battle was joined the morning of 2 March 1896. Within hours the Italian army had been literally decimated. Many of the Eritrean troops defected to the Ethiopians. Most of the Italian generals and many lower-ranking officers were killed, thousands of Italians were taken prisoner.

By telegraph and cable, news of the decisive defeat arrived in Italy in a day and word of the Ethiopian victory — the first of its kind by what is now called a Third World country against a European power — spread around the world. Menelik had secured Ethiopia's independence for another forty years. A Tigrayan emperor might have pursued the fleeing Italians to Asmara and helter-skelter down the escarpment to Massawa, expelling them permanently from Eritrea. But could he have succeeded? We will never know. In Rome the government fell, riots broke out in Italian cities, and political confusion ensued. Imperialist politicians and generals called for reinforcements to be sent to Eritrea to mount a new campaign against Menelik.

While Italians in Asmara panicked, fearing the Ethiopians would push them into the sea, Menelik held a victory parade on the Adwa battlefield on 7 March and had Italian officers witness 80,000 Ethiopians marching past. He told the Italians he would conclude a peace treaty if they would recognize the border between Eritrea and Tigray and permit free trade across it. He then embarked on a two-month triumphal march back to Addis Ababa. It took the Italians half a year to reconcile themselves to their defeat but the new government in Rome saw the advantage of peace with retention of Eritrea. Sober judgment prevailed on both sides. Menelik sought reconciliation, not revenge. He still had to secure Ethiopia's eastern, southern, and western borders against other Europeans eager to expand their colonial holdings. Menelik concluded peace with Italy in the Treaty of Addis Ababa signed on 26 October 1896, leaving Eritrea to Italy. This gave Ethiopia a secure northern border in an unstable region that had experienced invaders from all directions since ancient times.

Victory at Adwa increased respect for Ethiopia in Europe. For the next three decades sensible Italians concentrated on turning Eritrea into a colony where Italians might profit. The process of colonial evolution, with Christian highlanders retaining close links to Ethiopia, began. Italian imperial aspirations had not completely died, however, but they had been contained. They were revived forty years later in the Fascist era when, after years of preparation, Fascist Dictator Benito Mussolini launched his scheme to conquer all of East Africa in 1935.

Eritrea as an Italian Colony

Rome sent an able governor, Ferdinando Martini, to Asmara. During the next ten years he put an end to colonization plans and encouraged peaceful development without disrupting Eritrea's existing social structure. Under stable colonial rule, traditional Eritrean chiefs administered the population and collected taxes. Italians permitted the chiefs to keep 5 percent of the tax receipts at each step upward as money went to Asmara. After 1908 the priority became creation of a Colonial Army to consolidate Italian control over Somalia and conquer and pacify Libya. Six thousand Eritreans had been recruited and trained by 1910; ten thousand by 1914. By 1925 over sixty thousand Eritreans were serving in the Colonial Army. The manpower drain resulted in a labor shortage in the colony. Migrant laborers from Tigray were welcomed. Many settled permanently in Eritrea.

Government schools were introduced in 1911 to train a limited number of low-level civil servants, clerks and workers but, like the Belgians in the Congo, the Italians permitted no middle-level or higher education. Barely fifteen hundred students were enrolled annually in government schools by the early 1930s. A few Eritreans obtained further education from Catholic and Swedish missions. While Italy encouraged the spread of Catholicism, it feared that the educational activities of missionaries encouraged Ethiopian nationalism and expelled the Swedish mission in 1932. Young Eritreans with intellectual inclinations found their way to Ethiopia for education and often stayed there. There were no native-language newspapers or magazines. No organizations were permitted that could foster the development of a native intellectual class.

Italy's routine racist practices did not originally differ markedly from those of other European colonial powers in Africa. White supremacy was taken for granted. Wages for native workers were about 15 percent of the Italian level. Most Eritreans were confined to menial employment. Efforts to curb *madamismo* (cohabitation between Italians and Eritrean women) were never very successful with the result that by the 1930s a sizable mixed-race group had resulted. Many of these were initially permitted to acquire Italian citizenship, but when Fascist racial doctrine – in imitation of the Nazis – was applied in the 1930s, they were reclassified as African and suffered discrimination.

Eritrea's total population was estimated at barely two hundred thousand in 1890. Seven censuses carried out between 1905 and 1939 recorded steady population growth. Highland Tigrinya-speakers accounted for 35 percent of the population in 1905. By 1939 their proportion had risen to

237

54 percent of a total that had increased more than threefold in fifty years. The Tigrinya-speaking increase reflected migration from Tigray. Almost all highlanders were Orthodox Christians and residually Ethiopian in sentiment. Only eight thousand Orthodox Christians were converted to Catholicism during the existence of the Italian colony.[93] In contrast to Tigrinya-speaking highlanders who formed a regionally compact group, other indigenous groups in Eritrea, mostly Muslim and pastoralist (except for the Baria and Kunama, animist agriculturalists), were scattered around the western, northern, and eastern periphery of the colony.

Population pressure in the highlands caused land shortage and outflow of settlers into more thinly populated lowland areas. This provoked Muslim resentment. The Italian administration officially observed a policy of complete equality between Islam and Christianity. Muslims were administered through local leaders in the same way as Christians. During the 1930s, however, Mussolini shifted to a more a pro-Arab and pro-Muslim policy.

Eritrea was always a deficit area from the viewpoint of budget, trade, and investment. The colony attracted little private Italian capital and that usually came in only under highly concessionary arrangements. Revenue collected in Eritrea never covered more than a third of the colony's budget. Exports, which always lagged behind imports, included coffee re-exported from Yemen and in some years a large amount of goods from northern Ethiopia. The most important Eritrean export was salt. Most imports, primarily textiles, came from Italy. During the 1920s Ethiopia imported goods through Massawa and Assab, but this traffic fell sharply in the 1930s. Italy kept its commitment to permit free trade across the Ethiopian border.

Characteristically, the Italians as heirs of the Roman Empire undertook an energetic road-building program into all parts of the territory. Even before the colony was officially proclaimed, a narrow-gauge railroad inland from Massawa had been started in 1887. A spectacular engineering feat, it was completed to Asmara in 1911, extended to Keren in 1922, and on to Agordat by 1930 with plans for extension to Kassala in Sudan which never materialized.[94] Telephone and telegraph lines were extended to most parts of the colony.

Asmara was a tiny village around a church when Ras Alula chose it as his seat in 1877. After Italy made it Eritrea's capital, it grew rapidly and had a population nearing nine tousand by 1905. It was laid out as a compact Italian town. The 1931 census counted 15,732 "natives" and 3,057 Europeans in Asmara. After 1932, as Mussolini began preparing his invasion of Ethiopia, more than 50,000 Italian laborers were brought to Eritrea. By 1939 Asmara had over hundred thousand people, more than half of whom were Italians. The Italian influx generated no significant resistance among Eritreans, for it brought vastly expanded opportunities for employment. Italian colonial policy had never envisioned a separate — let alone independent — Eritrea. There was no power-sharing with the indigenous population or preparation for self-rule. Haile Selassie's coronation in 1930 and his commitment to modernization and reform nevertheless excited Eritrean Christians and aroused concern among liberal-minded Italians, such as Governor Zoli who wrote in 1930:

> Since we have not even benefited from the modest degree of evolution which existed in the local institutions, we now find ourselves in a condition of inferiority in respect to the population of Ethiopia.[95]

Ethiopia was a safety valve for anti-colonialist Eritreans. They could migrate there if they became alienated from the colonial regime. The majority of highlanders thought of themselves as Ethiopians from a cultural and religious viewpoint, but their concerns were local and limited. Muslims in Eritrea, on the other hand, though equally oriented toward local concerns, did not share the same feelings toward Ethiopia. Neither of these sets of attitudes was sufficiently strong to affect Italy's plans for conquest of all of Ethiopia. They would become politically operative only after Italian defeat in 1941 when British occupation permitted and encouraged a politicization of Eritrean society.

War: Italian Victory and Defeat

By the early 1930s Mussolini was ready for conquest of Ethiopia, avenging the defeat at Adwa. Fascist propaganda denounced Ethiopia as a primitive country where slavery still flourished. Preparations for a military build-up in Eritrea began in 1932. Mussolini wanted a quick, easy war to show the world that Fascism was a factor to be reckoned with. He needed a pretext for mobilization and found it in December 1934 at Walwal, an obscure cluster of wells in the Ogaden. Though Ethiopian casualties in the clash at Walwal were three times those of the Italians, Mussolini demanded apologies and reparations. He whipped up a nationalistic frenzy that drowned out voices of caution and fears of failure in Italy. It frightened other Europeans. He gathered soldiers, equipment, and ships for full-scale war. By the end of May 1935, in merely four months, the number of Italians in Eritrea had quadrupled.

Colonia Eritrea was ready to serve the purpose Italian imperialists had envisioned ever since 1890.

The story of Mussolini's brutal invasion of Ethiopia is too well known to need repeating. Determined action by Britain and France could have deterred Mussolini, who had no allies, not yet having forged an alliance with Hitler. But while the League of Nations palavered in Geneva, Mussolini concluded Ethiopia would be a pushover. It was not. It took hard fighting, bombing, and poison gas for the Italians to overcome Ethiopian resistance and drive Haile Selassie into exile at the beginning of May 1936. The country was never fully subjugated. Plans for settling millions of Italians in *Africa Orientale Italiana* did not materialize. Eritrea and Somalia were combined with Ethiopia and the whole Italian African Empire was divided into six regions. As one of them, Eritrea absorbed Tigray.

On 19 February 1937 Governor-General Graziani held a ceremony in Addis Ababa to celebrate the birthday of the Prince of Naples and enticed Ethiopians to attend by promising a gift of two Maria Teresa dollars (then legal tender in Ethiopia) to the first three thousand who came. As the distribution began, two Eritreans who had mingled with the crowd hurled seven hand grenades at Graziani and his entourage. Chaos ensued. Italian Blackshirts went on a rampage of murder and arson. The Eritrean attackers escaped and disappeared. Graziani had his troops round up all educated Ethiopians they could find and shot them. He destroyed the monastery of Debre Libanos. What the Fascists had called their "civilizing mission" in Ethiopia reached its nadir during the year that followed. Ethiopian guerrilla activities spread.

When Mussolini joined Hitler after France was overrun in June 1940, the fate of the Italian East African empire was sealed. A year later (six months before the United States entered WWII) Ethiopia had been liberated by British and Commonwealth (primarily South African and Kenyan) forces and Eritrea and Somalia were occupied. After the United States joined the Allies, Eritrea became a major American staging area for support of campaigns in the Middle East and the Lend-Lease lifeline through the Persian Gulf to the Soviet Union. By August 1942 more than 3,000 American soldiers and civilians were stationed in Eritrea. An American consulate in Asmara was opened nearly a year before the legation was reopened in Addis Ababa.

Britain signed an agreement with Haile Selassie in January 1942 recognizing Ethiopia as once again a "free and independent state", but Eritrea, having been internationally recognized as an Italian colony for almost half a century, was considered occupied enemy territory and administered by Britain entirely separate from Ethiopia. British military administration in Eritrea lasted ten years. It was the most vital period of Eritrean development before the final decade of the twentieth century.

Finding a Solution for Eritrea

Evolution toward political modernization set in quickly under mild British military rule. A large Italian community remained and was well treated. Allied military installations at Asmara and port facilities at Massawa provided employment with good income for Italians and Eritreans. There was no friction between them and Allied military personnel. British officials encouraged labor unions to form, established a press, and let associations of many kinds develop. They expanded education. Wartime prosperity generated expectations of rapid economic expansion, for a good deal of new industry was established to serve Allied wartime needs. When the war came to an end in 1945, however, Eritrea entered an economic slump that exacerbated political, social, and religious tensions. The free political atmosphere continued, but Britain developed no plan for the colony's future. British officials were divided on what the future of Eritrea should be. Haile Selassie wanted Eritrea returned to Ethiopia and the ancient link to the sea restored. Italy surrendered all claim to the colony in the 1947 peace treaty and a Four Power Allied commission[96] was charged with arranging Eritrea's future "in accordance with the wishes of its inhabitants."

A majority of Christian highlanders favored reunion with Ethiopia. Muslim lowlanders, on the other hand, were divided ethnically and felt little inclination toward Ethiopia, though a few were willing to accept a form of union that guaranteed their interests. Many Muslims favored amalgamation of the northern and western areas of Eritrea with Sudan. Smaller groups advocated a continued British mandate, independence, and even restoration of Italian rule. Both Ethiopia and Italy subsidized factions favoring their interests. The four - power commission was unable to reach any agreement and turned the problem over to the UN in 1948. The UN appointed a five-man commission and charged it with determining the amount of support for each proposed solution and judging its economic viability. The population became increasingly frustrated. In late 1949 violence broke out in several Eritrean regions.

The UN commission finally visited Eritrea in early 1950. Much of its activity was poorly organized and members clashed with each other. It ended up making two separate reports and three sets of proposals. Tension among the population increased.

When it came to consider the Commission's report in September 1950, the [UN] General Assembly was no better informed as to what the inhabitants of Eritrea wanted, or the truth about Eritrea's economy, than it had been two years earlier.[97]

Britain had turned over all communications facilities in Eritrea to the U.S. after 1945. When the Korean War broke out in June 1950 they became a crucial link in the worldwide American military and diplomatic communications system. Haile Selassie offered Ethiopian troops to fight with UN forces in Korea. This convinced Washington that facilities in Eritrea would best be protected by Ethiopia. American diplomats secured approval of a resolution by the UN General Assembly on 2 December 1950 that Eritrea would become "an autonomous unit federated with Ethiopia under the sovereignty of the Ethiopian Crown." The formula envisioned a federal government with responsibility for defense, foreign affairs, finance, commerce, transportation and communications. It prescribed an autonomous Eritrean government with legislative, executive, and judicial powers, and responsibility for all matters not vested in the federal government, including police, taxes, and budgeting. An Eritrean assembly was to be democratically elected and an administration organized no later than 15 September 1952. Anze Matienzo, a Bolivian diplomat, was appointed to implement the UN resolution and draft an Eritrean constitution.

Disorders in Eritrea persisted as the economy stagnated. The British had to take strong measures to curb violence. Matienzo delayed starting work until July 1951. His lengthy consultations had the effect of magnifying and hardening differences between political parties and factions. Three major groups had coalesced by this time: strongest and best organized were the Unionists, supported by Ethiopia and the Orthodox Church. They wanted federation to be merely a veneer over full Ethiopian control. The Independence Bloc changed its name to Democratic Bloc to show it accepted federation. The Moslem League of the Western Province could not reach a unified position, but most of its members were eager to keep Ethiopian links as tenuous as possible. The small Liberal Progressive Party, supported by Britain, was probably the only group that was committed to a genuine federal system.

Federation appealed to the U.S. and its allies as a way out of a dilemma: how to settle Eritrea's future "according to the wishes of its inhabitants" when no majority could be found? In reality federating a small, economically more developed, politically effervescent, highly factionalized Eritrea with a far larger underdeveloped and autocratically governed Ethiopia was incongruous. Haile Selassie and the Ethiopian ruling classes would have preferred outright annexation, but membership in the UN and the close American relationship ruled this out. So Ethiopia argued that the Emperor should be empowered to appoint an Eritrean governor-general with the powers of viceroy. He would appoint all high officials and have veto power over legislation. The Unionists shared this view and advocated a single-chamber assembly. The Democratic Bloc advocated two chambers that would check and balance each other. The Moslem League wanted two regional assemblies which would partition the territory into Muslim and Christian halves, each to be federated separately with Ethiopia. There were lesser arguments over the status of half-castes, language, flag, and symbols.

Matienzo departed in November 1951. His constitution provided for a governor-general appointed by the Emperor with the function of promulgating legislation and reading an annual speech from the throne, and a single-chamber assembly empowered to elect its own President. Executive power was vested in a Chief Executive elected by the assembly who appointed heads of government departments and judges. A civil service commission was in charge of other appointments.

Preparations for elections of an assembly to approve the constitution started in January 1952. In Asmara and Massawa the vote was direct by secret ballot. In other areas village and clan groups elected delegates to regional electoral colleges which, in turn, elected representatives by secret ballot. Elections were completed by the end of March 1952; In the cities 88 percent of registered voters participated, in rural areas participation was almost 100 percent. When the votes were counted, the sixty-eight seats were divided between the Unionists and other major parties. The Unionists won thrity-two, the Democratic Bloc eighteen, and the Moslem League fifteen. Two minor parties and an independent won the remaining three.

When the Assembly convened, Unionist deputies approved the constitution without demur. The Moslem League joined them while the Democratic Bloc abstained. Rather than have another election, the Assembly transformed itself into the legislature provided for in the constitution. In the following months, all but 348 of·the 2,217 foreigners who staffed the British Military Administration were replaced by Eritreans. Eritreans were appointed as provincial governors and heads of departments, legal formalities and property transfers were arranged, and Haile Selassie signed the Federal Act on 11 September 1952.

On the evening of 15 September 1952 the Union Jack was lowered in Asmara and the Ethiopian tricolor raised.

Eritrea became "an autonomous state federated with Ethiopia." British official Trevaskis concluded his account of the transition, written in Aden, where he had been transferred, with these prescient observations:

> The [Ethiopian] temptation to subject Eritrea firmly under her own control will always be great. Should she try to do so, she will risk Eritrean discontent and eventual revolt, which, with foreign sympathy and support, might well disrupt both Eritrea and Ethiopia itself... The future of the Federation, and indeed of the whole group of young countries in Northeast Africa, is likely to be affected by the course that Ethiopia takes. She has acquired a great responsibility.[98]

He was all too foresighted.

Failure of the Federation

The Eritrean-Ethiopian Federation never became functional. Haile Selassie and most Ethiopians felt no deep commitment to the spirit or details of the UN arrangement.[99] The UN, busy with crises, took no interest in the working of the federation after it went into effect. No federal institutions were established on the Ethiopian side. Eritrea's autonomy was systematically eroded. An opportunity for modernization of Ethiopia's own political structure was thus lost, to be regained forty years later and only after immense suffering and bloodshed on both sides of the Mareb.[100]

It is surprising that the pretense of federation was maintained as long as it was. Haile Selassie's desire to retain international respectability was perhaps the main reason.[101] Within weeks after the federation was proclaimed, press freedom and party activities were curtailed. The largely ceremonial position of Governor-General was transformed into *Enderassie* ["Viceroy" in Amharic] and the man the Emperor chose to fill it, his son-in-law Bitwoded Andargchew Masai, did not confine himself to ceremony. The Eritrean Assembly elected the head of the Unionist Party, Dejazmach Tedla Bairu, Chief Executive. He resigned in August 1955. Haile Selassie appointed him Ambassador to Sweden; he later defected. The Enderassie replaced him with his own deputy who advocated complete integration into Ethiopia. Carefully managed elections in September 1956 produced a more pliant Assembly, but its Muslim president, Idris Mohammed Adem, resigned in 1957, went to Cairo and joined Wolde-Ab Wolde-Mariam, a Protestant Christian who had originally edited a British-sponsored Tigrinya newspaper, and then headed the Eritrean trade unions and the small Liberal Progressive Party. [102] Ibrahim Sultan, former head of the Democratic Bloc, also went to Cairo. They all joined the Eritrean Liberation Movement (ELM) which had had a very modest beginning in Port Sudan in 1958, where the Sudan Communist Party helped five young Eritrean exiles organize it. [103]

In December 1958 the Assembly abolished the Eritrean flag. The next year Ethiopian law was introduced, and in May 1960, the Assembly changed the name of the government to "Eritrean Administration under Haile Selassie, Emperor of Ethiopia". The vote of the Assembly abolishing itself on 14 November 1962 surprised no one. Eritrea became Ethiopia's fourteenth province, governed like all the rest.

It is pertinent, however, to see these developments in the context of the time. Pan-Arabism and Islamic assertiveness had been on the rise for several years. Nasserist revolutionary fervor was sweeping the Middle East. The Soviet Union was increasingly supportive of all radical Arab movements. Some Arabs claimed Eritrea was an Arab country and Eritrean Muslims saw an advantage in pretending to be Arabs. With Eritrean exiles gathering in Cairo and other Arab capitals and broadcasting rebellion, it was not surprising that Ethiopia felt threatened.[104] The failed 1960 coup strengthened Haile Selassie's determination to act decisively to preserve his power.

In September 1961 Muslims in western Eritrea clashed with Ethiopian forces and eventually declared themselves to be the Eritrean Liberation Front (ELF). The EPLF celebrates this episode as the beginning of the thrity year fight for independence, though it attracted little attention at the time. The next year, directly across the Red Sea a radical revolution flared up in Yemen and Nasser sent an Egyptian expeditionary force to support it. Though worried, Haile Selassie took comfort from the fact that Ethiopia was calm and his international prestige was high. So great, in fact, that Nasser and the Soviets avoided denouncing him or challenging him directly. At the time, the abolition of the fictional federation arrangement in Eritrea enhanced rather than detracted from the Emperor's standing in the world.

After 1941, Eritreans had become active throughout Ethiopia as businessmen, officials, teachers, and traders. The process accelerated during the federation period. It continued after the federation ended. More economically developed than the rest of the country, Eritrea continued to attract investment and foreign aid. The enterprising Italian and half-caste population as well as the majority of highland Christians were pro-Ethiopian. American military installations continued to contribute substantially to the Eritrean economy. Eritrea remained peaceful until the mid-1960s and more prosperous than the rest of Ethiopia.

Rebellion and Response

Dejazmach (soon Ras) Asrate Kassa was appointed *Enderassie* in Eritrea in 1964, replacing General Abiye Abebe.[105] Asrate was strongly disliked by Prime Minister Aklilu Habtewold who was glad to see him removed from the capital and exiled to Asmara. Rebel activities in Eritrea were becoming bothersome. Asrate appointed Tigrinya-speaking Eritreans to most major offices and brought them together periodically as an advisory council. He continued the use of Amharic, however, for educational and official purposes. His tense relationship with Prime Minister Aklilu centered on two major problems: control of Eritrean revenues and control of the Army:

> The Ethiopian armed forces in Eritrea were... inefficient, brutal, and corrupt. Their activities lacked planning and coordination. Furthermore, the army was led by generals and colonels who considered military power the only proper way to deal with dissident Eritreans. Whenever the army was given a free hand in the province, the result was a bloody escalation and reinforcement of anti-Ethiopian emotions among Eritreans, Christian and Muslim alike.[106]

As a counterweight to the military, Asrate set up two groups under his direct control financed from the Eritrean budget: one, a commando force made up mostly of Christian Eritreans trained by Israelis; and two, an Eritrean security service, which benefited from both Israeli and American support. Rebel activities in Eritrea increased, but Addis Ababa developed no coherent policy to deal with them. A coordinating committee Asrate established in 1967 made little difference. Neither did the Emperor's periodic visits to Asmara when each high official reported separately to him and Haile Selassie sometimes gave contradictory advice. Rebel strength was not great, and much of Eritrea remained unaffected by their activities. To attain greater impact, rebels turned to sabotage, assassination and hijacking of airplanes. Mounting violence led Aklilu to order the army to take harsh action. [107]

Economic stagnation after the closing of the Suez Canal in 1967 depressed the Eritrean economy and enlarged the pool of unemployed young men for insurgents to draw from. Nevertheless the great majority of Eritreans during this period remained oriented toward Ethiopia, where many found employment because they had the advantage of skills, experience, and relatives and friends already working there. At the end of the 1960s three to four hundred thousand Eritreans lived and worked in other parts of Ethiopia as technicians, teachers, officials, lawyers, and businessmen. Eritreans occupied 19 percent of high positions in the central Ethiopian government, second only to Shoans, during the period 1941-66.[108]

Eritrean politicians and intellectuals who went into exile had sympathy but few active followers at home. Despite efforts to represent themselves as united, exiled Eritreans were rent by tensions and rivalries. These were reflected in competition among fighters in the field. Radical Arabs and various Soviet proxies began to provide arms in the late 1960s. Cubans, communist Chinese, and Syrians began taking young Eritreans for guerrilla training. Isaias Afewerki and Ramadan Mohammed Nur were trained in China during this period.

Rivalries did not prevent insurgents from gradually expanding their operations on the ground, Rivalries encouraged them, in fact, to resort to violence to overcome competitors. By 1968 they were fighting pitched battles against Ethiopian military forces and carrying out spectacular acts of sabotage and urban terrorism. Israeli advisers had difficulty countering the tendency of Ethiopian commanders to use brutal search and interrogation methods and tactics which drove civilians to seek rebel protection. Still no more than half of Ethiopia's forty-five thousand man army was ever deployed in Eritrea.[109]

Haile Selassie authorized a major military offensive in early 1970. In response in April Isaias Afewerki assassinated two Ethiopian judges in Asmara. The emperor gave his commanding general, Teshome Irgetu, authority to act without consulting Asrate, his viceroy. Asrate put his Eritrean deputy, Tesfa-Yohannes Berhe, in charge and left for London. Tesfa-Yohannes was ignored by the army which began a "pacification" campaign punishing villages judged to be rebel safe havens. Meanwhile Isaias and Ramadan Mohammed Nur drew together a stronger guerrilla organization with fighters who had returned from training in Syria and China: the Popular Liberation Forces (PLF). On 21 November 1970 the PLF succeeded in ambushing General Teshome and killing him. On Aklilu's advice, the Emperor removed Asrate, declared martial law in Eritrea, and appointed General Debebe Haile Mariam military governor in Asmara.

While Qaddafy embraced the Eritrean cause after he came to power in 1969 and Syria kept up support for the insurgents, funneling in supplies from Soviet-related sources, Moscow stayed in the background. Eritrean movements kept fragmenting and regrouping.[110] Prospects for a quick outcome of the Eritrean struggle were receding when the Marxist Eritrean Popular Liberation Front (EPLF) was formally proclaimed in February 1972.

During 1972 and 1973, the Ethiopian army gained control of all major Eritrean towns and highways. The Eritrean economy experienced a modest revival. The provincial government organized Expo '72, a commercial exposition that ran for several weeks in grounds on the edge of Asmara. Politically the situation remained stalemated. Though Chinese assistance for the insurgents ceased after Haile Selassie's October 1971 deal with Mao Zedong and Sudanese supply lines contracted after Nimeiry and Haile Selassie reached an agreement, Qaddafy's support and supplies from Soviet and East European sources funneled in from Syria and South Yemen sustained rebel groups. Cuba continued to train Eritrean fighters and conduct anti-Ethiopian propaganda.

During the spring and summer of 1974 expectations of a negotiated settlement grew in Eritrea, for the population was eager for peace and wanted to take advantage of economic opportunities made possible by reopening of the Suez Canal in late 1973. The situation looked propitious. The Marxist EPLF considered itself the "unified" competitor of the Revolutionary Command of the older, largely Muslim, Eritrean Liberation Front (ELF-RC). All Eritrean movements lacked cohesive leadership and were susceptible to fragmentation, for they were coalitions that reflected the ethnic and religious diversity of Eritrea's population. The Marxists included many young men from families who had converted to Protestantism in the nineteenth century.

Competition among Eritrean exile leaders and the propaganda they broadcast from various Arab capitals magnified the impression of the size of the insurgency. Serious guerrilla fighters of all factions probably numbered no more than two thousand at the beginning of the 1970s. In effect, the situation in early 1974 boiled down to a stubborn but unimaginative Addis Ababa government trying to subdue fractious coalitions of insurgents sustained primarily by foreign money and supplies. Neither side was doing well. Neither side had leaders with the breadth of vision to attempt to escape from a vicious circle of violence. The population felt victimized by both sides, but most Eritrean highland Christians still remained passively loyal to the Ethiopian state.

The Derg and Eritrea

Stalemate in Eritrea was one of the factors which enabled an improvised military committee that became known as the Derg to gain power and overthrow Haile Selassie on 12 September 1974. Eritrea was bound to test the political skill of any new Ethiopian government. More than any other single factor, Eritrea determined the Derg's fate. Eritrea owes the independence that was formally confirmed in May 1993 not only to the lengthy armed struggle of Eritrean guerrilla fighters and the endurance of its population, but to the Derg – and specifically to dictator Mengistu Haile Mariam. His decision in the fall of 1974 to bring the province to heel by force eventually propelled the whole population into favoring independence. The manner in which the Derg dealt with the Eritrean problem, more than any other aspect of its performance, also predetermined its own disastrous end.

When the Derg deposed Haile Selassie in September 1974, it needed an acting head of state. No Derg member had enough rank to step into this role. A reputable general of Eritrean origin, Aman Andom, was chosen. In fighting against Somali-backed insurgents in the Ogaden in the 1960s, Aman had made a name for himself as both a good commander and a champion of the common soldier. On Derg recommendation, Haile Selassie appointed him Chief of Staff of the Armed Forces in early July 1974. Before the end of the month he became Minister of Defense. Aman had hoped to persuade Christians in the EPLF to cooperate with the government against the predominantly Muslim ELF. He had a broad concept of Eritrean-Ethiopian reconciliation and had Christian Eritreans appointed as both governor-general of the province and chief of police. The population of Asmara showed strong support for Aman's program, but Eritrean exile politicians rejected his overtures.

Unfortunately, intense rivalry among Eritrean exile leaders had spread into Eritrea, where Tigrinya-speaking Christians, newly recruited into the Marxist EPLF, began an assassination campaign against Eritreans regarded as collaborators with Addis Ababa. Several prominent Muslims were killed. Violence blocked compromise among the rebels. During his weeks as Minister of Defense, Aman had devoted most of his time to his home province. He returned from a trip there on 9 September to present a nine-point plan for settling the insurgency calling for:

> ...general reform of the administrative system, removal of all obstacles which had impeded social progress... amnesty of political prisoners... return of exiles and their resettlement, promotion of foreign investments... lifting the state of emergency, punishing officials guilty of misconduct... [and] safeguarding Ethiopian unity. [111]

Eager to gain credit as an Ethiopian nationalist, Mengistu mobilized the Derg against Aman. On 23 November 1974 he sent troops to Aman's house in Addis Ababa to arrest him. In the ensuing firefight, Aman was killed. That night fifty-nine former imperial officials were summarily shot. All had surrendered or been arrested during the previous summer and were being held for investigation. Thus, in a single night the Ethiopian revolution turned bloody. Blood never ceased to flow for the next seventeen years. Mengistu's uncompromising approach not only hardened the Eritrean insurgents' will to resist. It drove the Eritrean populace into a more negative position toward Ethiopia than had ever occurred in imperial times. Shocked by Aman's violent death and no longer obligated by his 1971 agreement with Haile Selassie, Sudanese President Nimeiry soon let aid flow again to Eritrean insurgents through Sudanese territory. The Ethiopian revolution immediately took an openly pro-Soviet turn. Nimeiry let other Ethiopian resistance groups build up military forces in Sudan. By 1976, he was convinced that Mengistu and Qaddafy were collaborating in an effort to oust him and gave even greater support to the Eritreans.

With Aman gone, an Oromo general, Teferi Banti, was made head of state while Mengistu dominated the Derg. Efforts to negotiate with the rebels were abandoned. ELF-RC leader Osman Salih Sabbe issued a call from Beirut for intensified offensive action. EPLF forces on the ground could not afford to be less militant. All major actors concerned with Eritrea succumbed to the fatal illusion that they could impose their will by force. So the tragedy was doomed to play out over the better part of the next decade and a half.

In spite of Derg offensives, Eritrean rebels gained ground steadily during 1975-76, but rivalry among factions grew and new splinter groups appeared. There were three axes of tension: one, between exiles and guerrillas in the field; two, between fighters in various regions of Eritrea along ethnic and religious lines; and three, between exile leaders abroad. It is difficult to summarize the situation because at any given time the strength of sub-factions and individual leaders' hold over their followers were uncertain. The Derg announced a nine-point program for settlement in Eritrea in May 1976. Rivalry among Eritrean factions deterred all of them from considering any aspect of it.

The EPLF's "National Democratic Program" proclaimed in January 1977 contained more hard-line Marxism than the Derg's. Both the Soviet relationship and Eritrea may have been among the contentious issues that provoked the Derg shoot-out that resulted in the killing of seven men, including Derg Chairman Teferi Banti, in February 1977. Mengistu now came into the open as head of state and the Russian and Cuban ambassadors called immediately to congratulate him. Somali strongman Siad Barre concluded Ethiopia would soon fall apart and decided to invade and speed up the process. As the Somali offensive began in the summer of 1977, Eritrean insurgents captured the important towns of Keren and Decamere, but military success heightened competition between different groups. [112]

The fact that Eritrean insurgents of various factions were able during the remainder of 1977 to expand the area under their control while factional struggle intensified was due to diversion of Ethiopian manpower to fight the Somalis. By the end of 1977, only 5 percent of Eritrea remained under Derg control. Massawa was under siege, Asmara was preparing for assault, and the Ethiopian lifeline to the south

257

was under attack. But competing and mutually hostile insurgent organizations could not agree on a plan for consolidating victory:

> On the threshold of victory... young leaders... lost their chance to implement their goals. They had pushed aside older leaders in exile, but their radicalism prevented them from benefiting from what was fundamentally a pro-Eritrean process in the region... The neighboring Red Sea Arab states [now] conceived an independent, radical Eritrea as a great threat to their interests. Thus the stronger the EPLF became, the more isolated it became. [113]

Sudanese President Nimeiry brought Eritrean rebel leaders together at a meeting in Khartoum in March 1978 in an attempt to persuade them to unify, but he was unsuccessful. Meanwhile, with the aid of Soviet air and naval bombardment which inflicted heavy damage, Derg forces relieved the siege of Massawa. Transferring manpower from the south and benefitting from vast amounts of Soviet weaponry, advice, and air support, Mengistu was able to regain control of major Eritrean cities and communications routes by the end of the summer of 1978 by mounting a Russian-style, massive, slow-moving offensive.

The Demise of the Derg-Guerrilla Victory

The embrace of the Soviet Union, which supplied Derg Ethiopia with $12 billion worth of arms in the thriteen years 1977-1990, gave Mengistu hope of triumph over the rebels in Eritrea and Tigray. To please his Soviet beneficiaries he attempted to turn the country into a model of Stalinist "socialism". Most of the economy was nationalized. Peasants were forced into state farms and collective villages. As agricultural production declined and rebellion spread across most of northern Ethiopia, famine developed. When international aid groups began to send in food and medicine, Mengistu tried to keep supplies from reaching rebel-held areas. When the situation was publicized abroad and became an international scandal in late 1984, he was forced to relent.

Foreign aid groups were permitted to operate while Mengistu secured Soviet help to launch a program to haul hundreds of thousands of people from rebellious regions to lowland resettlement sites along the Sudan border. He staged a great celebration in Addis Ababa to inaugurate his communist-type Workers' Party on the tenth anniversary of the revolution in 1984. Three years later, with Soviet and East European hardliners as honored guests, he proclaimed Ethiopia a "People's Democracy". It was the last example of this kind of state in the world. Nevertheless, Mengistu's revolution kept unravelling. Hundreds of thousands of young soldiers and vast quantities of Soviet-supplied equipment were thrown against the Tigrayan and Eritrean rebels. The rebels kept defeating Derg offensives and capturing great quantities of the equipment the Soviets had supplied.

Applying organizational principles taught in China and lessons learned from the disasters of 1977-78, Isaias Afewerki turned his EPLF into a tightly organized professional guerrilla force in the early 1980s and gained dominance over all other factions in Eritrea by mid-decade. Foreign supplies became less important as the EPLF captured more and more Soviet-supplied arms and ammunition from Derg forces. The Derg kept pouring more soldiers into Eritrea. Many surrendered and were captured. By the end of the 1980s the Derg was able to hold onto only Asmara and Massawa and, during daylight, the highway in between.

A group of Tigrayan students who left Addis Ababa University in 1975-76 built a peasant-based movement in Tigray. They got occasional support from the EPLF but relations were often uneasy, with the Eritreans looking down on the Tigrayans as provincial amateurs. The Tigrayans, who adopted the name Tigray Popular Liberation Front (TPLF), relied on grass-roots mobilization of the rural population. They neither sought nor received significant foreign aid, and though they professed Marxism, they did not try to force peasants into collective life or interfere with their attachment to religion. In time they, too, benefitted from captured arms and equipment and, like the EPLF, developed supply and communications lines through Sudan. As the EPLF became more vocally anti-Ethiopian, the TPLF evolved in the opposite direction — capitalizing on Tigrayans' pride as heirs of ancient Ethiopian civilization and feeling a sense of responsibility for the country as a whole.[114]

While the Soviets paid no attention to the TPLF and the Tigrayans did not seek Soviet support, the EPLF maintained links with Cubans, East Germans, and Italian communists, among others, and Soviet operatives refused to give up hope that Mengistu and Isaias could be reconciled. Almost until their own state collapsed, the Soviets kept trying to bring Isaias and Mengistu together to solve their Ethiopian conundrum. Successive meetings in Rome and East Berlin between EPLF and Derg representatives proved futile.[115] But these efforts for a time seem to have maintained Isaias' hope that the Russians might eventually abandon Mengistu and shift to supporting Eritrean independence.

Both the EPLF and the TPLF became increasingly aware of the changes taking place in the world in the late 1980s. Evolution toward recognition of the consequences of the collapse of Marxist socialism proceeded faster within the TPLF, especially after Meles Zenawi emerged as the leader in 1988. Both northern movements sought contacts with Americans. The stunning defeat of Derg forces at Enda Selassie in early 1989, where the EPLF gave the Tigrayans some help, resulted in withdrawal of Derg forces from Tigray. The Derg's land links to Eritrea were cut. By this time the TPLF had elevated a satellite Amhara organization, the Ethiopian People's Democratic Movement (EPDM), to partnership in the Ethiopian Popular Revolutionary Democratic Front (EPRDF). This front, which attracted other supporters as well, became the vehicle for defeat of the Derg. Meanwhile the EPLF had decimated a huge Derg force at Afabet in northern Eritrea in March 1988 and captured huge numbers of prisoners, along with supplies of arms, and equipment. In March 1990 it took Massawa, cutting all Derg communication with its forces in Eritrea except by air.

At heart TPLF leaders would have preferred to see Eritrea enjoy a high degree of autonomy as a component of a new democratic Ethiopia but, though the two movements cooperated during the final stages of their struggle against the Derg, the EPLF was adamant about going its own way after the Derg's defeat. Only in the final stages of Derg collapse in May 1991 were American diplomats successful in helping Meles Zenawi persuade Isaias Afewerki to defer a declaration of independence until an internationally supervised referendum could be held by the spring of 1993. The TPLF needed this assurance to counter widespread feeling among Ethiopians that loss of Eritrea should not be accepted lightly.

Two days after Mengistu slipped away from Addis Ababa and flew to Zimbabwe, Derg armies in Eritrea surrendered unconditionally on 23 May 1991. The EPLF designated itself the Provisional Government of Eritrea on taking over Asmara.

EPRDF forces surrounded Addis Ababa but did not enter it until 28 May. The EPRDF convened a national conference in the first days of July to establish a Transitional Government for Ethiopia. Isaias refused to participate except as an observer. Many Ethiopian anti-Derg groups as well as exile organizations took part in the conference which involved five days of open debate on many issues, including the status of Eritrea. The conference devised a Charter which served as an interim constitution until 1995.

To the dismay of the EPRDF, which was preoccupied with gaining control and maintaining security in all parts of the country, the EPLF in June and July 1991 summarily expelled more than two hundred thousand defeated Derg soldiers across the border into Tigray along with tens of thousands of Ethiopian civilians, including women and children, who had been resident in Eritrea. The EPRDF lacked the means of dealing with this influx of men, women, and children, many of whom were wounded, starving, or sick. International relief organizations came to the rescue and USAID arranged for more than $15 million worth of food, blankets, and medicine left over from the Gulf War to be flown into northern Ethiopia.

Independence and Aftermath

By the end of the summer of 1991 expulsions from Eritrea ceased and, in the months that followed, practical arrangements were worked out for Ethiopian use of the

Eritrean ports of Assab and Massawa, international and internal air service, transit of goods and people across the border, and for continued Eritrean use of Ethiopian currency. Despite periodic frictions the outlook for cooperative relations between Addis Ababa and self-governing Eritrea looked good. The agitation that developed in 1992 and early 1993 in Ethiopia and among conservative Ethiopian exiles abroad about Eritrean independence was doomed to be futile. The EPRDF had no choice. The United States did not give Eritrea away in May 1991, as resentful exiles charged. Neither did the TPLF. Neither had ever held or had any means of holding it, and neither was foolish enough to try. EPLF leaders were determined to lead Eritrea to independence. Sustained Derg brutality had convinced the Eritrean people that independence was desirable.

Adhering fully to previous agreements and under conditions approved by the UN with international observers stationed throughout the country, the EPLF held an elaborately organized referendum on independence in the last week of April 1993. Voters were given only two choices: to be for or against independence. 1.2 million voters were registered; 99.8 percent of these approved independence, with fewer than two thousand negative votes being cast. Nevertheless, observers reported no intimidation or obvious illegality.[116] The country was formally declared independent on 23 May 1993. Agitation over Eritrea ceased almost immediately among opposition politicians in Ethiopia and legal aspects of the separation were efficiently accomplished.

The political evolution of Eritrea has been much slower and in a much more authoritarian direction than in Ethiopia. The EPLF transformed itself into the Popular Front for Democracy and Justice (PFDJ) at the end of 1994 and a constitutional commission was appointed. It engaged in elaborate study and consultation before producing a draft in 1996 which was then presented to the public for lengthy discussion and review. It provides for a unitary state based on geographic regions into which the Eritrea was redivided in 1996. Eritrea's nine major ethnic groups, in contrast to Ethiopia, were accorded no formal political recognition. As of mid-2000, the constitution had not been put into effect.

The EPLF has permitted no political parties or independent newspapers. Thus it has avoided the heated political debates and journalistic ferment that characterized Ethiopia after 1991. It also avoided international criticism for jailing journalists and oppressing politicians because none were permitted to operate.

Eritrea accused Sudan of abetting subversion in 1994 and broke relations in 1995. It provoked a quarrel with Yemen over the Hanish islands soon after and subsequently quarreled with Djibouti. In spite of these problems with its other neighbors, relations with Ethiopia remained close and cooperative through 1997. Eritrea used Ethiopian currency until November 1997 when it replaced it with its own legal tender, the nacfa, initially valued at par with the Ethiopian birr. Ethiopia henceforth required that hard currency be used in trade.[117] Ethiopia had already stopped drawing on the Assab refinery for part of its petroleum supply. Tensions over trade, border controls, and ports subsequently developed. In May 1998 Eritrea suddenly occupied several districts along the border which had been under Ethiopian administration. Residents were evicted and military clashes followed. The Ethiopian government appealed for international assistance in clarifying the situation. Alleging Ethiopian aggressive intentions, Eritrea refused to agree to inspection or negotiation under international supervision until Ethiopia mounted an offensive in the Badme sector in February 1999 and recaptured a portion of the territory Eritrea had seized. The rest of this history is the main subject of this book.

THE FUTURE:

PROBLEMS AND PROSPECTS

CHAPTER VIII

WHITHER ERITREA?

The Future: Problems and Prospects

Eritrea was decisively defeated by Ethiopia. As of this writing, Isaias Afewerki has only grudgingly recognized this defeat. His officials and propagandists continue to deny the extent of their defeat and the consequences for their political survival. It is not difficult to describe their predicament, but it is still not possible to foresee how they will cope with it. The problems Eritrea faces nevertheless are clear. They all relate to facing reality.

Foremost comes the question of the survivability of the leader and his ruling group. An authoritarian leader who embarks on a disastrous military adventure and fails seldom survives long in power. Examples in history are numerous. However, in recent years the world has witnessed the defeat of Saddam Hussein in Iraq and Slobodan Milosevic in Yugoslavia. Both remain dictators in control of their beleaguered countries. Isaias Afewerki apparently aspires to the same outcome. And so do those who make up his immediate entourage.

Often, however, a defeated dictator must face disaffection among his closest associates which may culminate in efforts to replace him. Can Isaias be sure that none of the men around him may not try to oust him and set Eritrea on a new course? Some may be thinking such thoughts. An atmosphere of suspicion must prevail in the inner EPLF group. Whether and when this might lead to action only time will tell. During his final decline Mengistu Haile Mariam was faced by an attempted coup by disillusioned generals. He thwarted it and proceeded, months later, to execute several of the generals, even though his power was visibly waning. Could Isaias repeat this kind of performance if faced with a coup?

Isaias will probably try to revive the notion that EPLF Eritrea is a bulwark against Islamic fundamentalism. He has already made accusations against Sudan. Sudan appears to have handled the awkward problem of dealing humanely with fleeing Eritrean soldiers and refugee civilians, but Isaias could find pretenses for accusations against Sudan if he judged it useful to pick a quarrel again in order to try to attract American or European backing.

Another tactic available to Isaias to improve his international status would be to try to ally himself with any country judged to be in some way a rival of Ethiopia. Egypt comes to mind in terms of controversy over Nile waters. Eritrea accounts for only a miniscule proportion of the water that flows into the Blue Nile. Eritrea is nevertheless entitled to participate in international discussions about Nile waters. In these, Eritrea could act as spoiler to frustrate Ethiopia. Egypt, however, can hardly be regarded as an enemy of Ethiopia. Other concerned powers urge both Ethiopia and Egypt to cooperate in planning future utilization of Nile waters and both countries are committed to peaceful resolution of Nile issues. Thus Eritrea's chances of gaining support for harassment of Ethiopia appear poor. Ethiopia has no real enemies either among neighbors or further afield. Isaias attempted to use Somalia as a base for harassing Ethiopia and gave support to OLF dissidents that enabled them to operate from Somali territory. This maneuver was notably unsuccessful.

Does Eritrea have the capacity to encourage opposition to the EPRDF inside Ethiopia? Before he sent his army into Ethiopia Isaias apparently let himself be convinced that the TPLF-led EPRDF government in Addis Ababa lacked widespread support. He failed to understand that multiple political parties and a lively private press function as a safety valve for political dissent in the democratizing climate of Ethiopia. Contrary to what he said to me about the OLF in April 1993 (see Chapter six above), he fell into the illusion that the OLF could create instability in Oromo-dominated regions of Ethiopia. As I have stressed repeatedly in preceding chapters, the most significant effect of the Eritrean incursion into Ethiopia was to reinforce national feeling and dampen political dissidence. Has Isaias recognized his faulty judgment? Persisting in this course of action would seem to be futile. A post-defeat Eritrean effort to continue fomenting disaffection in Ethiopia is likely to have quite the opposite effect. It will continue to reinforce Ethiopians' appreciation of their present leaders. If Meles Zenawi and his colleagues capitalize on the victory over Eritrea by offering encouragement to critics and potential dissidents to join into the governing and development process they should have little difficulty maintaining the high standing they presently enjoy with the country's entire population.

Defeated Eritrea's standing among African countries is not high. Like Siad Barre's Somalia in 1977, Isaias Afewerki violated one of the OAU's most important principles: that border changes between African countries be effected only by peaceful means and agreement of the parties affected. During the two-year confrontation with Ethiopia Isaias and other high - level Eritrean officials have often lashed out against the OAU and accused it of subservience to Ethiopia. It will take a long period of reasonable behavior on the part of Eritrea to live down its negative reputation. All its other neighbors have reason, given past history, to be skeptical of EPLF actions and intentions.

We now hear of manifestations of resistance among Eritreans to EPLF rule and, in particular, opposition to continued drafting of young men and women for military training. Losses of life among young Eritreans have been heavy. Their families want to be assured of the safety of sons and daughters who have survived. Beni Amer in some areas are reported to be refusing to let young men be taken for training. Ethnic groups that have a long record of skepticism about the EPLF – for example, the Afars and the Kunama – have already organized groups abroad advocating democratization of the Eritrean political system. Several long-existing groups of Eritreans in Europe and America have been energized to attempt to undermine EPLF dominance. How effective they will be, remains to be seen. History demonstrates that dictatorial regimes are usually toppled from within rather than by exile pressure from abroad. If resentment of EPLF rule in Eritrea grows, however, pressures from both the outside and inside could force the EPLF to moderate its rigid control, or even bring it to an end.

Can the EPLF convincingly change its colors? Moderation looks improbable in light of EPLF history. The EPLF attained dominance over other Eritrean guerrilla movements in the 1980s by employing strong tactics including assassination of rivals and pitched battles with guerrilla opponents, driving rivals into Sudan or more distant exile. Even incidents of EPLF betrayal of competing Eritrean fighters to the Derg have been reported. Disillusioned foreign advisors have reported use of oppressive and punitive measures by the EPLF to deal with manifestations of dissatisfaction after independence. Isaias' expulsion of NGOs from Eritrea in 1995 is explained by some observers as an effort to prevent outsiders from awareness of the EPLF's style of rule in rural and provincial areas. Can the present embarrassed and defeated ruling group remake itself to be taken as genuine benefactors of the people? It retains strong police and security services even if much of its military strength has been decimated. The temptation to use these to enforce uniformity and suppress dissidence will be hard to resist.

Isaias has mobilized the Eritrean diaspora to press Europeans and Americans for sympathy and emergency relief. Eritrean propaganda presents the country as the victim of Ethiopian invasion and stresses alleged Ethiopian atrocities against simple citizens, destruction of property, and theft of valuable goods. There is little substantiation for Eritrean claims. Warfare inevitably results in damage to property and dislocation of people. Ethiopia claims that its forces were under clear instructions to minimize destruction and do as little harm as possible to civilians. There is no reason to doubt this claim. Ethiopia did disarm all captured Eritrean soldiers and took possession of Eritrean military equipment and supplies. Many of the allegations of Ethiopian misbehavior that are spread by Eritrean media, Eritrean embassies and EPLF sympathizers abroad are intended to counteract the doubts of both the Eritrean population within the country and the diaspora. The aim is to create an illusory impression of continued EPLF vitality, and, above all, to keep the diaspora sending money. Evidence was already accumulating by early 1999 that the flow of money from the diaspora was slowing. It would be surprising if it has not slowed further since Eritrea's defeat.

The myth of Eritrean guerrilla invincibility is shattered. It is apparent to military professionals and students of military affairs that Eritrea relied on outdated and ineffective tactics in its assault on Ethiopia. On the other hand, Ethiopia's offensive that resulted in Eritrean defeat was brilliantly conceived, for it was based on understanding of the most successful principles of modern warfare. Eritrea does not have the resources to rebuild its military forces. Who would give it the funds to replace lost and destroyed equipment? Eritrea has lost its attractiveness to international arms merchants, for it is bankrupt. The twent-five kilometers border zone will hem Eritrea in and prevent future military harassment into Ethiopia. If Eritrea persists in harassment or evasion of the controls of UN peace-keepers, its non-compliance will immediately become an international issue. Though Isaias Afewerki has placed military preparedness above all other priorities since independence, this judgment has lost all logic. Who threatens Eritrea? While it threatened all its neighbors from 1993 onward, no neighbor took any action that amounted to a credible military threat against Eritrea. Like all authoritarian dictatorships Isaias had to invent threats and crises to justify maintaining an oppressive system over his own people.

An Eritrea that continues to be led by Isaias Afewerki and his EPLF will have difficulty again integrating itself into regional organizations promoting cooperation in the Horn of Africa and the Red Sea area. A new Eritrea, committed to a responsible course of independent development in harmony with the rest of the region will be welcomed back into IGAAD, the Nile Basin community, and economic arrangements benefitting the whole area.

The Eritrean economy was functioning poorly when the attack on Ethiopia was mounted in May 1998. Two-thirds of its trade was with Ethiopia. Repeatedly Eritrean propagandists have claimed economic successes during the past two years. These claims defy common sense. Nevertheless, Eritrea may now be exaggerating the degree of hardship its population has suffered as a result of Ethiopian military action as a technique for obfuscating the fact that its economy had already been reduced to a state of severe crisis before the final Ethiopian action began. The World Food Program and the emergency aid programs of many governments and NGOs are now engaged in a major effort to sustain affected Eritreans. Prospects for a successful agricultural year are poor. Even in good years Eritrea has a food deficit. Drastic emergency measures and careful management will be needed to prevent starvation and disease in Eritrea during the coming months – and perhaps years.

More could be said, but even brief contemplation of Isaias' current predicament demonstrates that he faces formidable problems. Bluster and a continuing barrage of propaganda of denial will not ease them. A less stubborn man would consider stepping aside and letting new leaders take charge, admitting that the EPLF's approach to managing Eritrean independence and setting the country on a positive course – as the whole world hoped would occur – was mistaken. New leadership in Eritrea genuinely committed to democratization of the country would enjoy wide international support and qualify for substantial development – not merely emergency assistance. No one threatens Eritrea's independence. There is no reason to doubt

Ethiopia's disavowal of any desire to obtain Eritrean territory or regain control of Eritrea as a whole. Why would Ethiopia or any of Eritrea's neighbors want to absorb a country whose leaders have made a wreck of it?

Could Isaias be taken seriously if he announced adoption of a new democratic, peaceful course? Could the EPLF undergo a convincing transformation into a party promoting democracy and justice? Could Isaias permit a multi-party system to develop? Or a free press where Eritreans could debate solutions to the difficult tasks which now confront them? It is difficult to give a positive answer to any of these questions.

What, then, is to be Eritrea's future? I commented at the end of the 1980s (cited in Chapter Three above) that for too long the EPLF appeared to be offering the population of Eritrea only two choices: one, to join the Arab world or two, to become an Albania on the Red Sea. Neither of these choices made much sense and neither is available to Eritrea now. While some Arabs are reported to have given the EPLF monetary support in the recent confrontation in response to Isaias' pleadings, Arab leaders know that the great majority of Eritreans are not Arabs. Even the wealthy Arab states now lack money to squander on losers. As for the Albanian "model"? It was always an illusion. Communist Albania collapsed more decisively even than Ceausescu's Romania and is now in worse condition than some of the most debilitated regions of the former Soviet Union.

Perhaps the best future Eritrea could anticipate would be to become, in effect, an international protectorate. If a formal international trusteeship could be devised for post-EPLF Eritrea, the country would be assured of the breathing space and the international support to overcome the most serious disabilities Isaias and the EPLF have brought upon it. Isaias' pride and stubbornness are probably too great to make such a formal arrangement possible. *De facto,* however, this may be what will come about. A status approximating a period of international trusteeship would probably be welcomed by the majority of the population. Even an informal arrangement of this kind would give the Eritrean population the opportunity to focus on economic and social development and evolution toward a democratic political system.

The peoples of Eritrea have proven during the past half century that they are resilient. Over and over again, they have endured hardship and devised successful survival strategies. The million-strong diaspora represents an enormous resource for Eritrea that can be mobilized for positive purposes. The EPLF has made the diaspora an ally in supporting its oppression and military adventurism. The money Eritreans living abroad have sent to support Isaias Afewerki has been wasted. The bonds Eritreans abroad have bought will have to be cashed at a drastic discount or simply thrown away. The arms and ammunition money from the diaspora paid for are now in the hands of the Ethiopian army. Mothers, fathers, and relatives to whom diaspora Eritreans sent money for support are suffering severely as a result of the disaster Isaias brought upon the country.

The affection Eritreans in the diaspora have for their homeland can be transformed into a positive force. The diaspora can be mobilized to support democratic reconstruction of Eritrea; the diaspora can help set Eritrea on the road to recovery and prosperity. If the possibilities I sketched in "The Economic Challenge" (Chapter Four above) could be realized, Eritrea could, indeed, become the hub of the Red Sea region and a constructive example for all of Africa. But if the EPLF continues to delude the diaspora and exploit it to prolong its hold on power, the next generation of Eritreans abroad will lose interest in their homeland and be lost to it as the country itself sinks into despair.

Ethiopians and Eritreans know that they are basically the same people. Their fates have been intertwined for three thousand years. The Addis Ababa government has refrained from stirring up hatred of Eritrea.[118] Many of its TPLF- derived leaders have blood ties to Eritrea. Some spent their youth there and went to high school in Asmara. Italian colonialism did not rupture connections between Eritreans and Ethiopians (as Chapter Seven demonstrates). Neither did British military administration. A significant portion of the Eritrean population is descended from Tigrayans who moved to Eritrea in the first half of the twentieth century. Movement of people in both directions between Ethiopia and Eritrea was normal until Eritrea invaded. The injustices that occurred on both sides when nationals were expelled can, with little lasting damage, be rectified. They need not be allowed to fester. If Frenchmen and Germans, Israelis and Arabs, Japanese and Koreans can be reconciled and live peacefully side by side, certainly this possibility is conceivable for Ethiopians and Eritreans.

Why should European and American governments have become obsessed with the notion of "rescuing" Isaias, a failed authoritarian leader who was not respectful of American and European values? The mistaken determination of American mediators to pursue a "balanced" approach to settling the confrontation left Ethiopians at all levels of society with the impression that there was some secret commitment to Isaias and the EPLF on the part of the United States. The suspicion is understandable in light of the irrational pressure to which Ethiopia was subjected. But the notion made no sense, and the pressure failed. There may have been a peculiar form of racial prejudice against Africans at work here. An African leader such as Meles Zenawi was not seen as entitled to insist on recognition of his country's territorial integrity when invaded. Ignorance of Ethiopia's history and the traditions of the country's leaders was common among officials of the Clinton Administration. So was ignorance of the nature of the EPLF regime in Eritrea. Europeans never seemed so unrealistic about the problem of bringing the confrontation to an end as the American mediators did. Neither did most Africans, especially those who sponsored the mediation effort of the OAU.

In the end Americans, Europeans, Africans, the UN and the OAU have no alternative to recognizing reality. Ethiopia found itself with no alternative and successfully took matters into its own hands. Ethiopia needs no special efforts to recover from the confrontation-only full resumption of the kinds of support and assistance it has enjoyed since 1991. It is fundamentally a strong country with excellent prospects for results now that it is again able to concentrate the energy and talent of its people on development and modernization. Eritrea, in contrast, is in tragic circumstances. Its people can, however, rescue themselves from the quagmire into which Isaias and his EPLF have led them. Their future is problematic, but not hopeless.

Washington, D.C.
August 2000

NOTES

CHAPTER I

[1] Essay II was featured in the Walta Internet service in Ethiopia in early May. It attracted an Eritrean response in an article by Tekie Fissehatsion entitled "Paul Henze Wrong Again" on 11 May 2000, the day before the Ethiopian offensive began.

[2] Letter from the Prime Minister's Office dated 16 December 1998, No. T80-PM/01/10.

[3] My "Record of Conversations with PM Meles Zenawi", Addis Ababa, March/April 1999. The following citation is also from this memorandum.

[4] My comprehensive history of the region, *Layers of Time*, is being issued in the summer of 2000 by Christopher Hurst & Co. in London and St. Martin's Press in New York. An English paperback edition is being specially prepared for Ethiopia. The book is in the process of being translated for publication in Ethiopian languages. *Layers of Time* includes a detailed history of Eritrea which has been condensed as an appendix to this book.

[5] EPLF propaganda has obscured the early history of dissident and separatist movements in Eritrea and the rise to dominance of the EPLF. The best attempts at objective analysis are in Haggai Erlich, *The Struggle Over Eritrea, 1962-1978* (Stanford: Hoover Institution, 1983); John Markakis, *National and Class Conflict in the Horn of Africa* (Cambridge: Cambridge University Press, 1987); and Ruth Iyob, *The Eritrean Struggle for Independence: Domination, Resistance, Nationalism, 1941-1993* (Cambridge: Cambridge University Press, 1995).

[6] These early, intense factional struggles are analyzed in detail by John Young in Chapter 4 of his *Peasant Revolution in Ethiopia, The Tigray People's Liberation Front, 1975-1991* (Cambridge: Cambridge University Press, 1997) pp. 106-117.

[7] Herman Cohen, Robert Frasure and Robert Houdek.

[8] For background and the events of this period see Paul B. Henze, "Ethiopia and Eritrea, the Defeat of the Derg and the Establishment of New Governments" in *Making War and Waging Peace: Foreign Intervention in Africa,* ed. David R. Smock (Washington, D.C.: U.S. Institute of Peace Press, 1993) pp. 53-77.

[9] I was an official observer assigned to a team in Om Hager on the Sudan border. I participated afterward in post-referendum activities in Keren and Asmara.

[10] In June and July 1991 the EPLF had summarily expelled all Derg soldiers and Ethiopian civilians considered Derg supporters across the border into Tigray. At least two hundred thousand soldiers and upwards of 50,000 civilians (including women and children) were ejected and a major humanitarian disaster threatened, for the EPRDF lacked means of coping with the influx. NGOs, church groups and Western aid organizations came to the rescue. USAID arranged for $15 million worth of food, medicine and supplies left over from the Gulf War to be flown in. Subsequently the World Bank funded a program which demobilized and resettled these and most other Derg soldiers. See "Case Studies in War-to Peace Transition" (Discussion Paper no.331, World Bank, Washington, D.C., 1996) pp. 25-123. Subseqently, however, considerable numbers of Ethiopians returned to live and work in Eritrea during the period after 1992.

[11] The EPLF transformed itself into the Popular Front for Democracy and Justice (PDFJ) in 1996, but little changed except the name. The party has remained monolithic and authoritarian.

[12] Eritrea had the potential to become the focal point of recovery and prosperity in the Horn of Africa. I outlined a vision of independent Eritrea becoming the "Switzerland of the Horn of Africa" in an address in Baltimore in November 1990 at a conference organized by "Eritreans for Peace and Democracy" (see Chapter IV). In spite of lip-service to the concept of becoming an "African Singapore" Eritrea evolved in the opposite direction, forbidding NGOs to operate and discouraging foreign investors and tourists by falling into quarrels with Yemen, Sudan and Djibouti before it invaded Ethiopia in May 1998.

[13] For a more detailed description and analysis of this evolution see Paul B. Henze, "Is Ethiopia Democratic? A Political Success Story," *Journal of Democracy* 9/4 (October 1998); Marc Michaelson, "Ethnic Federalism in Ethiopia - Transforming a Political Landscape," *Institute of Current World Affairs* (September 1999); and an interview with British Ethiopianist Christopher Clapham in *Press Digest*, Addis Ababa (16 December 1999).

[14] The nacfa has neither gold nor hard currency backing and rests on a deficit economy with few resources. Eritrea is unable to supply its own food needs and generates little foreign exchange from exports. In an era when twelve European nations have committed themselves to the euro and the worldwide trend is toward currency integration, it is difficult to find a rationale other than romantic nationalism for the Eritrean action. As of 1997 two-thirds of Eritrea's trade was with Ethiopia. See U.S. Embassy Asmara no.000684 (unclassified), *Eritrea's Economy: Challenging Structural Problems*, March 1998.

[15] See Wray Witten, *Bada, Further Background Information concerning the Eritrean Invasion of Ethiopia*, November 1998, a detailed e-mail report based on firsthand knowledge of the region by an American lawyer resident in Tigray.

[16] Ethiopia had long had a supportive relationship with the semi-independent Somaliland Republic. The EPLF attempted to cultivate the leaders of Somaliland to permit it to mount harrassment operations against Ethiopia but was unsuccessful.

[17] During a visit to Harar in April 1999 I personally observed the active condition of the economy of this region resulting in large part from the surge of traffic via Djibouti and heard of expectations of further development of import-export traffic through Berbera in Somaliland.

[18] Late 1999 data indicate that tourism in Ethiopia again began to rise.

[19] The reports of a German aid worker long active in the Irob region, Dr. Ann Waters-Bayer, have chronicled the destruction and brutality which have characterized Eritrean treatment of these people.

[20] A few story headlines from the weekly (English language version of the official *Hadash Eretra*) in November and December 1999 *Eritrea Profile* convey the spirit of Eritrea's propaganda: "How Ethiopia treats its 'heroes' and why this propels war"; "Need for concrete measures to break Ethiopia's naughty behavior"; "Deserter recounts atrocious rule of TPLF regime; TPLF regime's continued breach of humanitarian law; Ethiopia seeks to whitewash its larceny-[Eritrean] Presidential Adviser underscores; Ethiopia hindering peace, says member of British House of Lords; TPLF's belligerent style of survival; Ethiopia formally rejects OAU peace plan".

[21] It has led to articles in the private press which argue that the United States has always discriminated against Ethiopia – e.g., in 1935, in 1976-77, and in 1991. This emotional argumentation betrays lack of historical perspective. The United States was only on the fringes of the European diplomacy that permitted Italy to invade Ethiopia in 1935. The United States was among the very few countries that never recognized Italy's conquest of Ethiopia. From 1941 onward the United States was the major source of support for liberated Ethiopia. The United States never favored Somalia over Ethiopia but Mengistu Haile Mariam's actions against the United States prevented continuation of American support. American food and medicines kept millions of Ethiopians from perishing during the Great Famine of 1984-87. The United States and international lending institutions supported by it have been the major source of both emergency and development assistance from 1991 to the present.

[22] Misled American congressmen might even call for an embargo against Ethiopia, an action which was never undertaken against the Derg.

[23] See my essay "Who Lost Eritrea? What has been Lost?", privately circulated in May 1993 and reproduced in Chapter VI.

[24] Occasional anachronistic nationalists express such ideas from time to time in the private press. They represent no significant body of public opinion in Ethiopia.

[25] Cited from my Memorandum for the Record written shortly after the meeting.

[26] "Economic Sanctions Against Ethiopia: if Not Now, Then When?," *Eritrea Profile* (29 January 2000).

[27] A reliable Ethiopian source reports Meles as declaring "I could not get Holbrooke to listen; this egotistical man's only tactic is to try to threaten you with the power of the United States."

[28] Ethiopian Defense Forces were deployed primarily in the southeast and southwest of the country to deal with disorder spilling over from Somalia and Sudan.

[29] Approximately 1/3 of the parliamentary candidates did not claim party affiliation. Most candidates for regional councils did. Only a few major political parties put up candidates in large numbers of constituencies. Statistics are from a USAID pre-election survey, "List of Political Parties Running for the 2000 Elections."

[30] Officially called the Southern Nations, Nationalities and Peoples'State (SNNP).

[31] "Ethiopians and Eritreans Sign Cease-Fire", *New York Times* (19 June 2000).

[32] The same was true in the Organization of African Unity (OAU), the UN and countries of the European Union. As the crisis persisted, most officials of these organizations deviated less from their original understanding of the situation but tended to defer to the U.S. to devise a solution.

[33] The initial mediation proposal advanced by the U.S. and Rwanda and welcomed by the OAU was accepted by Ethiopia but rejected by Eritrea. Subsequent efforts to gain Eritrean acceptance seem to have had the effect of encouraging Eritrean President Isaias Afewerki to assume that by holding back he could eventually gain U.S. and OAU acquiescence in retaining some of the territory his forces had occupied in Ethiopia. This can hardly, however, been his entire aim.

[34] Media treatment of the crisis is the subject of the final essay in this series. If American officials had been more honest in briefing journalists abut the background and basic facts relevant to the situation, they would have

encouraged more complete and incisive press reporting and less inclination among journalists to echo Eritrean propaganda.

[35] In the present era when apologies for the past have become a routine feature of international discourse, Eritrean propagandists periodically maintain that the U.S. should feel obligated to atone for its guilt in failing to implement Eritrean independence at the end of World War II! Only ignorance of their own history can justify such a contention.

[36] For an account of this now largely forgotten sequence of events see Paul B. Henze, "Ethiopia and Eritrea, the Defeat of the Derg and the Establishment of New Governments" in David R. Smock, ed., *Making War and Waging Peace: Foreign Intervention in Africa* (Washington, D.C.: U.S. Institute of Peace Press, 1993).

[37] The primary reason, according to foreign advisors working in Eritrea at the time, was that NGO personnel had become too knowledgeable about suppression of manifestations of ethnic and religious dissatisfaction in the countryside.

[38] This assertion is based on continual contact with the American Embassy in Addis Ababa during the period 1995-1999. I spent several weeks as guest of Ambassador and Mrs. Shinn in 1997, 1998 and 1999. The Ambassador and his entire staff had a keen understanding of the entire region. Much of their reporting and advice was ignored by the State Department after Eritrea's invasion in May 1998.

[39] In apparent ignorance of how the war began, Karl Vick of the *Washington Post* referred to "the inscrutable war Ethiopia is waging with Eritrea" in a 14 February 1999 dispatch to his paper.

[40] Lt. General Tsadkan Gebre Tensae, Ethiopian Chief of Staff, declared in a briefing in late May 2000 that the ratio of forces in the region when Eritrea attacked in May 1998 had been 3-to-1 in Eritrea's favor. *Ethiopian Herald*, 29 May 2000.

[41] See editorials in the *Washington Post*, "A Foolish War" 8 February 1999; in the *New York Times*, "Africa's Futile War" 8 February 1999.

[42] *The Economist* gave its own "authoritative" confirmation to Eritrea's claims on 13 March 1999:

Eritrea's defenses on the Badme front had been thought impenetrable: the Ethiopian forces would find themselves running into a brick wall. They did, but they were prepared to sacrifice tens of thousands of men in an all-out bid to capture Badme. After their initial forays were repulsed, the Ethiopians launched a barrage of air strikes... They then threw division after division at the Eritrean frontline. Eventually the line buckled and the Eritreans were driven out of the Badme area. Ethiopia claimed victory.

The Economist description is an Eritrean propaganda formulation. The Badme operation was fought by five Ethiopian divisions against seven Eritrean. Far from mounting a "human wave", Western defense attaches in Addis Ababa confirmed to me in February 1999 that the Ethiopians used the same technique, based on surprise and mobility, they employed so successfully in May 2000: rapid, deep penetration by mobile task forces through the trenches, surrounding the Eritreans from the rear. In 2000 they still had plenty of manpower to effect an orderly and rapid penetration deep into western Eritrea.

[43] E.g., "Carnage On the Plain", *The Economist* (17 April 1999); and a dispatch by David Hirst from Eritrea called "Thousands of Ethiopians sent to deaths in border battle with Eritrea," *Washington Times* (24 May 1999).

[44] No journalist even expressed doubt that the Eritreans might be too comfortable resting on their laurels as successful guerrillas or noted that reliance on trenches in an era of mobile warfare is an outdated form of warfare.

[45] Among the best are the works of Erlich, John Markakis, Ruth Iyob and Young, already cited. Many books dealing with Ethiopia as a whole include important sections on the history of Eritrea since 1974; among the most useful are: Marina and David Ottaway, *Ethiopia, Empire in Revolution* (New York: Africana, 1978); David Korn, *Ethiopia, the United States and the Soviet Union* (London: Croom Helm, 1986); and Christopher Clapham, *Transformation and Continuity in Revolutionary Ethiopia* (Cambridge: Cambridge University Press, 1988). Readers must, of course, be wary of the immense hagiographic writing on the EPLF by a wide variety of journalists and some Eritreans.

[46] Through many permutations the ELF gradually gained adherents in Eritrea and money from Arabs. It broad.c.ast from several Arab capitals. It and groups allied with it were originally the principal competitors of Isaias' EPLF. He drove them out of Eritrea in the 1980s. After 1991 the ELF maintained a precarious existence in Sudan with representatives in some Arab capitals. Isaias' attack on Ethiopia has brought it back to life. It now claims to have adherents in Eritrea, but how effective it is remains to be seen. Ethiopia appears to have refrained from supporting it in contrast to Eritrean support of the outlawed Oromo Liberation Front to enable it to mount raids into Ethiopia.

[47] John Young's book is enlightening on the ups and downs of these relations, as is, of course, Medhanie Tadesse's.

CHAPTER II

[48] This paper is reproduced in Chapter IV of this book.

CHAPTER III

[49] I had already made five visits during the Derg era: in 1977, 1978, 1981 and twice in 1984.

[50] Viceroy.

[51] This figure is at variance with the two hundred thousand figure I was given in Kaffa. It is likely that no one had anything more than estimates at this point.

[52] In retrospect this Ethiopian National Exhibition, which ran for several months in 1972, is more remarkable than it seemed at the time. Held on spacious fairgrounds at the southern edge of Asmara, it featured exhibits by all Ethiopian provinces and by most industrial and trading establishments in the country with special emphasis on those in Eritrea. A number of foreign exhibitors, among them Italians and Israelis, participated too. In spite of some rebels' attempts to disrupt it, good security was maintained and several hundred thousand people visited the exhibition.

[53] The All-Ethiopia Trade Union Federation, a Soviet-style labor organization set up replace the ICFTU-affiliated and Western-supported Confederation of Ethiopian Labor Unions (CELU) in December 1975.

[54] Forbidden!

[55] A Semitic language of northern Eritrea, distinct from Tigrinya.

[56] Emperor Yekuno Amlak, who ruled from 1270 to 1285, restored the Solomonic dynasty which continued to occupy the Ethiopian throne without interruption through Haile Selassie I.

[57] The region around Asmara, now the most populous of the nine *awrajas* (provinces) of Eritrea.

[58] The Bilen are an Agau-speaking − i.e. non-Semitic − people who predominate in the Senhit, the region around the north-central Eritrean city of Keren. Many were converted to Roman Catholicism by missionaries in the 19th century and others to Protestantism.

[59] The old city of Massawa was severely damaged by Derg bombing after it was captured by EPLF forces in January 1990.

[60] National Tourist Organization.

[61] Between June and October 1986 I published a three-part series in the *London Encounter* under the title "Behind the Ethiopian Famine – Anatomy of a Revolution". These articles, discreetly circulated by USIS and the British Council, were widely read by Ethiopians both in the country and abroad.

[62] A locust-control specialist in the years following World War II, later a scholar and author of *Travels in Ethiopia* (London: Ernest Benn, 1949), and *The Abyssinians (*London/New York: Thames & Hudson, 1970).

[63] The Melottis were among Eritrea's prominent Italian entrepreneurs, famous for their brewery which produced excellent beer under the family name. Its trade mark was changed to "Asmara" after Derg nationalization but restored after the Eritrean victory in 1991. "Melotti" remains synonymous with commercially brewed beer throughout Eritrea and northern Ethiopia.

[64] Who defected to United States in the fall of 1985 and published *Red Tears* (Trenton, NJ: Red Sea Press, 1988).

[65] This curious of Ethiopian woman's name translates literally "You are a bed", but means figuratively "You are warm, comfortable, accommodating".

[66] The Church of St. Stephen which overlooks [then] Revolution Square. Its original name, Maskal [Holy Cross] Square was restored in 1991.

CHAPTER IV

[67] As I experienced it in 1990 this organization included an impressive group of highly educated professional Eritreans holding good positions in the U.S. I heard little of them when I visited Eritrea after 1991. I suspect that few of them returned, or remained if they did. I had no contact with the organization after the 1990 conference. It seems to have ceased to exist.

[68] Both these essays were printed by RAND and circulated widely in the U.S. and abroad. I recall sending them to Isaias to a post office box the EPLF maintained in Port Sudan. They were, of course, also available to the EPLF office maintained in Washington by Tesfai Ghirmazien.

[69] E.g. "Rebels and Separatists in Ethiopia," (Santa Monica:RAND R-3347-USDP, 1985); and "Eritrean Options and Ethiopia's Future," (Santa Monica: RAND 3021-USDP, 1989).

[70] "Ethiopia and the Challenge of Liberation" (address at the Eritreans for Peace and Democracy symposium in Crystal City, Virginia, 10 March 1990).

[71] "The Endless War," *Washington Quarterly* 9/2 (Spring 1986).

CHAPTER V

[72] I was sponsored by USAID's Democracy and Governance Project during this visit and officially accredited as an observer by the Eritrean Referendum Commission.

[73] Director of TDA.

[74] The book, my first on Ethiopia, was published in London by Ernest Benn in 1977.

[75] From USAID Addis Ababa, the Brookings Institution in Washington and the Carter Center in Atlanta, respectively.

[76] Elaberet was developed as a private Italian commercial farming and food-processing concession established in the late imperial period. Irrigated by dams on the Anseba river and its tributaries, it produced fruit, vegetables, wine, meat and dairy products. Nationalized by the Derg and occasionally fought over, it deteriorated.

CHAPTER VI

[77] Then in charge of Horn of Africa affairs in the State Department Washington, subsequently U.S. Ambassador to Eritrea, 1993-1996.

[78] The present author included; see, e.g., my "Eritrean Options and Ethiopia's Future," (Santa Monica: RAND N-3021-USDP, 1989).

[79] See Haggai Erlich, "The Eritrean Autonomy 1952-62: Its Failure and its Contribution to Further Escalation" *Models of Autonomy*, ed. Y. Dinstein (New York: Transaction Press, 1981).

[80] For an attempt to chronicle the complex interweaving of events that culminated in Mengistu's flight and the final victory of the EPRDF and ELF, see my "Defeat of the Derg and the Establishment of New Governments in Ethiopia and Eritrea," (Santa Monica: RAND P-7766, 1991).

[81] Germany was forced to surrender a quarter of its territory permanently to Poland and Russia and another quarter (the former so-called German

Democratic Republic) was lost for nearly half a century. At a minimum 6 or 7 million Germans were killed during Hitler's wars and at least 20 million displaced afterward. Material losses were enormous. Germany's western half was under foreign military occupation for ten years before sovereignty was restored. Germany is still making massive expenditures to restore its Soviet-ravaged eastern states to viability. Grave as Mengistu's damage to Ethiopia has been, it cannot compare in scale to that which Hitler caused Germany--or that which Stalin and his successors inflicted on Russia and most of the other nations of the ex-Soviet Union. Millions of German prisoners of war were kept for years as forced laborers, primarily in the Soviet Union, to repair damage caused by the Nazi invasion. The EPLF expelled all Derg soldiers and many civilians during the first weeks after taking power in 1991 under circumstances that were often relatively inhumane, but the international precedent of retaining prisoners of war for reconstruction seems never to have been considered.

[82] It is true that Eritrean independence deprives Ethiopia of revenue that would be gained from taxes and customs. For the years immediately ahead, however, the loss of revenue would appear to be more than offset by relief from the burden that reconstruction would place on Ethiopia's hard-pressed budget.

[83] I have elaborated these propositions at much greater length in several other places, e.g. my book *The Horn of Africa from War to Peace*, (London/New York:Macmillan, 1991); "Eritrea - the Economic Challenge" (a speech to Eritreans for Peace and Democracy at Baltimore, MD, November 1990); and" The Primacy of Economics for the Future of the Horn of Africa" (originally presented to a conference on the future of the Horn of Africa at the School of Oriental and African Studies of the University of London, November 1991 and subsequently published as RAND P-7763, 1992).

CHAPTER VII

[84] A highly readable edition *Periplus Maris Erythraei,* ed. Lionel Casson, (Princeton: Princeton University Press, 1989).

[85] The name survives as Zula, now a small village south of Massawa.

[86] Ge'ez is still used in both Ethiopia and Eritrea in the Orthodox Church. The name comes from one of the original South Arabian tribes that emigrated across the Red Sea.

[87] Practically everything now known about Aksum is summarized in two recent books: Stuart Munro-Hay, *Aksum, an African Civilisation of Late*

Antiquity (Edinburgh: Edinburgh University Press, 1991); and David Phillipson, *Ancient Ethiopia* (London: British Museum Press, 1998).

[88] Tigrinya and Arabic were adopted as equal official languages in Eritrea after the fall of the Derg.

[89] Published on his return to Portugal as *The Prester John of the Indies* and translated into many other languages, Alvares' book is one of the greatest classics of travel in this part of the world. An English edition was published in two volumes by Cambridge University Press for the Hakluyt Society in 1961. It is still a useful guidebook to many historic sites in northern Ethiopia.

[90] Some of these Americans wrote memoirs. One of the best is William Dye, *Moslem Egypt and Christian Ethiopia...as Experienced by the American Staff* (New York: Negro Universities Press,1968).

[91] The Israeli Ethiopianist, Haggai Erlich, has published an excellent biography of this remarkable Ethiopian, *Ras Alula and the Scramble for Africa* (Asmara: Red Sea Press, 1996). A Tigrinya translation was published in Addis Ababa in 1998.

[92] Eritrean leader Isaias Afewerki made the same mistake in misjudging Ethiopia and its leader Meles Zenawi in 1998 when he invaded Tigray only to be stunningly defeated in May 2000.

[93] Orthodox Christians recognized the Ethiopian Patriarch and Eritrean monasteries considered themselves subordinate to the Ethiopian religious hierarchy. Eritrean monasteries sent representatives to the coronation of Haile Selassie in 1930. In 1929 Italy persuaded the Coptic Patriarch in Cairo to exempt Eritrea from the jurisdiction of the Ethiopian Orthodox Church.

[94] The British extended it to Kassala in 1940 but tore up the tracks later.

[95] Tekeste Negash, *Italian Colonialism in Eritrea*, doctoral dissertation at Uppsala University, Sweden, 1987, p. 130, the best study of the colonial period that has yet appeared.

[96] With representatives of Great Britain, the United States, France, and the Soviet Union.

[97] G.K.N. *Trevaskis, Eritrea, a Colony in Transition* (Oxford: Oxford University Press, 1960) p. 109. This book remains essential to understanding Eritrea.

[98] Op.cit., p. 131.

[99] See Haggai Erlich, "The Eritrean Autonomy, 1952-1962: Its Failure and its Contribution to Further Escalation, in Ethiopia and the Challenge of

Independence," *Models of Autonomy*, ed. Y.Dinstein (New York: Transaction Press, 1981) pp. 213-24.

[100] Tekeste Negash, *Eritrea and Ethiopia, the Federal Experience* (Uppsala, 1997) is the best study available.

[101] No pressure was brought to bear on Ethiopia to live up to the commitments it had made to the UN by the countries who had devised the federation arrangement. The United States enjoyed full cooperation in Asmara and operations at Kagnew Station expanded steadily during the 1950s as the Cold War intensified.

[102] He returned to liberated Eritrea in 1991 and was honored by the EPLF as the founding father of independent Eritrea. He died in Asmara in 1995 at the age of 90.

[103] Ruth Iyob, *The Eritrean Struggle for Independence: Domination, Resistance, Nationalism, 1941-1993* (Cambridge: Cambridge University Press, 1995) pp. 99-100. This book provides an immense amount of detail on Eritrean exile personalities and their complex interrelationships but has relatively little information on developments in Eritrea itself during the period.

[104] Dissident Eritreans were also welcomed in Mogadishu after Somalia became independent in 1960.

[105] After Ras Kassa's death in 1956 Asrate took his father's place as one of Haile Selassie's closest confidants.

[106] Haggai Erlich, *The Struggle Over Eritrea, 1962-1978* (Stanford: Hoover Institution, 1983) p. 39.

[107] Erlich's summary of this period is based on information from official Israeli sources, Haggai Erlich, *The Struggle Over Eritrea, 1962-1978* (Stanford: Hoover Institution, 1983) pp. 36-42.

[108] Christopher Clapham, *Haile Selassie's Government* (London: Longmans, 1969) p. 77.

[109] Ethiopia's armed forces were all volunteer and made up almost entirely of men and officers from the center and south of the country. Few young Eritreans found military service appealing.

[110] Rivalries among rebels in the field as well as among leaders abroad during this period defy simplification. See Ruth Iyob, *op.cit.*, pp. 113-117.

[111] As cited in Haggai Erlich, *The Struggle Over Eritrea, 1962-1978* (Stanford: Hoover Institution, 1983) p. 49.

[112] Two hundred ELF-RC fighters were killed in factional fighting in July. The EPLF arrested hundreds of its members for opposing its National Democratic Program.

[113] Haggai Erlich, *The Struggle Over Eritrea, 1962-1978* (Stanford: Hoover Institution, 1983) p. 95.

[114] While the EPLF attracted a large contingent of journalistic and academic admirers who produced a vast volume of sycophantic writing, the TPLF attracted little attention abroad and did little to publicize itself. A German, Dieter Beisel, published a small paperback on it *(Reise ins Land der Rebellen* (Hamburg: Rowohlt, 1989). A Canadian John Young, has produced a comprehensive history based on extensive interviews: *Peasant Revolution in Ethiopia–the TPLF, 1975-1991* (Cambridge: Cambridge University Press, 1997). Jenny Hammond's *Fire from the Ashes* (Lawrenceville, NJ: Red Sea Press, 1999) provides a vivid account of life with the TPLF in the field during the late 1980s.

[115] Soviet and East German documents provide insight into this process. See, e.g., *The Cold War in the Third World...* (Bulletins 8/9, Cold War International History Project, Wilson Center, Washington, D.C., 1996/97).

[116] I served as an official referendum observer in Om Hager on the Sudan border.

[117] The U.S. Embassy Asmara reported that during the previous year 67percent of Eritrea's external trade had been with Ethiopia (Cable, "Eritrea's Economy: Challenging Structural Problems", 3 March 1998).

[118] Unfortunately it is difficult to attribute the same good sense to EPLF propagandists. Their press and media have been filled with "anti-Woyane" invective, characterizing Ethiopia's leaders as depraved and blood-thirsty autocrats eager to commit atrocities. It is to be hoped that most ordinary Eritreans have been little affected by these diatribes.